D0790158

The Coral For Life Society

The first time that I ever went to Hawaii, I went swimming off the beach at Waikiki. It was breath taking! Hundreds of colorful fish were swimming all around me, and I was floating over the most beautiful coral imaginable. I was mesmerized. I had not realized that there was such a beautiful place on Earth. The experience remains with me, and every time I think of coral, I think of Hawaii and the most beautiful ocean on Earth. Ironically, a few decades later I would learn that not only does the coral make the oceans clean and pristine, but some coral when eaten can have almost magical curative power. Currently, I am known by many as the King of Coral Calcium.

Thus, I have a passionate interest in preserving the coral reefs of the world. The harvesting of the coral calcium is done from the deep open ocean trenches many miles from the coral reefs which are protected by the Japanese Government and the people of Okinawa. However, every time a pound of coral is consumed, I worry about replacement, even though more coral calcium is produced naturally by the oceans than can possibly be consumed. The problem is that the coral reefs are super sensitive and just mild changes in temperature or salinity and runoff pollution can destroy them. Over the past decade, more than 30% of the world's coral reefs have been destroyed. The world is obviously facing a crisis. What can be done?

Because of my passion for the coral reefs, I was recently contacted by a representative of the "Russian Academy of Science" Apparently, over the past decade they have perfected a process to re-grow coral reefs at a rapid rate. The technology is currently being held by a non-profit organization, *"The Coral For Life Society."*

The Russian technology uses a coral ball made of porous concrete specially formulated to induce the rapid growth of coral reefs. Just one month in any ocean water and coral is growing profusely from the ball. Imagine if you live in Los Angeles and could go down to the beach to swim in the new coral reefs in clean and pristine water. The same will one day be true for all ocean side cities all over the world.

Currently, technicians are being trained and the bugs are being removed from the production technology. A new and improved world awaits, but first the public has to get behind the technology. Just imagine not only being involved in curing humanity, but also in curing the oceans. A more noble cause has never before existed. Bob Barefoot intends to purse the technology in hope that it can be developed to make a better world. Let's remove the horror, pain and suffering that degenerative disease causes humanity. Let's cure humanity, and let's grow coral reefs all over the world. Let's cure the oceans.

Plea for Help !!!

Please join Bob Barefoot in supporting the Coral For Life Society. Let's cure humanity, let's cure the ocean.

Let's Cure Humanity

This publication is intended to direct the attention of both physician and patient to the torrent of scientific research being carried out on the significance of biological calcium. It is for educational purposes. It is not intended to replace the orthodox physician-patient relationship. If you are sick, you are advised to consult a physician, and together, along with your newly gained knowledge, work towards the resolution of your illness.

However, since 1982, I have watched as nutritional therapy was used to help people cure themselves of diseases when doctors said that there was no hope. The truth being was that there was no hope as long as conventional medicine was applied. God made the human body miraculous so that if it gets what it needs, it can cure itself. And, the body does not need the white chemical killer drugs, but rather it needs only God's natural nutrition. The DNA in our bodies allows us to replicate damaged body parts, but the DNA only works when smothered in calcium, something doctors would rarely recommend. The scientific community, on the other hand, has produced thousands of documents extolling calcium's ability to alter disease. Thus, the only hope to reverse the deadly course modern medicine has put mankind on is to begin the use of God's nutritional therapy, medicine of the 21st Century. It is against the law in America for a anyone to claim that they can cure anything. I have never cured anyone, but I have watched many times as the deathly ill have cured themselves. Now, after reading this book I ask that America and the world join me in witnessing these miracles of life and together we will shout to the world, "Let's cure humanity."

Robert R. Barefoot
928-684-4458

I am Guilty

My name is Bob Barefoot. You have seen me on television, heard me on the radio or on my audio tapes, or you may have read my books on the subject of coral calcium and its health benefits. I have been studying biological calcium for about 40 years now, long before it became a popular subject. And for that reason many seek out my council on this important subject. I also have sold and endorsed my own brands of coral calcium as well as other brands that I believe to constitute high quality marine coral calcium. I am a very proud graduate of the Northern Alberta Institute of Technology, NAIT, 1967. Since graduation I have, with fellow Ph.D. co-authors, seven scientific publications and have written three books, "The Calcium Factor," "Death By Diet," and "If It Glitters," the first two of which are best-sellers. I have worked in the petroleum and gold industries for years and have several international patents. My recent infomercials, with Kevin Trudeau, were the most watched infomercials in television history. In the infomercial I continued my discussion regarding coral calcium. As such they have become extremely controversial. The FTC subsequently and incorrectly deemed that claims were being attached to the calcium product, coral calcium, discussed in the infomercial. I did not claim that the product itself cured anything, as can be verified by an examination of the verbal text of the show.

Bob Barefoot does admit guilt to the following:
1. Never charging the sick
2. Never charging for talks
3. Potentially saving thousands of lives with the message of the disputed infomercial
4. Never being paid for services rendered
5. Picking bad business partners
6. Trying to end pain, suffering and death for humanity

LET'S CURE HUMANITY

THE BOB BAREFOOT STORY

BY

ROBERT R. BAREFOOT

Let's Cure Humanity

The Relationship Between Nutrient Deficiency and Disease
By
Robert R. Barefoot

Published By:
Pan American International Nutrition Ltd, Publishing
Post Office Box 21389
Wickenburg, AZ 85358 U.S.A.

Copyright 2008 by Robert R. Barefoot,
First Printing October 2004, Second Printing June 2008

Library of Congress Cataloging in Publication Data
Barefoot, Robert R.
Let's Cure Humanity. The Relationship Between Nutrient Deficiency and Disease by Robert R. Barefoot --- 1st edition
Bibliography
Includes subjects:

1. Scientific and Medical Trends in History
2. Calcium and Disease
3. Launching Nutrition
4. Changing History
5. The Bob Barefoot Story
6. June 10, 2003, FTC D-Day
7. Appeal for Congressional Action
8. Bob Barefoot's Newsletters
9. Calcium and Cancer
10. Calcium and Heart Disease
11. Coral Calcium
12. Testimonials
13. Scientific References on Calcium and Disease

Library of Congress Catalog Card Number, C.I.P. 92-90529
ISBN 978-0-9633703-0-3
Printed in the United States

Table Of Contents

Chapter	Title	Page
	The Coral For Life Society	1
	Let's Cure Humanity	3
	I am Guilty	4
	Table of Contents	7
	Endorsements	8
	Forward	16
	Preface	22
	Acknowledgement	26
	Notation	26
	Disclaimer	27
	Post Script	27
ONE	Scientific and Medical Trends in History	28
TWO	Barefoot and the Calcium Factor	36
THREE	Calcium and Disease	45
FOUR	Launching Nutrition	57
FIVE	Changing History	61
SIX	Bob Barefoot	67
SEVEN	D-Day	79
EIGHT	Appeal For Congressional Action	85
NINE	Bob Barefoot's Newsletter.Com	104
TEN	Calcium and Cancer	118
ELEVEN	Answer to Cancer	131
TWELVE	Calcium and Heart Disease	133
THIRTEEN	Coral Calcium	145
FOURTEEN	Testimonials	155
FIFTEEN	Summary	181
SIXTEEN	Scientific References	191

Endorsements

"Mr. Barefoot is one of the Nation's top Nutritional Therapists, a chemist, scientist in the fields of biochemistry, hydrocarbon extraction and metal extraction from ores, inventor and holder of numerous patents, public speaker, writer, and outstanding business entrepreneur, a man of great integrity, enthusiasm, determination, loyalty, and tireless energy, coupled with a great personality. Mr. Barefoot has achieved wide acclaim in recent years for his biochemistry research into the inter-relationship between disease and malnutrition, espousing that degenerative diseases are caused by mineral and vitamin deficiencies," Howard W. Pollock, Congressman (Alaska) Retired, Past President Safari Club International, Ducks Unlimited, and The National Rifle Association.

"I have been a practicing physician for the past 25 years. I am a fellow of the American College of OB-GYN and a diplomat of the American Board of OB-GYN. Mr. Barefoot has helped me immensely to understand the complex chemistry of how calcium and other minerals contribute to overall health and preventive medicine. I personally know of many individuals who are much healthier today because of Mr. Barefoot's nutritional advice, including myself.," Wayne Weber M.D., Family Planning Associates Medical Group Inc., Los Angeles, California.

"I am a heart surgeon at Westchester Medical Center in Valhalla, New York, one of the largest open-heart surgery centers in the United States. I have had a special interest in nutrition over the past 30 years and have lectured on this subject throughout the United States, particularly its relationship to heart disease and other degenerative diseases. It is in this capacity that I have come to know and respect Robert Barefoot.

8

He is an internationally known chemist with numerous international patents. His use of bio-chemistry in the field of hydrocarbon extraction and the field of metal extraction of ores led him to pursue a different line of research over the past two decades, elucidating the intimate relationship between nutrition and disease," Richard W. Pooley, Professor of Surgery, New York Medical College, New York.

*"I am a physician, President and Executive Medical Director of Health Insight, S.B.S. and Health Advocate Inc. in the State of Michigan. I have extensive credentials and honors that reach the White House and Heads of States in other countries. Mr. Robert Barefoot is a remarkable gentleman and a scholar who works endlessly to complete his mission to cure America. He has worked over the past 20 years with many medical doctors and scientists across the United States and in other countries doing Orthomolecular Research on various diseases. The information has been culminated in two books, **The Calcium Factor** and **Death by Diet** which have been used technically as Bibles of Nutrition. Many people I know have thanked Mr. Barefoot for both saving their lives and returning them to good health. Mr. Barefoot is an amazing and extraordinary man who is on a 'Great Mission' for all mankind. I thank God for Robert Barefoot,"* Liska M. Cooper, M.D., Detroit, Michigan.

"I am a physician practicing at the Molecular/ Biological level for over 25 years. I lecture extensively in the nutritional- medical field in Canada, the United States and internationally. I have attended hundreds of lectures and seminars covering the aspects of medicine including a number of those given by Robert Barefoot whose discourses easily classify as absolutely excellent! Personal conversations with this man, a highly moral and ethical person, have served to confirm his unusual knowledge in the field of biologically applied nutrition and immunity enhancement." C.T. Taylor, M.D., L.M.C.C., P. Eng.,Stony Plain, Alberta.

"I have been an attorney involved in very complex litigation involving natural supplements and their ability to treat or cure various types of illnesses, including cancer. I am well-known in Maryland as a litigator, repeatedly named as one of the outstanding trial attorneys, specializing in complex matters of all natures and have written concerning trial techniques. Mr. Barefoot was engaged as an expert in the use of natural supplements, specifically minerals, and their effect on various forms of cancers. He is a renowned author in this field. There have been many occasions when I found him to be extraordinarily knowledgeable in this field of expertise. My professional opinion is that Mr. Barefoot's knowledge and experience with minerals and other natural substances and their application for the treatment of illnesses is quite unique. In fact, I am not aware of any other individual who possesses the knowledge and expertise in this very important and expanding field as Mr. Barefoot," David Freishtat, Attorney, Freishtat & Sandler, Baltimore, Maryland.

*"Mr. Barefoot has been, and continues to be, an advocate for health and natural healing through nutrition and knowledge. He has championed the cause of well over 440,000 American women and children who have been exposed to the toxic effects of silicone implanted devices. Mr. Barefoot, one of the rare silica chemists in the world, has delivered a message of hope to these suffering individuals, who didn't have any hope before, but are now arming themselves with the books **The Calcium Factor** and **Death By Diet** and are spreading the word. The name Barefoot has become a household word. In the past three years, he has traveled to countless meetings and medical conferences throughout the country without charging for his services. Robert Barefoot is a humanitarian and his efforts to educate through his books, informational tapes, lectures and vast media appearances has set a standard of excellence that is well above the norm. His work with hundreds of scientists and*

medical doctors, researching diet, has elevated him to one of the top speakers on nutrition in the nation," Jill M. Wood, President Idaho Breast Implant Information Group, Boise Idaho.

*"I recently retired as President and CEO of Bioflora International Inc., a manufacturer of nutritional supplements, liquid mineral extracts, and liquid organic plant foods. I oversaw the formulation and production of what is considered the world's best selling mineral supplement. I was originally introduced to and very impressed by the work of Robert Barefoot, specifically **The Calcium Factor** in 1996 but was not afforded the pleasure of a personal introduction until 1998. By that time he had developed a reputation and a title, "The King of Calcium,"* G. Scott Miller, Past President & CEO, Bioflora Phoenix, Arizona.

"I graduated from Harvard University in 1942 (BSC Chemistry) and worked as a Research Director and in corporate management at Franklin Electronics Inc., and have been awarded two patents. Mr. Barefoot has been highly influential in my survival of prostate cancer, with which I was diagnosed in the fall of 1991. Because of his detailed knowledge of biochemistry, he has much more penetrating knowledge of the relationship between disease and nutrition, a knowledge not available to many trained dieticians because of their lack of biochemical background. With his expertise, he has aided me in not only arresting the progression of my disease, cancer, through diet and nutrition, but also reversing it. Mr. Barefoot is, simply put, an extraordinary individual," Philip Sharples, President, Sharples Industries Inc. Tubac, Arizona.

"I have known Bob Barefoot for three years during which time he has provided my spouse with critical information. As a result of this relationship, I was able to

introduce dozens of people to Mr. Barefoot's idea relative to critical illness and nutrition. The results achieved have been remarkable. It is my personal opinion that Mr. Barefoot is the absolute top of his field, nutritional therapy," W. Grant Fairley, The Fairley Erker Group, Edmonton, Canada.

"I am a chemist and have been involved in product development, specifically nutritional supplements. I have written numerous articles and lectured throughout the United States on these products and the benefits of utilizing alternative medicine and alternative medical products within the U.S. healthcare regimen. Over the past three years I have traveled and lectured with Mr. Barefoot on numerous occasions all over the United States. He is recognized as a world class expert on calcium and its nutritional benefits for the human body. Mr. Barefoot blends his prestige and uncanny ability to talk to the average person in a way that allows complicated scientific subjects to be completely understandable and accepted. I have seen Mr. Barefoot 's information help a lot of people," Alex Nobles, Executive Vice President, Benchmark USA Inc., Salt Lake, Utah.

"I have been associated with Mr. Barefoot since 1993. His Nutrition therapy is the result of twenty years of research into non-invasive treatment of generic diseases. In Canada we now have six M.D.'s practicing his protocols. I understand that numerous Russian M.D.'s in Moscow are also practicing his protocols. This number will increase exponentially as the testimonial success of hundreds of afflicted people becomes known. Mr. Barefoot's biochemistry and science brings credence to his recommended dietary and lifestyle protocols. He must be considered at the top of his field," Peter Epp. P. Eng., President Albritco Development Corporation, Calgary, Canada.

"I am the General Manager of an audio cassette tape manufacturer. Previously, I was the Vice President of an.

12

engineering consulting company specializing in nuclear technology analysis under contract to the U.S. government. With a BS degree in Electrical Engineering, graduate school work at UCLA and over 10 years of research at McDonnell Douglas, my technical and scientific tools are extensive. I currently specialize in the audio production of technical information specializing in nutrition and health. It is in this regard that I have come to know the reputation and work of Robert Barefoot. Our company actively seeks men and women with scientific and medical backgrounds in order to develop substantive resource material for our client base. Robert Barefoot's lectures, books and tapes support his position as a leading spokesperson for the benefits of nutrition for good health," Al Vendetti, General Manager, Exxel Audio Productions, Oceanside, California.

"I am the founder of a company that specializes in both mining and the export of health and nutritional products overseas. Mr. Barefoot has tremendous knowledge of biochemistry and his expertise in the field of calcium research has earned him recognition worldwide for both his lecturing and research. He has authored several books, which my company exports overseas as nutritional standards for people involved in the nutrition industry. He has also researched and developed calcium supplements, which are being exported to several countries abroad. His research of the relationship between disease and nutrition is gaining recognition worldwide and if properly implemented, could substantially reduce the devastating effects of degenerative diseases caused by mineral and vitamin deficiency," Brett R. Davies, President, Davies International, Denver, Colorado.

"I am well known in the area of nutrition. I am certified by the National Association of Health Care Professionals as a Health Care Councilor and have lectured extensively in the

United States, Canada, Russia, and the Ukraine. Mr. Barefoot is considered one of the most knowledgeable people in the world, on effects of calcium on health," Robert G. Bremner, Mechanicsville, Virginia.

"Mr. Barefoot is a man in pursuit of 'Excellence'" in all his endeavors. He has received wide recognition for his research in the biochemistry field dealing with malnutrition. I have the distinct privilege and pleasure of having known Mr. Barefoot for several years," Jerry R. Gallion, International Financier, Vaulx Milieu, France.

"I am a retired university professor, Ph.D., known in the field of Pharmaceutical Chemistry, having written and lectured extensively over a forty year period, publishing numerous scientific articles. Based on Mr. Barefoot's education, and background in chemistry and nutrition, along with his published books and lecturing, it is my professional opinion that Mr. Barefoot is near the top of his field," Jerry Rollins, Ph.D., Austin, Texas.

We have purchased two of your books, "The Calcium Factor" and "Death By Diet." INCREDIBLE BOOKS !!! Well worth reading by EVERY PERSON IN AMERICA OF READING AGE !! I HAVE READ THEM TWICE.

We totally discount the crap that the "fanatics" in other fields and in the government who discount your writings. It <u>does show how afraid they are of the TRUTH, doesn't it</u> ? Bob we feel that your sales of coral calcium have helped so many people (including ourselves) and should continue unabated. Our congratulations to you for writing the EXCELLENT information you have in those books, and, therefore, helping to benefit many, many, many people's health.

We wish unabated success for you continuing your writings, work and success in defeating the scared idiots. Mae and Al Schone, Felton, Pennsylvania.

After seeing you being interviewed on television and hearing your story about coral calcium, I bought your books and a supply of coral calcium. I read the books with much interest. I have taken vitamin and mineral supplements for years and have read a number of books to learn more about vitamins, etc. In the 70s I was able to rid myself of bone spurs in my neck by increasing my calcium intake, just like you said in your books, after a friend told me that it was a lack of calcium that caused bone spurs. However, it took me three years to do it. Your books woke me up to the fact that our body does not absorb nearly enough calcium, and most of us never give it a chance to do so.

The amounts that I was taking were "recommended" levels and in spite of the supplements, I have arthritis in my knee and bone spurs in my shoulder, and I have sinusitis and a long list of allergies.

After only three weeks on coral calcium I have eliminated 99% of the pain associated with arthritic left knee and a right shoulder with bone spurs. I walk naturally again, and for the past year I had required a cane to walk. The only thing that I have done differently since reading your books is switch to coral calcium. My energy level is much higher. I look forward to seeing my health improve even further. Thank you so much for getting the word out on coral calcium and giving us a chance to help us cure ourselves. The chemistry involved, explained in layman's terms in your books, showed me just how vital calcium is and encourages me to stay on the regimen. Kennith R. Davis, Nashville, Tennessee

Foreword

Let's Cure Humanity was written to both inform and instruct the general public about one of the hottest topics of research in the scientific community: biological calcium. Each scientist specializes in his specific and complex arena of interest much like a musician specializes in his specific musical instrument. The purpose of this publication is to unlock the information hidden within scientific technical jargon contained within thousands of publications, and to demonstrate to the layman that all of the thousands of scientific arenas of research can easily be orchestrated using *The Calcium Factor* to produce an understanding of the symphony of life.

Calcium has also become a hot topic for nutritionists who are extolling its virtues in promoting good health. The general public is being told that "calcium is good for you" and food producers are responding by fortifying numerous products with calcium. Since promoting calcium is becoming old hat — just ask the dairy industry — then why another book on calcium? The answer is simple. *Let's Cure Humanity* explains *why* calcium is superior to all other elements in performing the biological tasks that are required to prevent disease and maintain good health and why so many of the world's best scientists have joined in the research of calcium and disease. In doing so the book becomes controversial to orthodox medicine, which although it has an excellent track record in dealing with catastrophic illness, has a dismal record in both dealing with and accepting preventive medicine. *Let's Cure Humanity* was written to withstand scientific scrutiny and criticism. Criticism from those who benefit from the maintenance of disease only serves to endorse the importance of understanding calcium's role in nutrition. Historically, all great concepts that are currently accepted by those who criticize were initially vigorously opposed by their predecessors prior to their total acceptance by the world at large.

The historical resistance to change of the governing establishments in the scientific and medical communities, as well as the resulting negative effects on innovation and research, will be explained. Dr. Carl Reich will be shown to be one of these innovators who fell victim to the system. Quotes from world-renowned scientists, including several Nobel Prize winners, will be given in support of the significance of the calcium factor to human health. A explanation of the relationship of calcium to disease will be given to show how it has become the *king of the bioelements* or the common denominator of good health. All of the scientific and medical facts will be presented in an order that supports this *unified concept of disease*, with calcium being the *"supernutrient."* As further explained, experts recognize that most diseases *cannot survive in an alkaline medium.*

Calcium makes up 1.6 percent of the human body weight, making it the most abundant metallic element. As such, it plays a myriad of crucial roles both structurally and biochemically. Only recently have scientists begun to unravel the intricacies that make calcium the *King of the bioelements.* They found that a drop in the level of calcium in the body is intricately involved in the process of aging as well as a host of degenerative diseases such as osteoporosis, allergy, gallstones, cancer, heart disease and many more.

The most distressing aspect of medicine today is that the Recommended Daily Allowance **(RDA)** for minerals and vitamins, although ridiculously low and *disease-inducing* (the new **RDI's** will be set at half as much), is rigidly adhered to, even though our society is heading towards several medical disasters, as is witnessed by the staggering increase in AIDS and cancer. My co-author of **The Calcium Factor**, Dr. Carl Reich, M.D., used to tell everyone that the term RDA stood for *"recommended death allowance,"* implying that you took only the meager amounts recommended, you would surely die young. He was also disgusted that the Food and Drug Administration, the FDA, only tests drugs, many of which later turn out to be toxic, resulting in thousands of deaths. He said that since no one ever died from a mineral, why would the FDA never exercise its mandate to protect the public and test the minerals for health claims. He therefore referred to the FDA as the *"Food Disinformation Agency."*

Although medicine is winning a few battles, it is definitely losing the wars. For example, in the 1950's cancer was striking one out of every four people; by the 1980's cancer was striking one out of every three people; by the year 2010 cancer will strike *one out of every two people*. AIDS is also skyrocketing with virtually no hope with the current medical approach of packaging a solution in a chemical drug. Since the AIDS victims do not die from the disease directly, but from other diseases that are able to attack their defense-weakened body, it makes sense that although a person may carry the virus, high pH body fluids may strengthen the body's health to the point where the disease is not allowed to flourish. This is the case with cancer.

Fortunately, the medical pendulum is beginning to swing in the opposite direction. There is a growing movement that wants to do more than just use chemicals and drugs to block the symptoms of disease. By researching biochemical processes, calcium deficiency has been shown to be the trigger for a whole host of diseases. The road to the prevention for these diseases can be found in the knowledge expounded in *Let's Cure Humanity*.

The scientifically defendable suggestion that diseases can be prevented and even cured nutritionally will most certainly be received by both skepticism and *medicine's traditional cry of "quackery."* The authors hope that such is the case, as most major advances of medicine in the past have been greeted by the same chorus. For example, Dr. Ignas Semmelweis was run out of the medical profession for the "quackery" of advocating in 1847 that physicians wash their hands. The American Medical Association told doctors that believing in something that you cannot see is the same as believing in spooks and therefore any doctor who washes his hands will have license suspended. Thus, for the next 60 years under the direction of the AMA, doctors killed millions of people needlessly.

More recently, at the turn of the century the pioneers of electro-biochemistry who introduced the electro-encephalograph (EEG) and the electro-cardiograph (ECG) to medicine, were called *"electronic quacks"* by the American Medical Association, and American doctors were banned from using these devices that are so common in medicine today.

The examples given of the behavior of the medical and scientific communities are *historical facts*, and are not meant to demean either profession. All criticisms are directed at the few in the upper echelon administrations of the governing bureaucratic establishments who rigidly regulate the innovation of doctors and scientists while vigorously protecting their own prestigious status quo empires. Unfortunately, criticism of these elite and most respected men is often met with the blind and defensive cry, "*blasphemy*," thereby providing encouragement for the system to perpetuate its mistakes at the cost of human lives and suffering. Ironically, blasphemy is "the disrespect for persons or things regarded as sacred." This implies that such men are holy and therefore incapable of making mistakes. It is hoped that by our pointing out a few, the reader will be alerted to the fact that history may once again be repeating itself. More importantly, the implementation of the knowledge expounded in this publication, *Let's Cure Humanity,* could provide an innovative alternative for the frustrated physician and the disheartened patient.

Unfortunately, before the physician can practice preventive medicine, he must prove that nutritional therapy works to the satisfaction of the governing regulators who already have refused to examine the massive documentation available, most of which was provided by the world's best scientists, some of whom won Nobel Prizes for their efforts. In other words, the American Medical Association just refuses to listen to logic, preferring to tread the beaten path of escalating disease treated by unnatural and expensive man-made chemicals. The cost of this stance is massive human suffering, and the premature death of millions of Americans. The best remedy would be an amendment, such as the one below, to the American Constitution *enshrining medical freedom*; thereby allowing both doctors and patients the right to practice and to preach preventive medicine:

" Each and every American citizen has the right to choose and to practice the form of medicine that the citizen deems

most beneficial to personal health, without economic, physical, political, or verbal interference or abuse, and any institution or governmental agency assigned to protect the state of the individual's health should be empowered only to make recommendations that do not infringe or prevent the individual's right to choose and to practice any form of medicine."

However, amendments to the Constitution are very rare, and require years to succeed. The American public is desperate today, and cannot wait for this urgently needed change. Thus the best interim remedy would be for each state and the U.S. Congress to legislate an *Alternative Medicine Protection Act* to read as follows:

"A practitioner of traditional or alternative medicine, registered by an appropriate government authority, who engages in medical or nutritional therapy or in any relevant health procedure, including the recommendation or sale of health supplements, that departs from orthodox or conventional medical treatment, shall not be found to be unqualified, unprofessional, negligent nor guilty of assault upon a patient, nor be denied the right to pursue her or his professional practice or livelihood, solely on the basis that the therapy employed is an alternative remedy, or is non traditional or departs from prevailing orthodox medical treatment, unless it can be conclusively demonstrated that the therapy has a safety risk for a particular patient unreasonably greater than the traditional or prevailing treatment usually employed for the patient's ailment."

(Howard W. Pollock, Former Territorial Chairman of the Legislative Committee on Statehood for Alaska, and First Republican U.S. Congressman for Alaska.)

many of these cultures exist to this day. For example, it was well known, and documented, that the Eskimo culture never had degenerative diseases such as cancer and heart disease until the white man started feeding them. Also the Hopi Indians in Northern Arizona never got cancer, while cancer ravished all of the cultures surrounding them. However, it was decided that the scientific community would probably attribute the *gene factor* as the reason. Thus it was decided to look for larger and more distant cultures. An article in the January 1973 edition of **National Geographic** entitled *Search For The Oldest People* provided examples of many of these cultures including the Abkhasians from Georgia (high in the mountains), the Hunzas of Pakistan (high in the mountains), and the Vilcabambans of Ecuador (high in the mountains). This list was quickly expanded to include the Bamas in China (high in the mountains), the Azerbaijans (high in the mountains), the Armenians (high in the mountains), the Tibetans (high in the mountains), and the Titicacas of Peru (high in the mountains). To this list the Okinawans of Japan (sea level) were added.

With all of the above cultures, *disease virtually does not exist:* "almost" no cancer, no heart disease, no diabetes, no Alzheimer's, no arthritis, etc. For example,, the Okinawans have less that one fifth the heart disease that Americans do. These cultures have no mental disorders and no doctors. They also live much longer than we do in North America and their aging process is dramatically slower. For example the Okinawans live 8 years longer than mainland Japan who lives 4 years longer than Americans. And the elderly seem to have youthful bodies. The common denominator is that all of their water is loaded with mineral nutrients from melting glaciers high in the mountains, and from the disintegrating coral reefs in Okinawa. Japanese scientists have concluded that the good health and longevity of the Okinawans is due to their consumption of calcium rich coral water, and the Spanish Explorers filled their ship holds with coral calcium that they concluded was the source of the good health. One quart of Hunza water, in Pakistan, contains 17,000 milligrams of calcium (17 times the RDA at the time), and they drink several quarts each day. In general, the over-riding factor in their disease-free longevity is the fact that these cultures can consume almost *"one hundred times the RDA"* of everything, with the only side effect being great health and longevity. Also, they eat large amounts of everything we are told is not good for you such as butter, salt, eggs, milk and animal fat.

Another major factor is that these cancer-free people are in the sun, which we are told causes cancer, most of the day. Mr. Barefoot and Dr Carl Reich wrote the book, ***The Calcium Factor*** which detailed the scientific explanations for their remarkable health and youth. The book was published in 1992. Mr. Barefoot was immediately invited as a guest speaker at health shows and was a frequent guest on numerous radio and television talk shows. Ten years later, in 2002, he was to make two of the most watched infomercials in television history, making a dramatic impact on nutrition in America. The infomercials aired for over a year before the FTC took action, despite repeated request from Trudeau's lawyers as to whether the FTC had any objections. When the infomercials had run long enough to produce substantial earnings, the FTC moved. Apparently, protecting the American people from the message was not their goal, it was the money. Also, they only targeted the less offensive infomercial, but it was coincidentally the one that made the most money.

Acknowledgement

The author is grateful and wishes to acknowledge his appreciation for the dedication, contributions and efforts of Fay Harlin, Barney Woods, his best friend John Baker, and his wife Isabelle, Bruce and Carole Downey, and also his friend Steve Bailey who inspired the writing of this book and the title, Tim Matson for his support and inspiration, Ron Nagle, Brett Davies, Steven Sullivan, and Shawn Christopher for editing, and most of all, his cherished wife of 35 years, Karen Barefoot, in assisting the completion, critical review and editing of this publication.

Notation

Research being carried out on the significance of biological calcium, it is not the intention of the authors to provide an alternative to the orthodox physician-patient relationship. Rather, it is the objective of the authors to expand the dimensions of orthodox medicine itself, and help speed it towards medical practices of the twenty-first century where diet and lifestyle will play a predominant role in preventive medicine.

"If the doctors of today do not become the dieticians of tomorrow, the dieticians of today will become the doctors of tomorrow." Rockefeller Institute of Medical Research.

Disclaimer

This publication is intended to direct the attention of both physician and patient to scientific research being carried out on the significance of calcium supplements to health and to the concept that coral calcium from Okinawa is the best form of supplemental calcium in the opinion of Barefoot. It is for educational purposes. It is not intended to replace the orthodox physician-patient relationship. If you are sick, you are advised to consult a physician, and together, along with your newly gained knowledge form this book, work towards the resolution of your illness.

Postscript

Because so many people who are in suffering and pain have sought my help, I have become passionate about ending degenerative disease. I have seen the success of using God's nutrients and I know that the results can be explained in detail in scientific terms. Both God and Science are One. However, if we start to cure disease we should start with those most affected, the Black community in America. Because of my passion, many in the Black community have tried to get Oprah Winfrey to talk to me, but unfortunately, she has a wall of protection around her that decides for her what she should hear. If she would one day be able to listen, my message for her would be, "Let's cure humanity, starting with Black America first." I also would like to challenge each and every celebrity in America to look, listen and learn, and then to do what is right as America will eagerly follow you. Thus, you have the ability to end suffering and misery in America. All you have to do is to try God's nutrients after you read this book. You will discover the magic and when you tell your fellow Americans, they will gladly listen and follow your example. The result will be a disease-free America. You owe it to your country to try.

CHAPTER ONE

SCIENTIFIC AND MEDICAL TRENDS IN HISTORY

It is said that one of the most important reasons for learning history is because it repeats itself, and therefore to know history is to know the future. The reason for this phenomenon is that man is both a creature of habit and predictable emotions that preside over logic. Thus, we find that the trends in medical history both follow and parallel the trends in scientific history where many a genius has been destroyed by people of lesser talent defending the status quo. Therefore, before judging the medical innovator, it is necessary to put him in historical perspective so that our views are not clouded by the biased authoritarian establishment, whose track record, as you shall see, leaves a lot to be desired.

"*Innovation is a twofold threat to the scientific hierarchy. First, it threatens their oracle authority. Secondly, it evokes the deeper fear that their whole laboriously constructed authoritarian edifice may collapse.*" Arthur Koestler, **The Age of Velikovsky**.

The most famous doctor of all times was Dr. Hippocrates. He practiced medicine over 2500 years ago and is most famous for his literary works of establishing a code of ethics for the medical profession. Most Doctors take his Hippocratic oath. However most doctors have never realized what a great doctor he really was. Hippocrates lived in a time before drugs. This meant that he treated using natural nutrients. Hippocrates wrote that he treated his cancer patients by suggesting they expose themselves to a great deal of fresh air and sunshine, by making them eat lots of fruits and vegetables and by insisting they consume as much garlic and onions as possible. Hippocrates claimed great success with his cancer patients. In 1988 a team of American scientists visited a culture in China that had virtually no cancer and that consumed very large amounts of onions and garlic. After a one year study they concluded that both garlic and onions do indeed help to prevent cancer and they returned to America, not to tell people to eat garlic and onions, but rather to try to extract the active ingredients so that a drug could be made. Thus it appears that Hippocrates had a 20t^h century scientific claim for his theories. He was definitely a man ahead of his time and that was fortunate for him because if he were practicing medicine in the 20th century, the FTC and FDA would have him incarcerated for making unsubstantiated medical claims.

In 1808, Dalton, the father of modern chemistry, proposed the *"Atomic Theory,"* in which atoms were the basic components of all substances. The scientific establishment of the day threw scorn on his theory. More than sixty years later, in 1869, Professor Williamson, President of the Chemical Society, "humored" those who accepted the theory stating that *"for lack of any better theory, it would have to do for now."* Even after one hundred years had elapsed, prominent scientists of the day, such as the renowned Professor Ostwald, were publicly administering scathing condemnnations for Dalton's theories, while attempting to show that the theory of chemistry was independent of the theory of atoms. For other lesser known scientists of the day, such as Albert Einstein and Max Planck, the atomic theory was as correct and as natural as sunshine. In contrast, almost two hundred years later, almost every educated man in the world believes in Dalton's Atomic Theory, despite the fact that he was ridiculed and criticized by the experts of his day.

Albert Einstein, who was unquestionably the most famous scientist of the twentieth century, had to withstand more efforts by the establishment attempting to disprove his theory of relativity than has ever been made to disprove any other theory in the history of science. This was demonstrably shown by one of his opponent's publications entitled *One Hundred Against Einstein*, to which he remarked that *"if they were right, one would be enough."* Thus Einstein was also ridiculed and criticized by the experts of his day.

Max Planck, a father of modern physics and Nobel Prize winner in 1903, stated that *"An important scientific innovation rarely makes its way by gradually winning over and converting its opponents; it rarely happens that Saul becomes Paul. What does happen is that its opponents gradually die out and that the growing generation is familiarized with the idea from the beginning."* Max Planck was also ridiculed and criticized by the experts of his day.

And so, despite the uphill battle, road blocks, and mine fields maintained by the scientific hierarchy of the day in an attempt to defend their prestigious status quo, science managed to progress to the point where, by the 1950's, the scientific establishment arrogantly announced to the world that *"in this atomic age, all there is to know has already been learned and all future advancements would be simply rearrangements of current knowledge."* The old adage, *"the more we know, the less we know"* was certainly not believed by this incredibly arrogant group of scientists.

While all these impediments were being placed on progress in basic science, medical science was also experiencing similar resistance to progress. For example, in 1841 Ignas Semmelweis, a Hungarian physician who was horrified by the high death rate of women giving birth in hospitals, became obsessed with finding the cause of the disease. At that time mothers who had given birth at home or in carriages on their way to hospital had a far greater chance of surviving their childbirth than if they had been delivered in a hospital. Moreover, in that period it was common practice for doctors to go directly from the morgue, where they conducted post mortem examinations and anatomy classes using the bodies of deceased patients, into the maternity ward and attend maternity patients dressed in usual garb, without washing their hands. For these and other reasons, Dr. Semmelweis suspected that the doctors were carrying an agent on their hands that was causing the fatal disease. In 1847 Semmelweis instituted a procedure of scrubbing and dipping the hands in a chlorine solution before every procedure, the death rate fell from *thirty percent to practically zero*. The protective medical establishment of the day reacted by blocking Dr. Semmelweis's application for research funds and proceeded to vilify, ostracize, and finally have him discharged from his prestigious positions in maternity hospitals. Haunted by the fact that hundreds of thousands of women continued to die, Dr. Semmelweis eventually died of insanity in 1865.

By the 1880's, the advent of the microscope made the invisible microbe visible, and doctors began to universally adopt Semmelweis's procedures. Despite the eventual acceptance of the hand scrubbing technique in maternity wards, both Louis Pasteur and Joseph Lister encountered great difficulty in having the *germ theory of disease and antiseptic surgery* accepted because the leading physicians of the day adamantly refused to accept the theory.

A few years later, Theodore Boverie, the true father of genetic science, discovered almost every detail of cell division including chromosomes which, he concluded, transmit heredity. This idea was strenuously opposed by the protective establishment, led by Thomas Morgan. Years later, Morgan found that his own experiments agreed with Boverie's. Quietly disregarding his previous criticism of Boverie, Morgan went on to describe the chromosome structure in more detail adding specific positions called *"genes,"* for which he received the Nobel Prize in 1937.

While all this research was going on, a few brave scientists were attempting to correlate the existence of bioelectrical systems with biological functions. Traditional biologists were horrified, and were, for the most part, successful in removing the funding for such experimentation. The medical establishment was likewise so miffed by these proposals that it was determined to block the propagation of such nonsense. Even under this severe duress, electro-biochemistry was further researched and when the pioneers of "electro-encephalography," the recording of electrical brain impulses referred to as an *EEG*, employed the new procedure, they were called *"electronic quacks"* by the American Medical Association.

More recently, electro-physiologists such as Dr. Robert Becker, a research orthopedic surgeon, found, as others had before him, that he had to wage a constant battle against the *"frozen thinking of the establishment,"* who to this day continue to block the results and advancements in this field. One such example is the natural ability of children under puberty to regenerate chopped off fingers and toes when the skin is not sutured over the stump but is only dressed to allow the exposed tissue to remain electrically negative, a practice carried out in many hospitals outside North America. In fact most Western doctors refuse both to believe these results.

Likewise, acupuncture, a safe and natural procedure for pain suppression, is supposedly accepted by the medical profession, but practiced only in limited fashion. Instead, doctors continue to kill over 50,000 Americans each year with anesthetics, while acupuncture surgery without anesthetics could have saved them all. At the least, this is manslaughter, as is the use of the chemical blow torch known as chemotherapy, with a kill rate of 97%. By ignoring the fact that most biological functions are electrically controlled, the medical profession remains ignorant to the fact that the low frequency electromagnetic fields, generated by most of the electronic or electrical gadgetry of our day, will superimpose over these natural bioelectric fields, thereby altering their functions. The result is a host of potential medical problems. This type of *"electro pollution"* will become common knowledge to every child in the twenty-first century. However, back in the twentieth century, the doctors did not understand how a pulsed magnetic field from an electric appliance could possibly affect the health of his patients. Also, although it is difficult for a Western physician to understand how a needle inserted in the head can cure a pain in the stomach, as is done by the Eastern physician, he readily accepts that a pill in the stomach can cure a pain in the head. True logic will only prevail once the best of both worlds is permitted by the always intransigent medical cartels.

How does the intelligent, highly educated well-trained physician of today find himself in the same "head-in-the-sand" ostrich position that was adopted by his medical regulators? The answer is simple. His profession, like that of the scientist, is one of the most extremely regulated professions in the world. In addition, his time is largely consumed in attending to his patients and, as he is sensitive to the opinions of his peers, he succumbs to total control by his regulators, on whom he has become basically dependent for survival in this calling. There can be no doubt that each practitioner is quite eager to apply any new technology that is endorsed by his medical superiors in teaching and research institutions. There can also be little doubt these elite few have a vested interest in maintaining the status quo of ignorance. Their actions moreover are whole heartedly endorsed by the powerful drug, military, and electrical utility establishments, all of whom have a vested interest in maintaining economic control. Thus, just as scientific advancement is suppressed by the scientific hierarchy of the day, so too, the advancement of medical science is suppressed by the medical hierarchy. History teaches us that this system has been in effect for hundreds of years, with the individual scientist or doctor participating as an innocent and ignorant victim of the system.

Unfortunately, the general public of the day has also been purposely kept uninformed, and thinks of the medical profession in *"God-like"* terms. After all, each generation is impressed by the spectacular advances in medicine that are applied to challenging very limited selected areas of medicine, while the majority of the public remain silent victims of the untreatable diseases that affect the masses.

Thus, the trends of history are the same as human nature, never changing. *"Great spirits have always encountered violent opposition from mediocre minds"* (Albert Einstein), and *"Resistance to innovation is clearly demonstrated, not by the ignorant masses, but by professionals with a vested interest in tradition and the monopoly of learning"* (Arthur Koestler, **The Age of Velikovsky**). The frustrated innovators, working not in establishment orientated institutions, but at the grass roots of science and medicine which is the logical source of practical innovation, unfortunately, must all follow the same path. And so it was for Dr. Carl Reich, who, after a lifetime of discovery, innovation, and medical practice during which he satisfied thousands of grateful patients, found himself suspended by the medical authorities. His *"crime,"* after thirty-four years of practice with most of his patients loving him was the pursuit of the practice of *Preventive Medicine*, which included revolutionary, therapeutic advances employing *The Calcium Factor*. Dr. Reich was also chastised by the medical authorities for his claim that *"calcium can cure cancer,"* as well as several other degenerative diseases. A claim which they believed was too simplistic to have any medical credibility, and a claim which two decades later would be triumphantly published and endorsed in medical establishment's own journals (See Chapter Twelve).

CHAPTER TWO

BOB BAREFOOT AND THE CALCIUM FACTOR

The year was 1982, and Dr. Carl Reich, was pounding on my front door. I've got to talk to you!" he shouted as he pushed passed me and threw a heavy bag on my living room table. Unzipping his bag he continued, "But first you have to read this." He proceeded to make two stacks of paper on the table, one was 8 inches high and the other was about 1/8 inch high.

Now I had recognized Dr. Reich from pictures I had seen in the newspapers, but I had never met him. He had been reported by the medical establishment as a medical maverick who preferred to treat his patients with nutrition and frowned on the use of drugs. His patients, however, loved him. Other doctors were being warned at the time that if they followed in his footsteps they would lose their medical licenses. Reich, on the other hand, was the medical pioneer, who thirty years earlier had begun to give his patients large dosages of vitamins and minerals. Being the first doctor to do so, which later earned him the title, "Father of Preventive Medicine," the medical establishment did not know what to do so they resorted to the age old practice of name calling. Hence, Dr. Reich became the first medical maverick.

Dr. Reich stood at my table loudly proclaiming that this was a medical emergency and that "you absolutely must read this immediately!" I looked at the large stack and gasped,

"But I am not a doctor!" Reich snapped back, "But you are a chemist, and I need a chemist desperately! Besides," he said, "I only need you to read the small stack."

I could see that the small stack was made up of official autopsies. I protested again, "But I know nothing about autopsies." Reich snorted back, "You can read, can't you?" "Besides," he said, "I only need you to read the last couple of paragraphs." I picked up the stack of paper and counted five autopsies. I began to read the last paragraphs. "Died in her sleep, died of unknown causes, died peacefully, died without pain and died with a smile on her face." Reich interjected, "Well, what do you think?" I responded that, "it appears that five healthy people died." He yelled back, "EXACTLY!" "Now I need you to examine the large stack. You will find that it contains their medical records. You will find that all of these women were diagnosed with terminal cancer and were given only weeks to live. You will find, when you examine the dates of their autopsies, that these women lived over twenty years." I could see that the medical records were from the University of Toronto, Berkley, UCLA and the Mayo Clinic. Reich was right! All of these women with terminal cancer who were given only weeks to live had survived for over twenty years, and their autopsies showed no sign of cancer. I said, "Wow, all of these women had beaten cancer!" Reich smiled and said, "I've got more autopsies back at the office if you need more proof." I asked, "How many people have you seen beat cancer?" In a subdued voice he responded, "Hundreds." I blurted, "What did you do?" He responded, "I put them on a program of nutrition and changed their lifestyle."

I thought to myself that it was 1982 and here was a man that knew how to cure cancer. I asked him what he wanted from me. He responded that many people had told him that I was a chemical maverick and that we had a great deal in common. He said that although he knew how to cure cancer and a host of other diseases, he did not have the technical explanation as to why it worked. All he knew was that it was *The Calcium Factor*. He explained that for years he had given his patients large dosages of calcium and vitamins and their disease disappeared. He tried to publish his results but the medical authorities said that his approach was too simple and that he would demean the medical profession. He said however, that in 1962, he was allowed to present his paper at the Max Plank Institute in Berlin, Germany, where he met Dr. Otto Warburg, a two time Nobel Prize winner. Warburg explained to Reich that "when you have a fire, you dowse it with water, and when you have acid, you dowse it with calcium" He explained that when most people get old their bodies build up with acid due to the lack of ingesting and digesting minerals like calcium. He explained that this acid drives oxygen out of the body and that he won the Nobel Prize for proving that this lack of oxygen was the major cause of cancer.

Reich was in love, and he refused to leave until Warburg agreed to collaborate to write the book *The Calcium Factor*. Although Warburg agreed, their efforts took several years and Warburg died before the task was done. Reich said that he searched the world looking for a replacement, but that he could not find a chemist with vision. He said, "at least that was until now. Bob you are the man and you know that you have to help me." I was stunned. I took his hand and announced, "Ok, but on one condition. We are not going to write a scientific paper. We are going to write a book that the average person can read and understand. You have already made it simple, and that's the way we must keep it. If calcium consumption can help to prevent cancer, then there must be people in the world that consume large amounts of calcium and do not have cancer. All we have to do is find them."

It was not easy. We toiled for ten years and finally, in 1992 we published the book, *The Calcium Factor*. We indeed had found cultures around the world that were virtually free of cancer. This did not mean that cancer did not exist, but rather that it existed as a fraction of what Americans are used to. The other prominent factor about these people was the fact that they lived much longer than Americans and that the elderly had much more vibrant bodies.

The *common denominator* of these many cultures with longevity and good health is that their soils are being *constantly replenished* with the mineral nutrients, most of which are missing in our soils. Except for some of the Japanese on Okinawa, all these societies all live in mountainous regions. They are the Tibetans, the Hunzas of Northern Pakistan, the Armenian, the Georgians, the Azerbaijans, the Vilcabamba Indians in Ecuador, the Titicacas in Peru, and a few other cultures. They all have their soils replenished with mineral nutrients contained in *the turbid water from melting glaciers*. The contained glacial-crushed minerals are so abundant that the water is white and is known as *"milk of the mountains."* The islands of Okinawa were built up over the years from coral reefs. Rain erodes the coral reefs producing mineral rich *"milk of the oceans."* All of these cultures also drink their water turbid. The contained dissolved minerals are so abundant that when they drink their customary four quarts each day, *"all"* of these disease-free societies violate our doctor recommended daily allowances, RDAs, by massive amounts.

For example, the Hunza glacial water contains 18,000 milligrams of calcium per quart, and they drink several quarts daily. This means that they consume about *70 times* the RDA of calcium. They also consume about *22 times* the RDA of magnesium, *18 times* the RDA of potassium, *126 times* the RDA of iron, *120 times* the RDA of fluoride, and so on. And, to top it off, they continue to exceed these RDAs even further by eating foods which are rich in these minerals. Also they consume *"RDA unacceptable"* amounts of trace metals in their water while maintaining a supposedly harmful diet rich in eggs, fat, milk, butter and salt. Therefore, the only side effect of consuming huge amounts of minerals, and eating what your doctor says is bad for you, is good health and longevity.

The Hunza drink their 30 daily cups of tea, each with a large hunk of rock salt and two patties of butter. Our American *disease-doctors*, who die prematurely, ignorantly recommend that you *do not* follow the dietary example of the *youthful, energetic, and disease-free 135 year old Hunzas*. Nutrient trained veterinarians, on the other hand, have long recognized the importance of mineral, metal and vitamin supplements, and as a result, animal foods are full of these supplements. For example, horse food and dog food can contain as much as *60 nutrient supplements*. Meanwhile, human food remains almost totally depleted in these life sustaining nutrients. As long as the animals are fed only animal foods and not people food, they remain relatively disease-free.

Archeologists studying the cultures of the past 700,000 years have discovered that those who lived as hunting cultures had strong bones and were slim and relatively disease-free, while those from agricultural cultures (starting 10,000 years ago) had weak bones, cavities, and were disease prone. Diet was therefore the key factor. Agricultural cultures began consuming large amounts of carbohydrates which are readily converted to glucose. The pancreas must produce large quantities of insulin to convert the glucose into collagen and fat. The high insulin also causes the body to produce cholesterol necessary to construct new cells to store the fat. The result is high blood pressure, high cholesterol, acidosis from the sugar and fat storage. The hunting cultures are eating a high protein, low carbohydrate diet, resulting in a low glucose. This causes the pancreas to produce glucagon, which removes the fat from the cells to produce fuel for the body. The protein/carbohydrate (*procarb*) ratio of the disease free hunting cultures of the past was 1 to 1 (about 50% protein with 50% carbohydrates). In agricultural America today the procarb ratio is about 1 to 4 (about 15% protein with 60% carbohydrates). Noteworthy, the U.S.D.A recommends the 1 to 4 procarb ratio, which is the same diet used to *"fatten"* pigs. If the average overweight person would increase (for only 4 weeks) his protein and fat intake to 200 grams per day while lowering his carbohydrates to 40 grams per day (a procarb ratio of 5 to 1), the pounds would drop off, muscle tone (shape) would improve, the insulin level would drop dramatically, the glucagon level would increase dramatically, blood pressure would drop, the cholesterol level would also drop dramatically, and toxins would be purged from the body. Every 4 weeks the carbohydrates can be increased by 40 grams until a noticeable gain in weight occurs. At this point reduce the carbohydrates by 40 grams per day and you will have determined your ideal procarb ratio (about 1 to 2). Biologically, 10,000 generations are required to adjust to a major change in diet, but the human body has only had 500 generations to adjust from a natural procarb ratio of 1 to 1 to a procarb ratio 1 to 4. The human body is therefore not currently designed for this 1 to 4 procarb diet, resulting in over-worked organs (pancreas, liver and kidneys) and the inevitable diseases, such as diabetes and hypertension. What all of this means is that Dr. Atkins was absolutely correct with his high protein diet.

So, it appears that a procarb diet ratio of 1 to 2 combined with high calcium intake is the answer. The question then becomes, is the consumption of liquid ionized calcium a good for you ? The answer is *"yes,"* but only if you get about two hours of sunshine a day. This will result in the parathyroid gland producing lots of the hormone calcitonin which will keep the serum (blood) calcium level normal, around the 100 ppm level, while inositol triphosphate, INSP-3, which serves to regulate the extraction of calcium stored in the cells, is photo-synthetically produced by the skin. The cultures who never get sick and consume 100,000 milligrams of calcium each day, practically live in the sun, and therefore produce adequate calcitonin and INSP-3, thereby maintaining a 100ppm calcium serum level in their blood, while regulating the proper amount of calcium to be stored in the cells. However, most of us do not get this amount of sun exposure, and as a result, the consumption of liquid ionized calcium can result in *"hypercalcemia"* where the serum calcium can reach as high as 200 ppm. In the book "Warning! Calcium Deficiency," Kawamura and Taniuchi reported that a 30 year study with 20,000 case histories of over 40 over the counter calcium products, found that those taking liquid ionized calcium were suffering from acute hypercalcemia as evidenced by such symptoms as muscle weakness, polyuria, dehydration, thirst, anorexia, vomiting and constipation, followed by stupor, coma, and azotemia in severe cases. Due to the rapid increase of calcium in the blood, the kidneys will attempt to reduce the excess calcium by excreting it in the urine. This abrupt lowering of calcium may result in *"hypocalcemia"* causing muscle cramps, tetany, convulsions, respiratory distress, diplopia, abdominal cramps and serious metabolic disorders. How-ever, the authors discovered that *over 30 years of study, none of the hyper/hypo-calcemic symptoms occurred with those in the 20,000 who ingested coral calcium or other marine calcium products.*

Also worthy of note is a product that has been consumed by the Japanese for hundreds of years with a huge number of health benefit claims; it is known as *"coral calcium,"* and is currently being consumed by increasingly large numbers of people, millions in the Western World. Coral calcium, the disintegration by-product of old coral reefs, is mined from deep troughs found a few miles from the coral reefs of Okinawa, Japan. A significant amount of calcium, magnesium and other trace metals are downstream from the coral reefs in Okinawa.

A significant amount of calcium, magnesium and other trace metals are dissolved by water alone. What this means is that the minerals are already ionized before entering your acid rich stomach. This is especially beneficial to *the elderly* who over time, *produce less acid*. This, combined with the fact that the form of calcium carbonate in the coral is the mineral aragonite with over a thousand times the surface area of other carbonates, results in the minerals being *ionized longer* and being more bioavailable for absorption. This leads to greater overall mineral absorption by the body when the nutrient is coral calcium, Mother Nature's ***milk of the ocean.***

One should remember that consuming calcium as a supplement is like consuming dairy products: the magnesium is like consuming vegetables (magnesium in the chlorophyll is what makes plants green), and the vitamins A&D like fruits, vegetables and liquid sunshine. Also, *the vitamin-D dramatically improves the absorption of the nutrients by the small intestine.* Science has shown that, in the amounts recommended, these supplements cannot hurt you, but they can make all the difference to your health. Thus, Grandma was right when she said *"the secret of good health is milk, fruits, vegetables and sunshine."* But, unfortunately, Grandma was only half right, as when God made the Earth and all its inhabitants, he used *all of the basic elements*, and most these basic elements are *sadly missing from our mineral depleted soils* and thereby our food chain. The first humans had all of these elements in their bodies. The water that they drank and the fruits and vegetables which they ate also contained all of these elements.

The Biblical Patriarchs lived to an astounding old age: Adam lived for *930 years,* Methuselah for *969 years* and Noah for *950 years.* After the great flood covered their lands with nutrient depleted sand and clay, the Biblical Patriarchs did not live as long: Eber lived to *464,* while Issac only lived to *180* and Jacob to *147.* Today, except in rare areas of the Earth where degenerative disease does not exist and the average expectancy can be as high as 135 years, the soils are rich in mineral nutrients from the nutrient rich glacial waters. In other parts of the world, America for example, the soils, and therefore, the foods grown in them, are depleted of most of these minerals and the life expectancy is out in half. For example, the American doctor only lives for an average of *58 years,* according to Dr. Wallach, while the average American lives almost two decades longer for an average of *75 years.* The Japanese live to 79 years while the Okinawans (according to scientific study) because of their calcium rich coral water, live to an average of 87. This is about 12 years more than the average American and therefore this factor is extremely significant and it is up to the FDA to explain it to the American people.

Barefoot's explanation is "the calcium factor." He hopes that one day soon the *"calcium factor"* will be considered by the FDA as one of the most predominant factors of human health and longevity.

CHAPTER THREE
CALCIUM AND DISEASE

The human body is made up of all the most common elements in the world, with the exception of silicon and aluminum. Although all these elements are required to sustain life as we know it, in the final analysis, the presence of no one element can be said to be more important than any other element. However, what can be said is that some elements are more abundantly intertwined in the vast array of bodily functions than others. Therefore the abundance of these elements is crucial to the maintenance of good health and to life itself. Through its natural evolution over many millennia the body developed a survival defense mechanism which compensates for any changes in the concentrations of these elements. Excess elements are readily expelled from the body. Deficiencies, on the other hand, can only be partially overcome by the induction of biochemical reactions through the adaptive functions of organs in an attempt to best balance this loss. The result is *a physically weakened body that is prone to disease of these adapting organs*.

One of the most important of these integral elements is the element *calcium*. It can be found molecularly bound in the bones in abundance, and in almost all human cells. When freed from its molecular bonding by ionization, it can then readily combine with proteins. The inclusion of such calcium bound protein in the ion channel on every cell wall constitutes biological valving that regulates both cell nutrition and the important bioelectrical cellular discharging processes involved in all bodily functions. Vitamin D, produced in the skin by a chemical reaction induced by the ultraviolet radiation of sunlight (photosynthesis), has as its main function, the ionization of ingested calcium by the small intestine. Although the inside walls of the small intestines are very negatively charged, the positively charged ionic minerals have a hard time being absorbed *"through"* the intestine walls.

Fortunately the walls of the small intestine contain vitamin D receptors or VDR's, which allow the long chain vitamin D to *penetrate deeply* into the intestine wall and leave its negatively charged oxygen end exposed at the surface. This allows the positively charged calcium ion, and other positively charged ions, to latch on to the negatively charged oxygen on the end of the vitamin D and be drawn into and through the intestine wall. It is estimated that filling the VDR receptors with vitamin D allows the body to absorb up to 20 times more of the difficult to absorb calcium. Thus *photosynthetically produced vitamin D* (lots of sunshine) and/or vitamin D supplements are crucial to the absorption of nutrients. At the same time, photosynthesis also results in the production of *inositol triphosphate, INSP-3*, which serves to regulate the extraction of calcium stored in the cells. This process is triggered to supply the cell with calcium when insufficient calcium is ingested and ionized by the vitamin D process. If there is insufficient calcium stored within the cells, then the parathyroid hormone, stimulated by the deficiency of Vitamin D, induces the *extraction of calcium from the bones*. Finally, with bones severely weakened by this calcium depletion, the body begins to extract its ionic calcium from the proteins that are regulating cell functions. The resulting cell dysfunctions manifest themselves with a whole host of symptoms and diseases identified correctly by Dr. Reich as the *"ionic calcium deficiency syndrome and diseases,"* but most doctors know them only as chronic disease of unknown or obscure origin.

Sufficient ingested and ionized calcium can therefore not only prevent many diseases, but due to its involvement in cell nutrition, it can also maintain vigorous good health. Calcium's involvement in cell nutrition is three-fold. First, as mentioned, calcium bound proteins regulate both the size and the opening and closing of the ion channels of every cell wall. Secondly, the calcium ion, substantially more than any other ion, has the capability of attaching itself to a large number of nutrient radicals, which are molecularly stacked on the outer surface of the cell membrane. When these *"stacks"* become electrically detached (detailed discussion of this process in *The Calcium Factor*, Chapter Five) the calcium ion is capable of transporting them through the cell ion channel thereby delivering the greatest amount of nutrients for the healthy function of the cell. Third, calcium combines with the phosphates in the extra-cellular and intracellular fluids to create a slightly alkaline, buffered and oxygen rich medium necessary to sustain life. *Only the element calcium* is capable of creating and maintaining these critical conditions.

With such a vital role to play in human health and with all the current massive amount of research being carried out by the scientific community one would think that the medical profession would eagerly grasp the importance of *"the calcium factor."* However, as history has taught us, the medical profession has not been quick to respond to simple concepts, such as washing their hands, so the concept of the true importance of milk and sunshine supplements to good health should be equally as difficult for them to accept. In addition, history has also shown us that it takes the medical profession several decades to accept new and proven scientific advances.

Today, mankind is in dire need for the medical profession to study and apply the knowledge contained in the horde of readily available scientific publications so that they will be better able to understand the effects of the calcium factor on human health, and to begin participating in this advancement in medical science. It is time for the men of medicine to take a time journey from the twentieth century's mode of treating disease with drugs to the twenty-first century's mode of *preventing disease through nutrition.*

Calcium is obviously an essential nutrient in our daily diet and a key factor in a wide range of biological systems within the body. Its role in disease prevention and treatment has been studied, and continues to be studied, by numerous scientists around the world. A search on the US National Library of Medicine's PubMed system reveals more than 17,000 scientific articles on calcium and its relationship to cancer. In particular, clinical trials have examined the link between calcium consumption and its positive effects on colorectal cancer. While the study of calcium continues, its importance is becoming widely recognized even among the more conservative members of the scientific and medical Communities. The 2001 "Physicians Desk Reference for Nutritional Supplements' " chapter on calcium states that calcium has anti-osteroporotic activity and may also have anti-carcinogenic, antihypertensive and hypocholesterolemic activity. Our literature is full of references on the relationship of disease to calcium.

For example:

"The Prime Cause and Prevention of Cancer," Otto Warburg, lecturer at the meeting of Nobel Laureates, June 30, **1966.** Director, Max Planck Institute for Cell Physiology, Berlin, said *"There is no disease whose prime cause is better known, so that today ignorance is no longer an excuse that one cannot do more about prevention of cancer. But how long prevention will be avoided depends on how long the prophets of agnosticism will succeed in inhibiting the application*

of scientific knowledge in the field of cancer. In the meantime, millions of men and women must die of cancer unnecessarily. " (Note: in 1966 cancer struck 23% of Americans, whereas today it strikes 39% of Americans.)

"*How a Mineral Can Vitalize Your Health*," by Dr. James K. Van Fleet, in the book **Magic of Catalytic Health Vitalizers, 1980,** Parker Publishing.

"*According to nutritional authorities, the American diet is more lacking in calcium than in any other essential food. Dr. Henry C. Sherman, the noted biochemist, has stated in effect that **the prime period of human life could be extended by a moderate increase in calcium** in the diet. It would also be wise to get at least 400 units of vitamin-D daily to insure proper absorption of the calcium from the tract into the body where it can be utilized.* "

"**When the body does not get enough calcium, it will withdraw what little calcium it has from the bones to make sure there is enough in the bloodstream**, then the body does its best to bolster the sagging architecture by building bony deposits and spurs to reduce movement and limit activity*

"*Calcium in Synaptic Transmission*," by Rodolfo R., **Scientific American**, October **1982.**

"*The connection between the electrical activity of the cell and the release of the neurotransmitter is not direct; **an essential intermediary is the calcium ion.** *"

By 1985, Carafoli and Penniston had further studied the importance of the calcium ion in controlling biochemical processes. They found that a "***common trigger***" precipitates biological events as diverse as the contraction of a muscle and the secretion of a hormone; the trigger is *"a minute flux of calcium."* They described the array of proteins that are specialized to bind calcium creating the molecules that serve to regulate the concentration of calcium ions within the cell as well as mediating its effects. They also found that these calcium bound proteins were essential to the role of ionic calcium as an intracellular messenger. Some of the calcium bound proteins control calcium concentration in the cell, thereby producing electrical signals, while others serve to receive the signals.

"The Role of Calcium in Biological Systems," Volume I, **1985**, CRC Press Inc:

As a prelude to the quotations in this book, the following comments, are made to help the reader better understand the quotations: "**The Role of Calcium in Biological Systems**" is a compilation of dozens of scientific publications by academically recognized scientists. This book deserves particular note because world class scientists are *concluding* that there is a link between calcium deficiency and cancer. Also, the hundreds of scientific references contained in this book, as well as the other books quoted, could lead the reader to thousands of scientific publications on the importance of biochemical calcium. Although the first quote is self-explanatory, the second quote may be difficult for the reader to understand. Basically, it says that calcium deficiency in the body fluids outside and inside of the cell *stimulates the proliferation* of both virus and cell mutation (**cancer**) by regulating DNA synthesis. Furthermore, it concludes that calcium deficiency is the universal property of *all* cancer cells, the knowledge of which may be *the key to understanding cancer* The biochemical mechanisms that trigger and stimulate cancer will be explained in detail in Chapter Eight, *Calcium and Cancer*).

"Calcium must certainly be the major bio-element of the times. Only a generation ago the calcium ion was known to physiologists and biochemists as a component of bone mineral and as a blood plasma constituent required in heart function and blood coagulation, but little more. But, in the 1970's a crescendo of calcium ion research developed. Today we know dozens if not hundreds of different cellular and extra-cellular processes that are regulated by the changes in cytosolic or extra-cellular calcium ions. Indeed, the calcium ion is emerging as a most important and ubiquitous intracellular messenger," Forward, Albert Lehniger, Professor of Medical Science, John Hopkins University.

*"As we have seen, **calcium is central** to the ordered progression of replicating cells through their growth-division cycle. Neoplastic epithelia and mesenchymally derived cells can initiate DNA syntheses and proliferate normally in a low calcium medium, which does not support the proliferation of their normal counterparts. Besides needing calcium ions, normal cells must adequately spread out on a solid substrate before they are able to initiate DNA syntheses Calcium is **specifically required** for spreading. Lowering the extra-cellular calcium and preventing spreading both block the initiation of DNA synthesis, without stopping on-going DNA synthesis. The elimination of extra- cellular calcium requirement for proliferation of viruses can be mimicked by exposing proliferatively inactive calcium-deprived normal cells to calcium-independent-nucleotide protein kinases located in the plasma membrane. Thus, addition of such subunits to the medium of normal cells cause them to behave like neoplastic cells by initiating DNA syntheses in calcium deficient medium. It is clear that the proliferative calcium independence*

*in vitro is an universal property of neoplastic cells, the understanding of which may be **the key to understanding cancer**.*" (page 158, Volume #1)

By 1986, Moolenaar, Defize and Delaat had found that a sustained increase in cytoplasmic pH and a transient rise in the free calcium ions in the cytoplasmic cellular fluid was a necessary function of DNA synthesis and cell division, stating that "***the rise in calcium ions is indispensable for cell proliferation***."

Calcium in the Action of Growth Factors," by W.H. Moolenaar, L.K. Defize, and S.W. Delaat, **1986 Calcium and the Cell**, 1986, Wiley:

"*Proliferation of cells in vivo is regulated by polypeptide growth factors. Binding of growth factors to their specific cell-surface receptors initiates a cascade of biochemical events in the cell which ultimately leads to **deoxyribonucleic acid (DNA) synthesis and cell division**. The immediate consequence of receptor activation include a sustained increase in cytoplasmic pH and a transient rise in cytoplasmic free calcium ions. The platelet derived growth factor induced calcium ion signal is due to calcium ion release from intracellular stores, whereas the epidermal growth factor seems to activate a voltage independent calcium channel in the plasma membrane. These results suggest that the rise in calcium ions is **indispensable for cell proliferation.***

By **1988**, Marvin P. Thompson, in summarizing the work done to that date stated that "***calcium is a major regulatory ion in all living organisms, interest in calcium is in the logarithmic phase, and calcium related disorders are enormous***."

"The Calcium Connection," Dr. Cedric Garland and Dr. Frank Garland, **1989**, Foreside, Simon and Shuster Inc:

*"**Low cancer areas were far more frequent in the sun belt.** (This statement is contrary to the incorrect popular belief that sunshine causes cancer.) What was the significance of sunlight with regard to cancer rates? Sunlight reacts with cholesterol inside and on the surface of the skin to create vitamin D. Vitamin D helps the body absorb calcium and plays a major role in the body's ability to use the calcium that is available."*

"Treatment of Vertebral Osteoporosis," by Dr. Meunier in the book **Molecular and Cellular Regulation of Calcium and Phosphate Metabolism**, **1990** Alan R. Liss Inc:

*"When calcium and vitamin D are given in daily doses along with moderate amounts of sodium fluoride to patients with osteoporosis, there is a substantial increase in bone mass and a **significant reduction** in the incidence of further vertebral fractures."*

Intracellular Calcium Regulation," Felix Bronner, **1990**, Wiley:

*"One of the astonishing developments in biological research is **the recent widespread interest** in the role played by calcium in cellular metabolism."*

"Intracellular calcium regulation will be of interest to researchers and graduate students in the areas of biochemistry, biophysics, cell rheology and nutrition."

"Calcium Takes Its Place As a Superstar of Nutrients" Jane Brody, October 13, **1998**, New York Times:

"Calcium is fast emerging as the nutrient of the decade, a substance with such diverse roles in the body that

virtually no major organ system escapes its influence. A research team at the University of Southern California in Los Angeles reported in The American Journal of Clinical Nutrition that adding calcium to the diet lowered blood pressure. Dr. Susan Thy-Jacobs, a gynecologist at St. Lukes Roosevelt Hospital Center in New York believes that "a chronic deficiency or imbalance of calcium is largely responsible for the disruptive symptoms of PMS suffered by women." Dr. Martin Lipkin of the Strang Cancer Research Laboratory at Rockefeller University in New York said that "Animal research indicated that increasing calcium levels to protect epithelial cells from cancer might also help **prevent cancer** *in such organs as the breast, prostrate and pancreas."*

"Calcium's Powerful, Mysterious Ways," Jennifer Couzin, May 3, **1999**, U.S. News & World Report:

"Researchers are increasingly finding that the humble mineral, calcium, plays a **major role** *in warding off major illnesses from high blood pressure to colon cancer. You name the disease and it's beginning to have a place there,"* says David McCarron, a nephrologist at the University of Oregon Health Sciences University in Portland. *"In the past year, calcium has also been reported* **to reduce premenstrual symptoms, and it may protect against heart disease.**"

Since there are thousands of scientific publications on biological calcium, thousands of more quotes could be given supporting the crucial role of calcium in human health. However, in just the few that were given, statements by the most prestigious scientists in America have explained *how calcium is* **responsible for cell division and cell growth**, *and how calcium deficiency is* **the key to cancer** *and other degenerative diseases.*

In all of these statements made by these scientific and medical researchers, there is one common denominator, that is that they are all **adamantly convinced** about the importance of cellular calcium or the **Calcium Factor** in the state of human health. While thousands of scientific publications have been written in support of their convictions, thousands more are being prepared for the press. The research has gone from its first historic stage where the initial theorists were both inhibited and scorned by the scientific hierarchy, to the second stage where it now is not only academically acceptable to pursue this work, but a few others in the medical profession are beginning to experiment. The third state or research will occur when the medical hierarchy begins to enthusiastically support this research. And finally the fourth state will begin when the medical profession at large enthusiastically begin to apply the **Calcium Factor** in their daily treatment. The problem with this slow pace is that mankind has to suffer the painful and needless wait.

As two-time Nobel Prize in Medicine winner, Otto Warburg stated, *"As long as the agnostics succeed in inhibiting the application of scientific knowledge in the field of cancer, millions of men and women must die of cancer unnecessarily."* (1966) While the orthodox doctor both cures and kills with the painful procedures of the twentieth century, other brave nutritional pioneers have cured with the painless procedures of the twenty-first century, as **no patient was ever killed** by implementing a healthy change in lifestyle, including diet supported by moderate dietary supplements and vitamins.

Hippocrates who lived from 460 to 377 BC, was known as the "*father of medicine*." Orthodox doctors who take the **Hippocratic Oath** and who depend on man-made, and therefore unnatural, chemical medicines should note that

Hippocrates believed that "the body has a tendency to "*naturally heal itself*" and that "*food is the best medicine and the best foods are the best medicines*."

CHAPTER FOUR

LAUNCHING NUTRITION

When statements are made that are obviously very controversial, some means of measurement must be found in order to gauge the merits of the arguments. Since the importance of calcium as the *"king of the bioelements"* is a scientific argument, then statements by respected men of science, by their sheer numbers and emphatic conclusions, should convince any unbiased third party. Unfortunately, those involved in judging the argument are prejudiced by a vested interest in maintaining the status quo, and that is why the famous Max Planck said that the next generation will be allowed to accept the new concepts as soon as the older establishment *"gradually dies out."*

Although the quotes from some of the research being done on the calcium factor can provide some insight into these scientific advancements, they provide little or no information as to how these advances apply to your personal health. The information is *locked within the technical jargon* in the masses of available literature. However, there would be no doubt in your mind, once you began to review some of the massive research being done, about the significance that so many prominent scientists place on the importance of calcium in the human body. What is required before this technically garbled information can be put to use is for someone to present a total overview of the research in a more simple and understandable way. This would require a summary of the research by the scientific community that is followed up by integration with medical observations, and then, finally, recommendations to employ this knowledge about *the calcium factor* to maintain good health.

In 1992 the book *The Calcium Factor* was published and Bob Barefoot became instantly in demand as a speaker at health conventions and as a host on talk radio and television. His goal was to put the understanding of nutrition's role in disease into terms that the average person could understand. It worked as Barefoot was always asked for a return visit. On every talk show, the telephones rang off of their hooks as people appeared to be desperate for answers. People in America were suffering and dying horrific deaths. Conventional medicine was not addressing the problems that had been around for the past century.

For example, cancer only struck 3% of the population at the turn of the 20t[h] Century. Cancer was named by the ancients, after the great veins that usually surround the malignant growth, who compared them to the *"claws of a crab"* or *"cancer"* (Latin). Its origin was unknown and it was generally treated unsuccessfully with special potions, and on occasion, with local surgery. By the turn of the twentieth century, orthodox medicine believed that cancer was *caused by* a variety of factors such as *"irritating substances, external injuries, the abuse of stimulating potions, immoderate indulgence in venery (**sexual intercourse**), the depressing influence of moral afflictions, bad food combined with the debilitating effects of cold and otherwise unhealthy habitations, and the injurious influence of one or more of these causes on particular organs."* Also, *"the frequent occurrence of cancer in individuals for whom none of these predisposing causes seem to have cooperated in the production of the disease has led many pathologists to believe it as having an hereditary origin, the germ of the disease, or cancerous virus being transmitted from the parent to his offspring."* Remedies at this time included local bleeding (which could reduce the tumor to 1/4 of its original size) by means of leeches, local compression, application of mercury or various preparations of iodine, and the removal of new growths by knife or by *their destruction by caustic applications*. At this time in history, the use of caustics was proven to have provided a *"permanent cure"* in many cases. (**Health and Longetivity**, Joeseph G. Richardsom, M.D., University of Pennsylvania. 1909, page #378.) Also noteworthy was the use of caustics with potassium iodide to successfully treat rheumatism. Thus, at the turn of the 20th Century, doctors with surgical procedures *"cured cancer."*

By the 1950's, with cancer striking one out of every four people in North America, *the alkali treatments had long since been forgotten* and radiation was beginning to be used to kill the cancer and, unfortunately, the surrounding healthy tissue. Doctors were no longer curing cancer and most patients died. Chemotherapy was also used to kill the cancer and, unfortunately the surrounding tissue. Most patients died. By the 1980's, and with the incidence of cancer increasing, striking one out of every three people (see Table #1 US Cancer Deaths), chemical therapies (chemotherapies) were being perfected with the death rate rising. An extrapolation of the table show that by the year 2020, cancer should strike 50% of the population, and if the pattern continues, by the end of the century cancer will strike 100% of the population. Today, the *orthodox traditions and treatments*, which are firmly entrenched, are obviously *loosing the war against cancer,* even though they win some minor battles. In order to change the course of history, and save mankind, we must take medicine in another direction. The only hope, as expressed by our best scientists in thousands of scientific publications, is nutritional therapy. Also we would be wise to adopt the successful therapies of the past including Dr. Hippocrates nutritional cures for cancer.

Table #1 U.S. Cancer Deaths
(Source: The American Cancer Society)

Year	Deaths
1970	320,000
1975	365,000
1978	405,000
1985	482,000
1990	514,000

At present, although thousands of publications and books have been written extolling the importance of *the calcium factor* in the human body, few dare to recommend the practice of clinically employing nutritional therapy. Although the importance of cellular pH and calcium deficiency has been scientifically proven, medically, the jury is out! The jury is composed of the *old guard who, as history teaches us, have a vested interest in protecting the status quo, no matter the cost in human lives*. Unfortunately, we are going to be forced to stand idly by and watch as thousands of patients die painfully and as Dr. Otto Warburg said, *"die needlessly."*

With tens of thousands of scientific publications correlating lack of calcium with disease, there appears to be one avenue of hope where modern medicine has hopelessly failed. As Nobel Prize winner Otto Warburg told American audiences, "millions are dying needlessly" and the pain is horrific. Thus the time has come to launch nutrition and to make nutritional therapy the medicine of the Twenty First Century. It won't be easy as the richest establishments on Earth will not want to give up their powers and riches. Perhaps before we start, we should review the efforts of those who came before us.

CHAPTER FIVE

CHANGING HISTORY

In 1776, George Washington got together with the founders of our nation and made an unfortunate blunder, which would later contribute to the loss of his life. Almost every American is ignorant of the fact that medical freedom was tragically left out of the American Constitution. In 1776, Dr. Benjamin Rush, Surgeon General and the only American doctor to sign the Declaration of Independence, tried strenuously, but failed, to have *"medical freedom"* enshrined in the Constitution. It should be noted that Rush was successful in getting religious freedom enshrined in the Constitution. He stated *"The constitution of this Republic should make special provisions for Medical Freedom. To restrict the art of healing to one class of men and deny equal privileges to others will constitute the **Bastille of medical science**. All such laws are **un-American** and despotic."* Rush predicted that within 60 years the orthodox doctors would get together to form an organization that the Constitution would allow to destroy its medical competition. Sixty years later the American Medical Association was formed. He also warned Washington that one day he would pay for his mistake of giving in to the doctors. A few years later Washington woke up with a high fever. His men of medicine did what they usually would do, and that was to blood let. At first, the reduction of Washington's blood pressure made him feel better, but not for long, so the doctors removed more blood. Washington was getting sicker so they did their next medical procedure, and that was to pack his mouth with toxic mercury compounds so that it would swell and blister thus releasing the poisons. When this did not work, they let some more blood. By this time Washington was pleading for death. In desperation the doctors shoved toxic mercury up his annus. Now Washington really wanted to die. The last bloodletting solved the problem as Washington bled to death. Ironically, it could have been worse. Washington could have been treated by a modern day doctor who would burn his anus with radiation or kill him with toxic chemotherapy. The bottom line is that Washington did not have a choice as he was instrumental in making sure that Americans do not have medical freedom. The freedom to choose the medical procedure, including nutrition.

As was previously discussed, in 1808, Dalton, the father of modern chemistry, proposed the "*Atomic Theory*," that atoms were the basic components of all substances. The scientific establishment of the day threw scorn on his theory. Dalton was austracized and removed from his position in the university for fear that his ridiculous theories would discredit the university. He spent the rest of his life being mocked and ridiculed by the scientific community of the day.

As was also discussed earlier, 1841 Ignas Semmelweis, a Hungarian physician who was horrified by the high death rate of women giving birth in hospitals, became obsessed with finding the cause of the disease. At that time mothers who had given birth at home or in carriages on their way to the hospital had a far greater chance of surviving their childbirth than if they had been delivered in a hospital. Moreover, in that period it was common practice for doctors to go directly from the morgue, where they conducted post mortem examinations and anatomy classes using the bodies of deceased patients, into the maternity ward and attend maternity patients dressed in usual garb, without washing their hands. Because in 1846 Dr Semmelweis believed that a doctor washing his hands would remove invisible contaminenets he believed were responsible for the deaths of women having babies in hospitals, the American Medical Association, AMA, which was created just a few years earlier, warned all American doctors that believing in things that cannot be seen is the same as believing in ghosts and therefore any doctor washing his hands would have his license suspended. In the meantime the AMA lobbied other medical associations around the world and finally all descended on Budapest Hungary where they had Seimelweis discharged from his prestigious positions in maternity hospitals. Haunted by the fact that hundreds of thousands of women continued to die, Dr. Seimelweis eventually died of insanity in 1865.

By the 1880's, the advent of the microscope made the invisible microbe visible, and doctors began to universally adopt Seimelweis's procedures. Despite the eventual acceptance of the hand scrubbing technique in maternity wards, both Louis Pasteur and Joseph Lister encountered great difficulty in having the **germ theory of disease and antiseptic surgery** accepted because the leading physicians of the day adamantly refused to accept the theory. They pleaded with the AMA to examine the pictures of **"Dr Seimeilweis's spooks"** so that doctors could begin washing their hands as millions of people had been dying needlessly. The AMA decided to study the problem for decades to come. Millions more people died.

Albert Einstein, who was unquestionably the most famous scientist of the twentieth century, had to withstand more efforts by the establishment attempting to disprove his theory of relativity than has ever been made to disprove any other theory in the history of science. This was demonstrably shown by one of Einstein's opponent's publications entitled **"One Hundred Against Albert Einstein"** to which Einstein remarked that *"if* *they were right, only one would be enough."* Just the same, the scientific establishment of the day considered Einstein a **quack**.

$\mathbf{M}$ax Planck, a father of modern physics and Nobel Prize winner in 1903, stated that *"An important scientific innovation rarely makes its way by gradually winning over and converting its opponents; it rarely happens that Saul becomes Paul. What does happen is that **its opponents gradually die out and that the growing generation is familiarized with the idea from the beginning.**"* Max Planck was frustrated that his theories were considered quackery by the establishment of the day.

$\mathbf{A}$nd so, despite the uphill battle, road blocks, and mine fields maintained by the scientific hierarchy of every day in an attempt to defend their prestigious status quo, science managed to progress to the point where, by the 1950's, the scientific establishment arrogantly announced to the world that *"**in this atomic age, all there is to know has already been learned and all future advancements would be simply rearrangements of current knowledge.**"* The old adage, *"The more we know, the less we know"* was certainly not believed by this incredibly arrogant group of scientists.

$\mathbf{T}$oday, although scientists admit that they do not know everything, their arrogance remains intact. From 1952 to 1986 Dr. Carl Reich prescribed large dosages of vitamins and minerals to his patients with spectacular success. The medical authorities took the position that what he was doing was just too simple to be valid and therefore if they allowed him to publish he would degrade medicine. His 1986 statement that calcium supplements help to prevent cancer, which has now been confirmed by many scientific studies, was the last straw for the medical authorities who then removed his license.." Several years later Dr. Reich was written about in newspapers as *"a man ahead of his time"* and because he was the first medical doctor to prescribe nutrients in large doses, he was called *"The Father of Preventive Medicine."*

The publication of the book *The Calcium Factor* by Bob Barefoot and Dr. Carl Reich in 1992 brought international attention to the concept of nutritional therapy. Barefoot was in demand as a guest speaker for health conventions and he became a frequent guest on radio shows. For the next ten years Barefoot continued doing this, never charging for any service. Of course thousands of the hopelessly ill came to him, and by their own testimonies, many cured themselves. By 1999, Barefoot had made the audio tape, "Barefoot and Healthy" which sold millions. The word on nutritional therapy was spreading like wild fire, and Barefoot was given the title the "King of Calcium." Later, when coral calcium became popular, many referered to him as the "King of Coral Calcium." Thousands attended his talks and millions watched him on television.

Also, thousands and thousands of scientists, from the world's most renowned scientific institutions, were writing scientific publications extolling the health benefits of supplemental calcium. Barefoot had supported the use of coral calcium, which he discovered in the literature in 1982, and which, in his experience, he believed to be the best form of supplemental calcium for human consumption. Although he had never used the product before that time, he believed that 600 years of track record with tens of millions of people taking and loving the natural product that God had made, spoke for itself. Over the centuries, there seemed to be millions of testimonials. No other natural or man-made product had ever come close to this record. Scientific publications pointed to the fact that not only did it have about 70 trace metal nutrients, but the marine coral seemed to have the preferred 2:1 calcium to magnesium ratio. There were also publications, by Japanese scientists indicating that the calcium in the coral was much more absorbable than other calcium nutrients. The Japanese government scientists also discovered that the consumption of calcium rich coral water was the reason for the good health and longevity of the people of Okinawa. Also, in discussions with Swedish scientists, Barefoot learned that the coral contained marine microbes that were extremely beneficial to the human digestive system. Thus Barefoot backed coral calcium sight unseen. In the early nineties the coral came to Europe and finally by the mid nineties the coral came to America. The first thing that Barefoot noted was that almost 50% of those Americans taking coral had a testimonial within one month. Some of these testimonials were spectacular. Both Barefoot and coral calcium soon became the hottest names on the internet with Barefoot becoming synonymous with coral calcium.

CHAPTER SIX

BOB
BAREFOOT

In 1999, Barefoot met Dr. Steven Holt in Las Vegas. Both were serving on the board of a health nutrient company. Holt suggested that they join forces as with Barefoot's name and his marketing expertise they could sell a lot of coral calcium. Barefoot wanted a product that was less expensive than the current $40/bottle that was being sold so they agreed to produce a product for about $13/bottle. They signed an agreement and after several months of delays, Holt finally had a product for sale. He initially sold it to MLM companies, but their final price was not $13/bottle, but rather $40/bottle. When Barefoot complained Holt told him that he did not understand the business world. Barefoot, who knew that it cost much less for Holt to produce, became angry and disappointed in Holt. About a year later Holt came back to Barefoot offering to make amends. He suggested that Barefoot write a book on coral calcium which he would then publish. This he believed would universally increase the sales of coral calcium.

Holt offered to draft the contract himself to save money as he said that he had taken all the legal courses and could be lawyer. Unfortunately for Barefoot, Holt added the words that "the publisher would have the right to use Barefoot's name in a reasonable manner to promote the sale of the book *and associated items to be sold.*" This appeared at the time to be acceptable as in order to promote the sale of the book, other associated items such as brochures, tapes and other promotional materials are required. However, Holt used the contract to promote the sale of his coral calcium, even though coral calcium products had not been mentioned in the contract. In addition, tens of thousands of books "Barefoot on Coral Calcium" were given away to promote the sale of Holt's coral. Thus both book sales and royalties to Barefoot virtually did not exist, making the contract totally worthless to Barefoot.

   Barefoot immediately launched a lawsuit against Holt for fraudulently claiming that Barefoot had formulated Holt's product. Holt then launched a counter lawsuit against Barefoot. He then made extra efforts to have the jurisdiction transferred to New Jersey. The New Jersey judge dismissed Holt's lawsuit and ordered Holt to appear in Federal Court in Arizona to answer Barefoot's lawsuit. Finally, in March 2004, both sides agreed to an out of court settlement. Holt terminated the publishing agreement and Barefoot agreed to allow Holt to market his "Bob Barefoot's Coral Calcium Plus."

   Barefoot had made it his mission for years to put people and coral calcium together. He formulated his own brand, Barefoot's Coral Supreme™, to which he added large quantities of vitamins and other nutrients. Finally the big time marketers decided that it was time for an infomercial. At first they considered Dr. Joel Wallach of "Dead Doctors Don't Lie." However he did not have enough expertise on the subject. Finally, Kevin Trudeau, who was considered "The King of Infomercials" decided that he liked what he had heard from Barefoot, so he invited him to do a show.

   The invitation came through a young, and therefore inexperienced, individual named Donald Barrett of DMC who promised to take care of Barefoot. He offered to pay Trudeau to do the show and then give him a piece of the action. He would pay Barefoot a royalty per bottle of coral sold as well as the standard book industry royalty for the books sold. In addition the show would sell Barefoot's Coral Supreme™ for which Barefoot was already making a small production royalty. Barefoot agreed but decided to wait and hear Trudeau's opinion before signing a contract. Barefoot met Trudeau for for the first time in a Los Angeles studio in December 2002. They had a 20 minute discussion where Trudeau alleviated Barefoot's concerns about compliance, saying that he had a full time compliance officer and that he was just as concerned, and would make sure that that show was FTC compliant. Barefoot then found himself onstage with a Larry King Live setting. Trudeau seemed relentless in his efforts to extract a confession from Barefoot, who held his ground. It made for excellent television. Sixty minutes later it was over. Barefoot asked about the compliance and was told that it would be done after the market testing.

After a few weeks, Barefoot was told by Donald Barrett that the show was a spectacular success. It had scored an industry record of 180, which meant that for every $1000 spent on airing the show, 180 people would phone in. Donald was eager to get working on the contract, but insisted on adding terms that Barefoot could not agree with. In the meantime, Barrett was also having trouble closing his contract with Trudeau.

Barefoot then learned that his negotiations with Trudeau had broken down and that he had joined forces with another marketer, Triad Media. Triad began snow balling the television airwaves. They put in another order but because Barefoot had not received a royalty for the previous sales, he decided to wait instructing his bottler not to ship. Weeks went by and then Barefoot discovered that Triad had convinced the bottler to ship without his permission, so Barefoot ended the sales. Barefoot quickly learned that they had developed a knockoff cheaper version, called Coral Daily which did not use the high grade coral, and despite this, they were still using his name to promote it. Then he learned that they were claiming to be the publisher of his books and were having them printed, a clear violation of copyright law. Barefoot contacted a Canadian printer who agreed to cease and desist immediately, but Triad just went to other printers in America to get the job done. These printers refused to cease and desist. Also, his best selling tape, "Barefoot and Healthy," was also being illegally duplicated in violation of copyright law.

Ironically, Dr. Holt had seen the infomerical and decided to cash in. He demanded that Trudeau buy all of his product from Holt only. He said that he would produce Coral Supreme for less, but Barefoot was concerned. Barefoot and the Trudeau group decided to keep their current manufacturer. Holt then began to bash the infomercial. He told anyone who would listen, including the FDA and FTC, that Barefoot had made false medical claims. He said that people were offended by statements like "growing new brains" (a quote from Scientific American, May 1999 "New Nerve Cells for the Adult Brain"), in which the scientific publication demonstrated proof that parts of the brain can indeed re-grow.

Of course Trudeau and Barefoot launched a lawsuit against Donald Barrett and DMC and they countersued us. The problem was that law suits take years to settle. and Triad was making millions on the infomercial. Trudeau then decided that he would fight back by making his own infomercial. Once again Barefoot found himself in a studio in Los Angeles, only this time Trudeau had a beautiful co-host, Debbie. It was all over within an hour and Trudeau's staff was euphoric. Trudeau's lawyers drafted a contract that left Barefoot in total control of the production of the Coral Supreme while offering him five percent of gross revenues. Once again compliance had been discussed as the Triad group was still running the original infomercial, and once again Trudeau stated that it would be handled.

Over the next few months royalty checks began arriving. However, by this time Barefoot was involved in five lawsuits and I had about seven law firms to pay. Barefoot had also launched a lawsuit against Triad for copyright violations. Barefoot instructed Trudeau that the royalties be sent to the lawfirms to help offset the costs. Then came a whopping tax bill. All of the Trudeau money was gone.

Barefoot's friends and advisors advised that it was only a matter of time before the FTC launched an injunction against him. Barefoot believed that the offending material in the infomercial could be corrected, but Trudeau did not believe he was correct. If Trudeau were wrong it may have caused Barefoot enormous problems, so Barefoot launched a lawsuit against Trudeau to try to make the infomercial FTC compliant. Now Barefoot had lawyers having daily conference calls with lawyers and his remaining money was dwindling fast. Finally, Trudeau's lawyers got the message and agreed with Barefoot that the show should be made compliant. For the next three months we negotiated the terms. But, unfortunately, time had run out.

About this time, Dr. Holt, obviously joined forces with Dr. Steven Barrett, a nutritional quack buster who was urging the FTC to take action against Barefoot. Holt's lawyers also wrote several letters to the FTC requesting action against Barefoot. Barrett, a retired psychiatrist with no active license, began attacking Barefoot mercilessly and contacted ABC News. Barrett currently is being sued by many others for his slanderous attacks. A California court ruled in October 2003 that Dr. Barrett was biased, and *"beyond any credibility"* in the area of nutrition. Barrett appealed and lost again. Thus,

Dr. Barrett can and will be handled by the courts. In addition, Dr. Barrett uses as his "calcium expert," another quack buster called Robert Baratz, who is the owner of a hair removal and ear piercing salon in Braintree, Massachusetts which appears to be the head quarters for the quack busters operations. Both of these men did a hatchet job on Barefoot in a featured story in the Edmonton Sun newspaper where both were referred to as calcium experts, which would be considered a joke by the scientific community. Despite the fact that Barrett had been declared by the court to be beyond credibility and that the expert scientist was but a mere ear piercer, ABC ran a story attacking Barefoot while extolling Barrett as an expert. Barefoot disagrees with ABC television's characterization of Dr. Stephen Barrett as a "calcium expert" as there is no evidence that Barrett is an expert on calcium and its relationship to disease. Barefoot also suspects that Barrett has never published peer-reviewed literature based on original research concerning calcium, and there are no articles by either Barrett or Baratz in the calcium scientific literature. Thus the scientific community would not support any claims by these inexperienced quack busters and therefore by definition they become the real quacks. Barefoot would therefore willingly challenge these amateurs to a public debate, but unfortunately they appear to be hiding behind the anonymity of the internet. Barefoot also challenged ABC Television to a public debate, but to date they have refused. The Edmonton Sun is also not interested in correcting their erroneous story, as they said that the story was "old news."

On May 15 the Council for Responsible Nutrition (CRN), which has a good reputation for servicing the nutrient industry, requested that "the FTC and the FDA take appropriate enforcement action to end Mr. Barefoot's highly visible and deceptive marketing campaign for coral calcium and to prevent Mr. Barefoot from further fraudulent activity."

The CRN states that "many of the claims have no scientific support" a claim which Mr. Barefoot disputes. nevertheless, if many of these claims do not have scientific support, then they are claiming that many of these claims do have scientific support, a claim that Mr. Barefoot supports, and they should therefore list these claims that are not in dispute.

The CRN cites a renowned Okinawan Centenarian Study to prove that the calcium in the Okinawan water is not responsible for their longevity, as Barefoot suggests, which the CRN calls "egregious, false and unsubstantiated." However, this is contradictory to scientific study by the Japanese. For example Dr. Jun Sato, Professor of Okayama University presented his research at the academic society in 1985 where his investigation concluded that the lower rate of disease and the longevity of the Okinawans "was due to the calcium enriched coral water." Also, Professor Jun Kobayashi of the University of Okayama presented a paper in 1990 to the 55th Nipon Gakkai where he concluded that *"there was a correlation between the lower death rate and the coral rich coral water in Okinawa."* Professor Jun Kobayashi concluded that "longevity and good health was due to the mineralized water, and also the calcium rich fruits and vegetables cultivated from the calcium rich land and soil." Barefoot was correct!

Also, their disbelief that anyone could consume 100,000 milligrams of calcium daily is inconsistent with published facts. Certified analyses of the Hunza water, for example, contain 18,000 milligrams of calcium per quart and these people drink up to 30 cups of tea daily, which puts them in the 100,000 milligrams of calcium daily range. Their side effects are great health and longevity.

The scientific community is currently publishing results that calcium supplements can benefit a large number of diseases. There are dozens of scientific studies available. Thus no one is disputing the benefits of calcium. Barefoot, however, believes that coral is the best way to absorb calcium and a host of other nutrients, and welcomes the CRN, FTC and FDA to try to prove otherwise. As millions of lives are at stake, it is crucial that these organizations take up this challenge. If they do so millions of lives could be saved.

Barefoot believes that the CRN was reacting to pressure from the press, such as the ABC Good Morning America show, May 6, and the story in the Washington Post, May 20. Both contained the same misinformation that was reported by the CRN.

Barefoot was in his office one day when an ABC television crew arrived at his door. Barefoot recognized the fellow holding the microphone as a man who traditionally likes to do hatchet jobs on people so Barefoot refused to be interviewed by a surprise attack. The story was aired May 6, 2003 without any reasonable input by Barefoot or the opportunity to provide such input under appropriate conditions. The ABC television show was instigated by Dr. Steven Barrett, a retired psychiatrist who currently does not have a license. Also, the California courts declared him to be "biased, unqualified and beyond credibility." Had this information been aired, Dr. Barrett would have had no credibility with the audience or the CRN, and Barefoot would not have been maligned.

In the Washington Post story, they "claim" that the Okinawa longevity is due to such factors as "a diet rich in vegetables, grains and fish, an active lifestyle and strong social networks for the elderly." This is a major health claim that, sounds great but has no scientific validity, especially since there are dozens of cultures throughout the world that live the life described by the Post, but do not have longevity. Although the Washington Post's story suggest that "experts contest many of the claims made by Barefoot," Barefoot's response is that other experts, such as those referenced in his book "The Calcium Factor," fully support his claims.

The Post erred in its reference to Barefoot claiming that calcium makes the blood slightly alkaline and can change the blood's pH. Barefoot lectures that the blood pH can never change as it is biochemically buffered and always alkaline at a pH of 7.4, and that calcium plays a crucial role in maintaining this pH. The Post also has experts who "suspect" that coral calcium, the bone remnants of living sea critters, has the same chemistry as found in chunks of limestone. In other words they are claiming that "they suspect" a rock is the same as a dead critter, which is obviously ridiculous.

Barefoot's position is that his critics, many of whom are scientists, have provided no scientific substantiation for their claims against coral calcium, which is a natural nutrient made by God. None of the critics have published peer-reviewed literature based on original research concerning calcium, and I can find no articles by them in the calcium scientific literature. A real expert can see a huge difference between coral calcium and calcium carbonate. Coral calcium has the preferred calcium to magnesium ratio, 2:1, calcium carbonate does not. Coral calcium has about 70 trace nutrients, calcium carbonate does not. Coral calcium has marine microbes to assist in digestion, calcium carbonate does not. Coral calcium, an aragonite, has over 1000 times the surface area of calcium carbonate, calcite. Also, studies done by the Japanese show that most of the calcium from coral calcium is absorbed by the body while very little of the calcium from calcium carbonate is absorbed. Finally, coral calcium has hundreds of years of history with probably millions of testimonials, calcium carbonate does not. Millions of people all over the world who defy the critics and happily ingest it for health benefits. Regardless of whether this natural nutrient is to be unfortunately suppressed in America, the rest of the world is being introduced to its health potential. If history repeats itself, coral calcium will flourish and become the nutrient of the 21st Century, with Barefoot leading the way.

Unfortunately, due to the massive attention created by the Barefoot infomercials, Bob Barefoot has become the focus of public attack. However, there are thousands of medical claims by the consumer created by the consumption of coral calcium. For hundreds of years, people taking the coral have made such claims, and Barefoot personally believes most of them. He also believes that they should be evaluated by competent medical researchers. This will take a great deal of money and hopefully lead to the beginning of the cure of America. Most of the information contained can be acquired by reading his books, *The Calcium Factor*, *Death By Diet* or *Let's Cure Humanity* (800-884-1942).

Unfortunately, it has become an American pastime for lawyers to sue. In California, "The Teachers against False Advertising" have launched a class action suit against Trudeau and Barefoot, seeking to get the money that the FTC is also trying to get. Then in Texas, another mass action lawsuit has been launched against Trudeau and Barefoot for the same reason. Apparently, on behalf of the people, lawyers can sue and charge so much money for their services that there is nothing left for the people. It seems that the hyenas and vultures are circling. Everyone wants the money. Barefoot doesn't have any, but it will cost millions to defend himself. Trudeau has money, and he has been in the business a long time and I am sure that he is capable of protecting himself.

And if all this were not enough, rumors are spreading that Barefoot's coral is high in lead. This of course is not true as the coral has certified analyses in Japan, also when it arrives in America and also every batch is sent out for certified analysis. All prove that the lead content is below the allowable limit. The California lawsuit is using this misinformation.

To complicate matters further, Steven Holt is telling anyone who will listen that Barefoot is using "toxic cesium." Barefoot has several scientific publications that virtually conclude that cesium is not toxic, especially in the ridiculously low levels that are used by Barefoot. The scientific literature shows that hundreds of thousands of times the amount of cesium that Barefoot uses would be required to be toxic, and that this amount would only cause stomach upset, whereas this same stomach upset could be caused by consuming regular table salt in a fraction of this amount. Thus for Barefoot's critics, table salt, along with other nutritious foods are all toxic substance. For example, potassium, one of the most common and nutritious minerals found in our food, has been injected into the veins of criminals who have been sentenced to death to "terminate their lives." Once again, using the logic of Barefoot's critics, potassium would be toxic and therefore they would be urging the public to not eat the most nutritious foods. The reality of toxicology is that it is not the substance that is toxic, but rather *the amount of the substance.* Thus, cesium in the amount used by Barefoot is not toxic, and many scientists claim that cesium has anti-cancer properties and other health benefits. Unfortunately, just the threat is enough to effect sales.

The bottom line with the Barefoot/Trudeau and DMC infomercials was that many people made many millions of dollars. Unfortunately, the man responsible for their success,

Bob Barefoot, made nothing. The FTC action caused Barefoot to lose millions of dollars made from previous business transactions and has caused him economic pain. Although Barefoot has numerous differences and disputes with Trudeau, he does recognize that millions of people have been introduced to coral because of the infomercial. Barefoot believes that this has resulted in the saving of millions of lives. Thus, instead of persecuting Trudeau, the FTC should be giving him a medal.

And yet both men are still being persecuted, not just by the government, but also by the lawyers abusing the system and using the law to try to get rich quick. Trudeau previously was responsible for putting the famous Atkins diet on the map, a diet that has been touted as the best advancement in dietary medicine by the scientific community, but at the time was condemned by the government regulatory authorities. Also prior to the infomercial, only a few hundred thousand people were taking coral. By the time the FTC acted that number had risen to about 5,000,000. Thus millions of lives were saved. Also, the fact of the matter is that if Trudeau was saving millions of lives, as I believe he did, then the FTC interference preventing him from continuing to save lives means that the FTC is now responsible for terminating the lives of large numbers of Americans. As a result, a Congressional hearing may be necessary to rectify the problem, so that we can minimize the loss of American lives.

Thus, when it comes to American freedom, we have demonstrated to the world that America lacks medical freedom and that government agencies, like the FTC and FDA, can declare innocent men guilty without a trial. This gives the Arabs and the Russians a lot to smile about.

CHAPTER SEVEN

D-Day

Every American will never forget 9-11. That day changed all of our lives. However, for Bob Barefoot, his day of infamy was 6-10. On June 10, 2003, the Federal Trade Commission, FTC, filed a preliminarily injunction against Bob Barefoot, Kevin Trudeau and others. That action against Bob Barefoot virtually destroyed him economically and did serious damage to his reputation. Although the complaint contained only accusations and the accused is supposed to be innocent until the courts rule otherwise, in reality the target is guilty until he can prove himself innocent, a feat that usually requires millions of dollars. The claims made by the FTC were unfounded. Outside of a court of law they would be defamatory, however the guilty agents in the FTC are protected by the government. In other words, the FTC is allowed to bypass the American system of justice. This of course is totally *"un-American."*

Barefoot would also would like to set the record straight about this case brought against him and others by the Federal Trade Commission. Investigating what prompted the FTC to bring that suit, it has been learned that Dr. Stephen Holt was in communication with them, with his lawyers sending derogatory letters and from this we can only surmise that Holt had a major hand in pushing the FTC to act.

The FTC alleged that Barefoot had made unsubstantiated medical claims concerning coral calcium in the infomercial in which Kevin Trudeau and he appeared. In an attempt to fully cooperate with the FTC, and despite disagreeing with positions the FTC is taking in the case, Barefoot voluntarily agreed to a temporary injunction or agreement in which he has agreed not to make certain claims unless and until he has obtained appropriate substantiation. The temporary agreement in no way prohibits him from continuing to publish and speak on the subject of coral calcium, nor does it prohibit him or his authorized distributors from selling CORAL CALCIUM SUPREME™ or my other coral calcium products.

Barefoot has cooperated with the FTC, and has reached a final settlement with it. Under that settlement, we again expect that I will not be precluded from publishing or speaking on the subject of coral calcium, or from selling my coral calcium products.

On the other hand, my good friend Congressman Pollock, Alaska, advises that innocent men should never plead guilty. He said that he had seen the infomercial and in his opinion (Congressman Pollock is a lawyer) Barefoot is innocent of all charges. This was reiterated by another congressman, Congressman Dan Burton, Indiana who said that his lawyers had concluded that Barefoot did not cross the line and he is therefore innocent.

While Barefoot has an extensive collection of authoritative, peer reviewed studies and literature, from the "cream of the crop" in international research, supporting and substantiating his concepts and claims on biological calcium, (see 1000 scientific references at the end of this book), there are also thousands of average Americans who are making medical claims and for whom Barefoot will always be required to take responsibility, for which he does. Barefoot's position is that he fully supports the FTC's mandate that no product receive public claims until there is FDA approval to do so. However, Barefoot believes that in the near future, because of the hundreds of scientific studies and publications on the health benefits of calcium, the FDA will be forced to exercise its mandate and demonstrate that it is also responsible for **"food"** and not just drugs and begin to approve many of the claims that are currently being made by the American nutritionists and that are currently at issue in the FTC proceedings. In other words, if the FDA had done its job to protect the American public and directed its efforts towards the nutritional value in food for the American public instead of drugs for the drug industry, then the FTC would have no basis for any action against Barefoot. Instead, the FDA refuses to exercise its mandate by examining the available scientific evidence on the health benefits of food, resulting in the FTC taking action that harms the American public. Instead, the FDA continues to endorse several drugs one year and then later takes them off the market for killing people. **Vioxx** and **Celebrex** are but just a few examples. Other drugs from previous years are **Seldane, Rotashield, Latronex, Posicar, Resulin, Redux, Trovan,** and **Duract.** All of these drugs were medical disasters. It makes one wonder which of the drugs that the FDA currently endorse will they tell us next year are going to kill us. In the meantime Barefoot who never made the claims he is accused of making, will continue to avoid making such claims, and is working with the FTC to resolve the situation, for the best interests of the American public.

The problem, however, with working with the FTC is that they always seem to be playing games. The first thing they requested is that I sign their temporary injunction stipulating that I would refrain from making 6 claims (see next chapter). As I had never made any of the claims in the first place, I had little trouble with their request. Next they decided to depose me and my family.

I was not very happy that they wanted to bring my family into the mess, however, we had nothing to hide so I agreed.

Being deposed is an experience in itself. Two determined FTC and relatively inexperienced agents, Laura Sullivan and Daniel Kaufman, asked a series of questions, most times the same questions with different wordings, trying to establish if Barefoot had any money. Since negative publicity about the FTC action had brought him to the brink of bankruptcy, destroyed his business and destroyed his investments, there was no money to be had. Although the charges were slanderous, it is almost impossible to sue a government agency, especially the FTC or the FDA. Before 6-10, Barefoot had been receiving monthly royalty checks for books in the six-figure-per-month range. After 6-10, it immediately shrunk to about less than 1% of that amount. Then, to worsen Barefoot's financial situation even further, Trudeau stopped paying royalties and all others stopped paying for goods received in anticipation that the FTC action would drive Barefoot into bankruptcy. All of a sudden, even though there was no income, the lawyers lined up demanding to be paid, and many got offended when they realized that there was no money, as did the FTC agents deposing me. I answered most questions with "yes" or "no", but when they asked me how much I thought Trudeau had made on the infomercial I responded that I thought that he had made hundreds of millions of dollars. Trudeau's lawyer, listening to the deposition, began to howl and quiz me on what proof I had. I responded that I would be the last person that Trudeau would supply such information. I told them that my proof consisted of logic. I told him that the DMC group had told a judge a few months earlier that they had made $50 million dollars in primary sales and that Trudeau had told me to multiply that number by five to get the total sales. When the retail sales were added the number became staggering. When you add this information to the fact that Trudeau's infomercial was more successful according to the industry and also Trudeau himself, then hundreds of millions must have been made. The FTC agents were ecstatic, as they believed that they had found money to grab. But, unfortunately for these agents, in the end, Trudeau was forced to pay a meager two million dollars.

Shortly after the deposition the FTC agents told my lawyers that they were willing to settle and that as Barefoot had no money, they would not be seeking any. They said that they had to present the offer to the courts by October 2, 2003. Barefoot had invested earlier in the year in a product developed by the Russian Academy of Science that actually grew new skin. It would be fabulous for cosmetics and the stores lined up. Then came 6-10 and the stores disappeared as did Barefoot's investment. Similarly, Barefoot had invested substantially in a new television and radio network that offered him prime time advertising. After 6-10 there was no demand for the advertising and Barefoot's investment became worthless. What else could go wrong?

The question was answered on October 8, 2003, 6 days later, when the FTC submitted their final injunction proposal with a list of demands. Not only did they seek to tie up Barefoot's operation by demanding that Barefoot be restrained and enjoined from misrepresenting in any manner, expressly of by implication, including the use of endorsements, that such dietary supplement can prevent, treat or cure any disease, they also demanded, and they also ordered Barefoot to pay $45,000 within 20 days. They also demanded the title to Barefoot's home and they wanted assignment of any monies due from Trudeau, which would be or they thought a substantial amount of money. Then to add insult to injury, Barefoot learned that the FTC was only negotiating, and they did not really expect to get what they asked. As Barefoot's financial future was on the line he had not expected the FTC to play games, but they did anyway. Of course the offer was totally unacceptable.

In conclusion, despite the negative publicity that has been waged against me by competitors, and most notably Holt, very little has changed. Barefoot continues to endorse coral calcium as an important dietary supplement, and is continuing to publish my beliefs in this area. Also, sales of my authentic, high quality coral calcium products, including CORAL CALCIUM SUPREME™ are continuing well. Barefoot does not expect the negative publicity to suddenly end. So Barefoot requests that each of you carefully consider the source of this negative publicity weigh it accordingly. Remember that since Otto Warburg told American audiences that millions of Americans would have to die needlessly, over 20 million Americans have died needlessly from cancer including Michael Landon, Timothy Hutton and Steve McQueen.

CHAPTER EIGHT

APPEAL FOR CONGRESSIONAL ACTION

In the Spring of 2003, Congressman Dan Burton approached Bob Barefoot at a Health conference in Las Vegas and cautioned him that the FTC would soon be moving against him. Burton offered that if their actions were severe he would convene a session of Congress to help. A couple of months later, it happened and after three months of being abused by the FTC, Barefoot responded with an appeal for Congressional Action. Being a realist and knowing that at no time in history had Congress ever responded to rectify abuses by either the FTC or FDA, Barefoot, along with his lawyers, did not believe that this action would be effective. However, because of the sincerity of Congressman Burton to try to prevent the FTC from assisting the drug industry's effort to suppress the nutrition information Barefoot decided to participate. Also, the fact that had not only two responsible Congressmen determined that Barefoot was innocent of all charges, but also three expert consulting reports had determined the same. In addition, examination of the script of the show would demonstrate that Barefoot had not said any of the statements for which he had been accused. Finally, the FDA is currently considering aceptance for many of the health related calcium claims for which Barefoot is being charged and even though a Congressional hearing is more than justified, it will probably never happen due to the wavering nature of the political beast.

Congressman Dan Burton
2185 Rayburn Building
Washington, D.C. 20515

Appeal For
Congressional Action

My name is Bob Barefoot. You have seen me on television, heard me on the radio or on my audio tapes, or you may have read my books on the subject of coral calcium and its health benefits. I have been studying biological calcium for about 40 years now, long before it became a popular subject. And for that reason many seek out my council on this important subject. I also have sold and endorsed my own brands of coral calcium, i.e., CORAL CALCIUM SUPREME"-, CORAL CALCIUM SUPREME PLUS"-, and as well as other brands that I believe to constitute high quality marine coral calcium. I am a very proud graduate of the Northern Alberta Institute of Technology, NAIT, 1967. Since graduation I have, with fellow PhD co-authors, seven scientific publications and have written three books, *The Calcium Factor*, *Death By Diet*, and *If It Glitters*, the first two of which are best sellers. My recent infomercial, with Kevin Trudeau, was the most watched infomercial in television history. As such it has become extremely controversial because of my references to the claim that calcium supplements can reverse a host of diseases, which are supported by thousands of scientific publications. The FTC incorrectly deemed that the claims were being attached to the calcium product, coral calcium, being sold, even though I did not claim that the product itself cured anything, as can be verified by an examination of the verbal text of the show.

In my books tapes and shows I refer to hundreds of scientific documents that demonstrate that Calcium is an essential nutrient in our daily diet and a key factor in a wide range of biological systems within the body. Its role in disease prevention and treatment has been studied, and continues to be studied, by numerous scientists around the world. A search on the US National Library of Medicine's PubMed system reveals more than 17,000 scientific articles on calcium and its relationship to cancer. In particular, clinical trials have examined the link between calcium consumption and its positive effects on colorectal cancer, one of the most common cancers in America. While the study of calcium continues, its importance is becoming widely recognized even among the more conservative members of the scientific and medical Communities. The 2001 "Physicians Desk Reference for Nutritional Supplements" chapter on calcium states that calcium has anti-osteoporotic activity and may also have anti-carcinogenic, antihypertensive and hypocholesterolemic activity.

The Kevin Trudeau/ Bob Barefoot infomercial reflected these scientific views. The FTC's position is that the show claimed precisely the following:

1. Coral Calcium is an effective cure for any form of cancer
2. Coral calcium is an effective treatment or cure for multiple sclerosis, lupus, or other autoimmune diseases.
3. Coral calcium is an effective treatment or cure for heart disease and/or chronic high blood pressure.
4. A daily serving size of coral calcium provides the same bio-available calcium as two gallons of milk.
5. The body absorbs significantly more, and in some cases as much as 100 times more, of the calcium contained in coral calcium, and at a rate significantly faster, than the

calcium contained in other commonly available calcium supplements.

6. Scientific research published in the Journal of the America Medical Association, (JAMA), the New England Journal of Medicine, and other reputable medical journals prove that calcium supplements are able to reverse and/or cure all forms of cancer in the human body.

However, an actual examination of the verbal text of the show will demonstrate that all of the above FTC accusations are totally incorrect. Their actions to get a preliminary injunction combined with the generated publicity have forced me to the brink of bankruptcy. Unfortunately, in America when the FTC takes any action, American citizens are considered guilty until they prove their innocence, a process requiring millions of dollars. And even if they slander American citizens, FTC agents are protected by the courts. This activity is totally un-American, and I therefore seek redress from Congress. Using the text of the contentious show, the FTC should be made to prove to Congress their charges against me. As this will be impossible for them to do, they should be forced to issue a public apology and provide financial compensation. Furthermore, the FTC has demonstrated the height of pettiness by demanding that I give them my home, a mobile home which I purchased for less than $15,000 three years ago. They also want to muzzle me and to destroy the rest of my business and confiscate all of my assets. Their injunction froze my assets and by doing so, the FTC made it impossible to raise money to pay lawyers. Thus the FTC is allowed to deny legal council to its victims and wins by default. When I explained what had happened to Congressman Howard Pollock (Alaska), he declared that what the FTC did was un-American.

Despite the fact that I am innocent, my lawyers advise that, because FTC action can cost millions of dollars, I should plea bargain. My choice is to fight, as innocent men should not plead guilty. However, my lawyers informed me that even if I win, it will cost me millions of dollars that I will never recover, and I do not have the millions to spend. Thus, in mid December I reluctantly signed a settlement agreement whereby I pleaded guilty, and if the FTC ruled that in the future I made any unsubstantiated medical claims, they would immediately invoke the clause forcing me to pay them $3 million and I would have no legal recourse.

Trudeau, on the other hand has money to fight back, and of course I thoroughly support his efforts. He began by arranging for three expert consulting reports. The first report was by Kenneth E. Mulligan III, Ph.D. Pharmacy (Medical Chemistry) from Oregon State University. The conclusions of his report were as follows:

1. Compelling evidence exists which link dietary calcium and/or calcium supplementation to good health.
2. Compelling evidence exists which link dietary calcium and/or calcium supplementation to positive cardiovascular benefits.
3. Compelling evidence exists which link dietary calcium and/or calcium supplementation to the potential; risk reduction of contracting certain types of cancer, especially colorectal cancer.

Dr. Mulligan provides dozens of government documents to support his conclusions and also refers to the Sloan TrenSense Report of 2002 that stated that calcium had 80,000 medical counts and 4,000 consumer counts in media forums. The nutrition industry uses this data as a barometer for consumer awareness/exposure, popularization, and the ability to commercialize a product or ingredient. An ingredient is considered to be commercially successful at 500 medical and 200 consumer counts. Thus calcium has been introduced to the market at an astounding rate with more than 200 new products introduced per year for the last three years. Thus Dr. Mulligan concurs with the medical views on calcium's health potential that was expressed in the Trudeau infomercial.

The second expert report was by James T. Berger, Ph.D., Northwestern University. He begins by criticizing the FTC for not having the necessary consumer survey that probed how potential viewers would perceive the information that is communicated in the infomercial. He further states that "In my opinion, based on my teaching and professional experience as well as my analysis of the infomercial as a whole, I do not believe false and/or misleading allegations have been made. He then proceeds to refute all six claims made by the FDA by comparing their claims to the text of the infomercial. He concludes with "It is my opinion that in the absence of a consumer survey, there is no evidence of false or deceptive advertising. Also, court precedence requires the survey before the FTC can make the declaration that Barefoot "implied" any claims. Mr. Johnson concludes that Barefoot and Mr. Trudeau simply establish a relationship between calcium and various diseases. Mr. Barefoot does not contend that his product will cure or reverse any of these ailments, and as was clearly stated in the infomercial transcript, Mr. Barefoot says, 'We're not curing anybody, you're curing yourself'"

The third report was by Philip Johnson, M.B.A. University of Chicago, Chief executive Officer of Leo J. Shapiro and Associates, a market research and consulting firm that conducts surveys. Mr. Johnson conducted a survey to determine whether or not purchasers of Robert Barefoot Coral Calcium products were satisfied or dissatisfied with their purchase, as well as the reasons underlying their beliefs. On the survey of about 10,000 households, 70% report being very satisfied, with 58% reporting being extremely satisfied and with most respondents saying that "the product works for them, and really has changed their lives" and 75% saying that they would purchase the product again in the future. Johnson concludes that the purchasers have not been mislead by advertising claims and that Robert Barefoot coral calcium products are rated at the highest level of satisfaction.

Kevin Trudeau will use these reports to try to persuade the courts to permit the re-airing of the coral calcium infomercial. Bob Barefoot endorses Trudeau's position and will continue to fight the FTC's action in the press, the internet and in Congress. **JUST WATCH!**

Bob Barefoot does admit guilt to the following:
1. Never charging the sick
2. Never charging for talks
3. Saving thousands of lives with the disputed infomercial
4. Never being paid for services rendered
5. Picking bad business partners
6. Trying to end pain, suffering and death in America

In order to facilitate a quick understanding of the massive amount of scientific documentation on calcium and disease, a summary of scientific statements on several diseases will be given along with unaltered quotes from some of the world's best scientists. After reading them you will conclude that indeed all of the diseases mentioned can be cured with God's nutrients, even though every scientist was very careful not to use the "cure" word. You will also think that what Barefoot said on his infomercial was timid compared to what the scientists are saying.

Summary and Explanation of Scientific References

As there are over 17,000 scientific articles on calcium and its relationship to cancer in the US National Library of

Medicine, why has the FDA and FTC taken no action to protect the American public from disease. Unfortunately, doctors don't have time to read and the FTC and FDA don't read. This submission will provide dozens of these articles as well as provide scientific references for hundreds of others.

In the October 13, 1998 edition of the New York Times "Calcium Takes its Place as the Superstar of Nutrients," Dr. Martin Lipkin of the Strang Research Laboratory at Rockefeller University, New York, showed that *"calcium supplements could inhibit colonic cell proliferation in people susceptible to colon cancer."* Also in the same article, Dr. Peter R. Holt of St. Luke's Roosevelt published in the Journal of the American Medical Association that *"When consumption of calcium rich dairy products reached 1200 milligrams of calcium a day, cell growth in the (cancerous) colon became normal."* Now to the average person, that means that the cancer was "cured." Also in Exhibit 3, July 18, 1995 edition of the Reader's Digest, "Calcium that Magic Mineral, the Digests writes that the scientific community has discovered that calcium supplements lower your blood pressure, help to fight osteoporosis, helps to prevent kidney stones, helps to prevent heart disease, and eases menstrual woes. The February 1999 edition of the Reader's Digest in an article entitled "The Superstar Nutrient" writes that dozens of scientific studies since the early 1980's have suggested that calcium affects blood pressure and that *"It is the low intake of calcium that accounts for the high rate of hypertension among African Americans."* The article also told of Dr. Peter Holt's research that showed that *"calcium rich foods make cell growth in the colon improve toward normal."* The same article quotes Dr. Susan Thys-Jacobs, an endocrinologist and clinical director at the Metabolic Bone Center at St. Luke's Roosevelt Hospital as saying she *"believes a chronic deficiency of calcium is largely responsible for the disruptive premenstrual syndrome."*

Thus the American press has written about the scientific explosion of information on the association of dietary calcium and disease. In this submission dozens of scientific articles on calcium deficiency and its relationship to cancer, high blood pressure, kidney stones, bone fractures and menstrual disorders, will be provided to demonstrate the tip of the iceberg in information available. Below, find direct quotes from the documents provided. Unfortunately, the FTC is either unaware of this information or chooses to ignore it. Ironically, the FDA, on the other hand, is currently reviewing for many of the claims for which the FTC is prosecuting Barefoot. However, until this is done, medical pioneers expounding these claims will continue to be persecuted by the FTC and FDA. It is therefore imperative, in the best interests of the health of Americans, that Congress take action to quickly right this wrong and thereby save millions of lives

Scientific Publications on Calcium and Cancer Health Claims:

"Coral Calcium Exhibited an inhibitory effect on the growth of cancer cells."
Yuji Hirota, Ph.D., Takashi Sugisaki, Ph.D., *Medical Preventive Group Laboratory, MPG Co., Ltd. 2-41-18 Sumida, Sumida-ku, Tokyo, Japan 131*

"A protective effect of calcium on colorectal cancer, one of the most common malignancies in Western societies, has been supported by results of in vitro animal studies."
Maria Elena Martenez and Walter C. Willett, *Arizona Cancer Center, University ofr Arizona Health Sciences Center, Tuscon, Arizona. And the Channing Laboratory, Harvard Medical School, Department of Nutrition, Boston Massachusetts, 10/30/97.*

"Adding dietary calcium markedly suppressed the diet induced hyper proliferation of epithelial cells (cancer)."
Lexun Xue, Martin Lipkin, Harrold Newark, Jiarmin Wang, *Influence of*

Dietary Calcium on Diet Induced Epithelial Cell Hyperproliferation in Mice, Memorial Sloan-Kettering Cancer Center, Strang Camcer Prevention Center, New York, Cell Biology laboratory, Henan Medical University, China.

"Higher calcium intake is associated with a reduced risk of distal colon cancer."

Kana Wu, Walter C. Willer, Charles S. Fuchs, Graham A. Colditz and Edward L. Giovannucci, "Calcium Intake and Risk of Colon Cancer in Women and Men," Department of Nutrition, Harvard School of Public Health, Boston MA, Department of Nutrition and Epidemiology, Harvard School of Public Health, Channing Laboratory, Harvard Medical School.

"The results of the present study show that there is a significant protective effect of calcium intake from drinking water against colon cancer"

Chun Yuh Yang, HuiFen Chiu, Shang Shyue Tsai and Ming Fen Cheng, "Calcium in Drinking Water and Risk of Death from Colon Cancer," School of Public Health, Department of Pharmacology, Kao, Hsiung Medical College Taiwan.

"The results of the study show that there may be a significant protective effect of calcium intake from drinking water on the risk of rectal cancer."

Chug Yuh Yang and Hui Fen Chui, "Calcium in Drinking Water and Risk of Death from Rectal Cancer," School of Public Health, Department of Pharmacology, Hsiung Medical College, Taiwan.

Higher levels of calcium intake were associated with reduced colon and rectal cancer risk."

Pamela M. Marcus and Polly Newcomb, University of Wisconsin Comprehensive Cancer Center, Madison WI, International Journal of Epidemiology, 1998; 27;788-793.

"These data support the hypothesis that higher calcium intake may decrease risk for colorectal neoplasms (cancer)."

Sonia M. Boyapati, Robert M. Bostick, Katherine McGlynn, Michael Fina, Walter Roufail, Kim Geisinger, Michael Wargovich, Ann Coker, and James Hebert. Center for Health Services Research, Vanderbelt University, Nashville, TN, Department of Epidemiology, Norman J Arnold

School of Health, University of South Carolina., Wake Forrest University, University of Texas.

"Both men and women who died of colorectal cancer had a lower mean calcium intake compared to the rest of the population."

Ingrid Slob, Johannes Lambregts, Alberine Schuit and Frans Kok, *"Calcium Intake and Cancer Mortality in Dutch Civil Servants, Department of Epidemiology and Public Health, Agricultural University, The Netherlands.*

"Supplemental calcium has been shown to reduce the recurrence of colonic adenomatous polyps in patients at increased risk for colonic neoplasm (cancer)."

Peter Holt, Carla Wolper, Steven Moss, Kan Yang and Martin Lipkin, *Comparison of Calcium Supplementationon Epitheleal Cell Proliferation and Differentiation," Nutrition and Cancer, 41(1&2), 150-155, Department of Medicine, St Luke's Roosevelt Hospital, Strang Cancer Prevention Center.*

"Dietary calcium may inhibit colonoc carcinogenisis promoted by high fat and low fiber diets."

P. Rozen, Z Fireman, N. Fine, Y. Wax and E. Ron, *"Oral Calcium Suppresses Increased Rectal Epithelial Proliferation of Persons at Risk of Colorectal Cancer," Department of Gastroenterology, Tel-Aviv Medical Center, University of Isreal, National Cancer Institute Bethesda, M.D.*

"Our data suggests that high calcium intake may lower colorectal cancer risk."

Paul Terry, John Baron, Lief Bergkvist, Lars Holmberg, and Alicja Wolk, *"Dietary Calcium and Risk of Colorectal Cancer: A prospective Study in Women," Nutrition and Cancer, 43(1), 39-46, Department of Medical Epidemiology, Karolinska Institute, Stockholm, Sweden.*

"Calcium was found to significantly reduce tumor multiplicity."

G. Ranhotra, J. Gelroth, B. Glaser, P. Schoening, and S. Brown, *"Cellulose and Calcium lower the Incidence of Chemically-Induced Colon Tumors in Rats," Plant Foods for Human Nutrtion 54: 295-303, 1999, Kansas State University.*

"The article by Lipkin in the November 28 issue of the New England Jouranal of Medicine strongly suggests that calcium intake may play a part in the incidence of colorectal cancer."
Genaro Palmieri, M.D., *New England Journal of Medicine, University of Tennessee Medical Center.*

"The ability of oral calcium supplementation to suppress rectal epithelial proliferation supports its potential to prevent development of colorectal carcinoma in high risk individuals."
M. Thomas, J Thomson, and R Williamson, *"Oral Calcium Inhibits Rectal Epithelial Proliferation in Familial Adenomatous Polyposis" Br. J. Surg, 1993, Vol 80, April, 499-501, Department of Surgery, Royal Medical School, St Marks Hospiatl, London, England.*

"The chemo -preventive activity of calcium was suggested by epidemiological studies associating high dietary calcium with decreased colon cancer risk or mortality."
Chemoprevention Branch and Agent Development Committee, Clinical Development Plan, Calcium.

"Habitual dietary calcium may contribute to nutritional modulation of colon cancer risk."
Mirjam Govers, Denise Termont, John Lapre, Jan Kleibeuker, Roel Vonk and Roelof Van Der Meer, *"Calcium in Milk Precipitates Intestinal Fatty Acids and bbb, Thus Inhibits Colonic Cytotoxicity in Humans," Cancer Research, 3270-3275, July 15, 1996, Department of Nutrition, University Hospital Groningen, The Netherlands.*

"These inhibitory effects on metabolic factors suggest a preventive effect of dietary calcium on colon carcinogenisis."
R. Van Der Meer, J. Lapre, M. Govers, J. Kleibeuker, *"Mechanisms of the Intestinal Effects of milk products on Colon Cancer," Cancer letters 114 (9197) 75-83, Department of Nutrition University Hospital Groning, The Netherlands.*

In human subjects at increased risk for colon cancer, hyper-proliferation of colon epithelial cells was reduced after oral dietary supplementation with calcium."
Harold Newark, and Martin Lipkin, *Cancer Research (suppl) 52, 2067-*

2070, April 1, 1992, Sloan Kettering Cancer Center, New York, Rutgers University College of Pharmacy, New Jersey.

"Recent findings have indicated that dietary calcium can modulate and inhibit colon carginogenisis."

Sergio Lamprecht and Martin Lipkin, *"Chemoprevention of colon cancer by Calcium," Strang Cancer Prevention Center, New York.*

"Mediating effects of extra cellular calcium on cellular proliferation could provide a rationale for the use of calcium supplements for intervention in early phases of colon cancer."

Eniko Kallay, M. Bajina, Friedrick Wirba M.D., Stephan Kriwanek M.D., Meinrad Peterlik, Ph.D., M.D., Heide Cross Ph.D., *"Dietary calcium and Growth modulation of Human Cancer Cells," Department of Experimental pathology, Department of Clinical pathology, University of Vienna Medical School, Vienna, Austria.*

"Recently we have shown that supplemental dietary calcium inhibits colonic epithelial proliferation which may decrease the risk of colon cancer."

Mirjam Govers, Denise Termont, and Roelof Van Der Meer, *"Mechanism of the Antiproliferative Effect of Calcium Supplements on Colonic Cancer," Department of Nutrition, Institute for Dairy Research, The Netherlands.*

Scientific Publications on Calcium and High Blood Pressure

"These data suggest that supplementation of dietary calcium may contribute to a reduction of blood pressure in elderly patients with hypertension."

Yasuyuki Takagi, Masaaki Fukase, Scoichiro Takata, Tadao Fujimi, and Takuo Fujitta, *"Calcium Treatment of Essential Hypertension in Elderly Patients," Department of Medicine, Kobe University Scholl of Medicine, Kobe, Japan.*

Treatment with oral calcium represents well tolerated non-pharmacologic intervention that lowers blood pressure in patients with mild to moderate hypertension."

David McCarron, M.D., Cynthia Morris PhD., *"Blood Pressure Response to Oral Calcium in Persons with Mild to moderate Hypertension,"* Annals of Internal Medicine, December 1985, Volume 103, Number 6, Published by the American College of Physicians, Portland Oregon.

"If calcium intake of the general population were to increase to above 1200 mg the incidence of hypertension in the elderly might be decreased."

Ihab Hajjar, M.D., Clarence Grim, M.D., Theadore Kotchen, M.D., *"Dietary Calcium Lowers the Age-Related Rise in Blood Pressure in the United States,"* The NHANES Survey, Division of Geriatrics, Department of Internal Medicine, Palmetto Health Alliance University of South Carolina and the Department of Medicine, Medical College of Wisconsin, Milwaukee, WI.

"Conclusion: Dietary calcium is inversely related to systolic blood pressure in young children."

Matthew Gillman, M.D., Susan Oliveria, MPH, Curtis Ellison, M.D., *"Inverse Association of Dietary Calcium With Systolic Blood Pressure in Young Children,"* From the Evans section of Preventive Medicine and Epidemiology, Boston School of Medicine, Dr. Gillman is the recipient of a Physician Investigator Award, American Heart Association.

"The results of our investigation show that the high calcium diet blunts the development of high blood pressure and may protect against the development of hypertension."

Wasswa Semafuko, and David Morris, *"Effect of High Calcium Diet on the Development of High Blood Pressure,"* Department of Pathology and Laboratory Medicine, The Miriam Hospital Division of Biology and Medicine, Brown University, Providence Rhode Island, USA.

"The systolic and diastolic arterial blood pressures of rats fed calcium were significantly lower compared to rats of the other groups."

N Buassi, *"High Dietary Calcium Decreases Blood Pressure in rats,"* Department de Ciencias Fisiologicas, Centro de Ciencias Biologicas Universidade Estadual de Londrina, Brasil

"The results of our research indicate that calcium restriction accelerates salt-induced hypertension."

M. Nakamura, M.D., H. Suzuki, M.D., H. Yamakawa, M.D., Y. Ohno, M.D., T. Saruta, M.D., *"Calcium Restriction Accelerates Salt-Induced Hypertension,"* Department of Internal Medicine, Scholl of Medicine, University of Tokyo, Japan.

"Calcium intake has been implicated as being important in the development and treatment of hypertension."

R. Schieffer, and A. Gairard, *"Blood Pressure Effects of Calcium Intake in Experimental Models of Hypertension,"* Institut de Recherche contre les Cancers, Hopitaux Universitaires, Strasburg, Faculte de Pharmacie, Universite Louis Pasteur, France.

"More than 80 studies have reported lowered blood pressure after dietary calcium enrichment in experimental models of hypertension."

D.C. Hatton and D.A. McCarron, *Dietary calcium and blood Pressure in Experimental Models of Hypertension,"* Hypertension, 1994, April 23, (4):513-30, Division of Nephrology and Hypertension, Oregon Health Sciences University, Portland.

"Low calcium in the diet is a mechanism increasing systolic blood pressure."

K.J. Lai, K. Dakshinamurti, *The Relationship Between Low-Calcium-Induced Increase in systolic Blood Pressure,"* Department of Biochemistry and Molecular Biology, Faculty of Medicine, University of Manitoba, Canada.

"Dietary calcium supplementation normalizes blood pressure in rats and may prevent hypertension."

T. Butler, J. Cameron, K. Kirchner, *"Dietary calcium Supplementation Restores blood Pressure in Rats,"* Jackson State University, Mississippi, Am J. Hypertens, 1995 June 8 (6):615-21.

"High levels of dietary calcium attenuate the elevation of arterial blood pressure induce by salt in dogs."

Emmanuel Bravo and Yo Kageyama, *"Dietary Calcium Supplenmentation Prevents the Development of Hypertension in Salt-Treated Dogs,"* Endocrine/Hypertension Research Laboratory, Research Institute Cleveland, Department of Internal Medicine, Nationaal Tochigi Hospital, Japan.

"The blood pressure-lowering effects of dietary calcium is associated with blunting of thrombin-induced increase in platelet cytosolic calcium."

Ramachandra Rao, Youxhen Yan, and Yanyuan Wu., *"Dietary Calcium Reduces Blood Pressure" Calcium Hypertension Research Lab, Charles R. Drew University of Medicine and Science, Los Angeles, California.*

Scientific Publications on Calcium and Kidney Stone Claims:

"Two powerful prospective observational studies have suggested that increased dietary calcium reduces the risk of kidney stones."

H. Heller, *"The Role of Calcium in the Prevention of Kidney Stones," University of Texas Southwestern Medical Center at Dallas, Texas. J. Am Coll Nutr, 1999 Oct 18, (5 Suppl):373S-378S.*

"Recent evidence suggests that dietary calcium restriction may actually increase the risk of kidney stones and dietary restriction of calcium should be avoided in patients who have kidney stones."

G. Curhan, M.D.,*"Dietary Calcium and Kidney Stone Formation," Channing Laboratory, Department of Medicine, Brigham and Women's Hospital, Boston, Mass.*

Dietary calcium intake was inversely associated with the risk of kidney stones."

Gary Curhan, M.D., Walter Willet, M.D., Eric Rimm, Sc.D., and Meir Stampfer, M.D., *"A Prospective Study of Dietary Calcium and the Risk of Kidney Stones," Department of Epidemiology and Nutrition, Harvard School of Public Health, Veterans Affairs Medical Center, Boston, Mass.*

Scientific Publications on Calcium and Bone Fracture Claims

"In 12 of the 19 studies on bone loss in which calcium intake was controlled, all 12 studies showed that calcium conferred a significant benefit."

R. Henley, *"Calcium and Osteoporosis: How Much is Enough,"* New England Journal of Medicine, 1993;328:503-505, Pharmaceutical Information Associates Ltd.

"The capacity of compensatory mechanisms to provide sufficient calcium to offset daily losses from the body declines with age, hence, increasingly the body tears down bone to access its calcium."

Robert Heaney, M.D., FACN, *"Calcium Needs of the Elderly to Reduce Fracture Risk,"* Creighteon University, Osteoporosis Research Center, Omaha, Nebraska, Presented at the 41st Annual Meeting pf the American College of Nutrition at Las Vegas, Nevada, Oct 12, 2000.

"This review supports the current and public health policy of recommending increased calcium intake among older women for fracture prevention."

Robert Cumming and Michael Nevitt, *Department of Public Health and Community Medicine, University of Sydney, Austrailia, Hournal of Bone and Mineral Research, Vol 12, Number 9, 1997.*

"A preventive effect on the risk of hip fracture may partly be achieved by using calcium supplements for a late prevention in elderly people."

P Meunier, *"Prevention of Hip Fractures by Correcting Calcium Insufficiencies in Elderly People,"* Dept. of Rheumat and Bone Disease Hopital Edouard Herriot, Lyon, France.

"In elderly women low calcium absorption and intake increases the risk of hip fracture."

Kristine Ensrud, M.D., Tu Duong, Jane Cauley, Robert Heaney, M.D., Randi Wolf, Ph. D., Emily Harris, Ph. D., Steven Cummings, M.D., *"Low Fractional Calcium Absorption Increase the Risk for Hip Fracture in Women With Low Calcium Intake,"* Study of Osteoporotic Fractures Research Group, Ann Intern Med, 2000;132:345-353.

"Thus, oral calcium supplements prevented a femoral bone mineral density decrease and lowered vertebral fracture rate in the elderly."

T. Chevalley, R. Rizzoli, V. Nydegger, D. Slosman, C. Rapin, J Michel,

H. Vasey, and J. Bonjour, *Effects of Calcium Supplements on Femoral Bone Mineral Density and Vertebral Fracture Rate in Patients," World Health Organization for Osteoporosis and Bone Disease, Department of Medicine, University Hospital of Geneva, Switzerland.*

"Intake of 1000mg of calcium seems necessary to maintain bone health in postmenopausal women and if this level cannot be achieved by diet, calcium supplements should be given."

Anthony Albanese, Ph. D., *Calcium Nutrition in the Elderly," Burke Rehabilitation Center, White Plains, New York.*

Scientific Publications on Calcium and Menstrual Disorders

"Based on available evidence, a strong statement can be made regarding the importance of ensuring calcium intake in all women, particularly those in post-menopause."

The North American Menopause Society (NAMS), *"The Role of Calcium in Postmenopausal Women: Consensus opinion of the North American Menopause Society," Menopause 2001, March 8 (2):84-95.*

"Calcium supplementation is a simple and effective treatment for premenstrual syndrome."

Susan Thys-Jacobs, M.D., Silvo Ceccarelli, M.D., Arlene Bierman, M.D., Henry Weisman, M.D., Mary Cohen, M.D., Jose Alivir, M.D. Ph.D., *"Calcium Supplementation in Premenstrual Syndrome," Department of Medicine Metropolitan Hospital, New York Medical College, New York, Society of General Internal Medicine in Washington, D.C.*

"Within two months of calcium therapy, two pre-menopausal women with a history of menstrual-related migraines and premenstrual syndrome both cited a major reduction in their headache attacks as well as premenstrual symptoms."

Susan Thys-Jacobs M.D., *"Vitamin D and Calcium in Menstrual Migraine," Division of General Internal medicine, Mount Sinai Hospital, April 11, 1994.*

"Calcium supplementation, 1200 to 1600mg daily, should be considered a sound treatment option in women who experience premenstrual syndrome."
Michael Ward and Teresa Holimon, *"Calcium Treatment for Premenstrual Syndrome,"*

"Calcium supplementation reduced the negative effect, water retention, and pain, during the menstrual phase."
Jose Alvir, M.D. Ph.D., and Susan Thys-Jacobs, M.D., *"Premenstrual Symptom and Response to Calcium Teatment,"* Hillside Hospital, Division of LonfIsland Jewish Medical Center, Glen Oaks, New York, Vol 27, No. 2, 1991.

"Clinical trials in women with PMS have found that calcium supplementation effectively alleviates the majority of mood an somatic symptoms."
Susan Thys-Jacobs, M.D., *"Micronutrients and the Premenstrual Syndrome: The Case for Calcium,"* Clinical Director, Metabolic Bone Center, St. Lukes Roosevelt Hospital, Columbia University, New York.

CHAPTER NINE

Bob Barefoot's Newsletter.Com First Edition-1

September 3, 2003

My name is Bob Barefoot. Many of you have seen me on television, heard me on the radio or my audio tapes, or you may have read my books on the subject of coral calcium and its health benefits. I have been studying biological calcium for about 40 years now, long before it became a popular subject. And for that reason many seek out my council on this important subject. I also have sold and endorsed my own brands of coral calcium, i.e., CORAL CALCIUM SUPREME™, CORAL CALCIUM SUPREME PLUS™, as well as other brands that I believe to constitute high quality marine coral calcium.

Recently, however, I have received a great deal of negative publicity, mostly from competitors who have financial motives and economic interests in attacking my reputation, the quality of my products, and the message I bring to the public about coral calcium. Among those competitors are Dr. Stephen Holt and his companies, including Nature's Benefit. Many of these competitors have engaged in unscrupulous business practices, in some instances amounting to nothing more than outright fraud and misrepresentation.

In view of all of this false and misleading information being spread around about me and my products, I would like to take this opportunity to set the record straight.

Stephen Holt, His Companies, and His Newsletter

Holt and his companies, most notably Nature's Benefit, have been committed adversaries to both me and my message regarding coral calcium for well over a year. Holt indeed has made a spectacle of himself in the industry, at trade shows, and in the marketplace. He has steadfastly misrepresented and falsely stated to the public and to industry participants that he owns my entire interest in my own name and likeness. He has made false and misleading statements about me and about my products. In his attempts to disparage my coral calcium products, he has falsely stated and misrepresented throughout the industry that they are toxic and dangerous because, according to him, they contain cesium and lead, subjects that I will address below. Ironically, while that Holt denigrates me and my products, he continues to place my name and my photograph on his own products.

Holt's outrageous behavior left me with no alternative but to file a lawsuit in federal court in Arizona to stop him. That suit is now pending, and we are hopeful that it will go to trial early in 2004. Holt retaliated with his own suit against me in New Jersey, but the judge dismissed the case. Now he must answer to a Federal Judge in Arizona.

A number of parties have falsely stated or represented that I formulated their product or endorse their product. Holt is one of these. Holt initially indicated on the label of his coral calcium product, "BOB BAREFOOT'S CORAL CALCIUM PLUS," that I formulated the product. He has also publicly misrepresented that I collaborated with his staff to formulate the product. Both statements are false, and he knows they are. After I filed the lawsuit against him, he changed his label to read "physician formulated." It is interesting to note that he doesn't claim to have formulated the product himself.

In public, Holt has taken a high moral stand against both the Kevin Trudeau infomercial and my CORAL CALCIUM SUPREME ™ product on what he insists are "ethical" grounds. In private, however, Holt solicited Mr. Trudeau and attempted to take commercial advantage of him and the infomercials he now attacks, offering and at one point even demanding to become the exclusive supplier of coral calcium sold through the infomercials. Only after his commercial proposals and demands to profit from the infomercials were rejected did Holt begin his "ethical" assault on them.

Lastly Barefoot uses only the highest grade marine coral from Okinawa, Japan. Steven Holt chooses to use cheaper versions, while claiming to protect the public and pocketing the profits.

Having suffered several important setbacks in his litigation with me, Holt resorted to flagrant and repeated public attacks against me and my products, including campaigns to falsely convince the public that my products contain dangerous and toxic substances, most notably cesium and lead. Many of these attacks have come through Holt's newsletter, "Welcome to Coral Calcium News.Com." Under the guise of news, but in reality purely to obtain unfair commercial advantage, he propagates misinformation. His website has become a forum for Barefoot bashing, and little else. Examples of misinformation can be found in his recent edition, Volume 2, Number 4, where he falsely states that the FDA impounded CORAL CALCIUM SUPREME™ because of its belief that the product contained potentially toxic amounts of lead.

It is Sufficient to say that Holt has made a wholesale assault on me, my products, and the message I bring to those who have faith in coral calcium. The court systems do not work quickly, but Holt will be brought to justice.

Bob Barefoot's Newsletter.Com First Edition-2

September 3, 2003

My name is Bob Barefoot. Many of you have seen me on television, heard me on the radio or on my audio tapes, or you may have read my books on the subject of coral calcium and its health benefits. I have been studying biological calcium for about 40 years now, long before it became a popular subject. And for that reason many seek out my council on this important subject. I also have sold and endorsed my own brands of coral calcium, i.e., CORAL CALCIUM SUPREME TM, CORAL CALCIUM SUPREME PLUS TM, and as well as other brands that I believe to constitute high quality marine coral calcium.

Dr. Stephen Barrett and His "Quackwatch" Web Site

I received a substantial amount of criticism last fall when Dr. Stephen Barrett disparaged me and my product on his website "Quackwatch.com." Holt lost no time in publishing the Barrett disparagements industry-wide, and added a few insults of his own. We are still investigating Barrett's real motives, but it is interesting to note that a California court found Barrett to be biased, financially motivated and in certain respects unqualified as an expert witness, and dismissed his testimony as beyond belief. The California court reported that Barrett, a former psychiatrist, retired in 1993, nearly ten years ago, and let his medical license lapse. Barrett clearly has his own agenda, and that agenda unfortunately came to include an unwarranted attack on me and my products. Barrett often uses a "calcium expert" Robert Baratz, who runs a hair removal and ear piercing salon in Braintree, Massachusetts. Barrett was the key witness in an ABC television special that depredated Barefoot. Also the program had another doctor declare that he had lived in Okinawa for 6 years and had never heard of coral. This implied that Barefoot did not know what he was talking about. However, there are Japanese scientific studies sponsored by the Japanese government which conclude that "the longevity and good health of the Okinawans is due to their consumption of the calcium rich coral water." Someone should tell Oprah. Thus, in conclusion, despite the negative publicity that has unfairly been waged against me by competitors, and most notably Dr. Stephen Holt, very little has changed. I continue to endorse coral calcium as an important dietary supplement, I continue to publish my beliefs in this area, and sales of my authentic, high quality coral calcium products, including CORAL CALCIUM SUPREME ™ are continuing well. I do not expect the negative publicity to suddenly end, at least not until I have a court judgment against Holt and maybe not even then. So I ask each of you to carefully consider the source of this negative publicity, and weigh it accordingly. I welcome your questions and comments. Here's to a healthful and happy future.

Bob Barefoot's Newsletter.Com First Edition-3

September 3, 2003

My name is Bob Barefoot. Many of you have seen me on television, heard me on the radio or on my audio tapes, or you may have read my books on the subject of coral calcium and its' health benefits. I have been studying biological calcium for about 40 years now, long before it became a popular subject. And for that reason many seek out my council on this important subject. I also have sold and endorsed my own brands of coral calcium, i.e., CORAL CALCIUM SUPREME™, CORAL CALCIUM SUPREME PLUS TM, and as well as other brands that I believe to constitute high quality marine coral calcium.

The Misinformation About Cesium

Holt began a campaign in about March of 2003 to attack my CORAL CALCIUM SUPREME™ product and thereby bolster his own sales of coral calcium by trying to scare the public into believing my product contained dangerous and toxic levels of cesium. Cesium is a naturally occurring element found in coral calcium. CORAL CALCIUM SUPREME™ in fact includes a small amount of it, about three milligrams per roughly 1000 milligram tablet. The literature includes support for the potential benefits of cesium, but we are not aware of any that indicates cesium at this low dose has any dangerous or toxic effects. We enlisted an independent medical expert who studied the literature on cesium and concluded that, not only is there no support in the medical literature for Holt's claim of toxicity at these levels or anything approaching them, but that

Holt had misrepresented the literature in concluding that it was. When challenged on this point, Holt was unable to produce any responsible literature supporting his claims of toxicity at these levels. He was merely trying to scare consumers away from CORAL CALCIUM SUPREME™ and increase sales of his own product using reprehensible and indefensible tactics.

Thus, Holt's contention that cesium is toxic is not supported by the scientific word and borders on fear mongering, as every element on Earth is toxic in the appropriate amounts. For example, the common element potassium, found in large quantities in potatoes and bananas, is used as a lethal injection to terminate criminals. It would therefore be toxic, by Holt's definition, and it would therefore be dangerous to eat potatoes and bananas. This, of course, is ridiculous as is Holt's contention that the 3 milligrams of cesium found in Coral Supreme is toxic. Most studies done on the toxicity of cesium find it to be basically non-toxic and that it takes huge amounts to cause any discomfort. Dr. Holt refers to a study that "suggested" that huge quantities of cesium "may" cause problems with the rate of your heart beat. The study was done on rats and the researchers concluded that the problems of heart beat may have not even been caused by the cesium, but rather by the lack of potassium which has been proven to effect the heart beat, as we can stop the hearts of criminals with large injections of potassium. The amount used in the studies was equivalent to 180,000 milligrams compared to the three milligrams used in Coral Supreme, which experts conclude is harmless to humans.

Bob Barefoot's Newsletter.Com First Edition-4

September 3, 2003

My name is Bob Barefoot. Many of you have seen me on television, heard me on the radio or on my audio tapes, or you may have read my books on the subject of coral calcium and its' health benefits. I have been studying biological calcium for about 40 years now, long before it became a popular subject. And for that reason many seek out my council on this important subject. I also have sold and endorsed my own brands of coral calcium, i.e., CORAL CALCIUM SUPREME™, CORAL CALCIUM SUPREME PLUS™, and as well as other brands that I believe to constitute high quality marine coral calcium.

<u>The Recent Misinformation About Lead</u>

More recently, in his "Newsletter," Volume 2, Number 4, Holt falsely alleges that CORAL CALCIUM SUPREME™ contains lead and is therefore dangerous, and that the FDA impounded CORAL CALCIUM SUPREME™ because of its belief that the product contained potentially toxic amounts of lead.

CORAL CALCIUM SUPREME™ does not contain lead. The product is manufactured by reputable suppliers, and is analyzed and quality tested on a routine basis by certified American laboratories. We have not found any lead in the product. If it were there, we would know about it. It isn't.

Moreover, the FDA did not impound any of my CORAL CALCIUM SUPREME™ based on a belief that it contains lead, or for any other reason. It is my understanding that the FDA impounded a single batch of Kevin Trudeau's coral calcium product because he bad put on the label "As Seen On TV," which tied it to the infomercial the FTC found to be objectionable. This is further addressed below.

Holt's misrepresentation regarding lead is merely another of his disreputable attempts to undermine fair competition. If the FDA had truly found lead in my products or in Kevin Trudeau's, they would have impounded all of the product, not just one batch. Holt has no evidence of lead in my product. If he had such evidence, he would have included it in his "Newsletter."

Bob Barefoot's Newsletter.Com Second Edition-1

September 25, 2003

My name is Bob Barefoot. Many of you have seen me on television, heard me on the radio or on my audio tapes, or you may have read my books on the subject of coral calcium and its health benefits. I have been studying biological calcium for about 40 years now, long before it became a popular subject. And for that reason many seek out my council on this important subject. I also have sold and endorsed my own brands of coral calcium, i.e., CORAL CALCIUM SUPREME™, CORAL CALCIUM SUPREME PLUS™, and as well as other brands that I believe to constitute high quality marine coral calcium.

Bad Press - Canada

In the August 22, 2003 edition of the Edmonton Sun, Staff Writer, Jeremy Loome, wrote an article entitled "Cancer Scam Alleged" with "former city man at center of accusations over infomercial." The article was written as a hatchet job on Bob Barefoot, a very proud graduate of the Northern Alberta Institute of Technology, NAIT, 1967. Since his graduation Bob Barefoot has, with his fellow Ph.D. co-authors, seven scientific publications and he has written three books, *The Calcium Factor*, *Death By Diet*, and, *If It Glitters*, the first two of which are best-sellers. His recent infomercial with Kevin Trudeau was the most watched informercials in history. As such, it has become extremely controversial. Because of Barefoot's references to the claim that calcium supplements can reverse a host of diseases, which are supported by hundreds of scientific publications. The FTC deemed that the claims were being attached to the coral calcium product, being sold, even though Barefoot did not claim that the product itself cured anything, as can be verified by an examination of the text of the show. Barefoot believes that the FTC is just doing its job and exercising its mandate. The restrictions of the United States' laws on what can be said concerning a nutrient's relationship to a disease when stated in conjunction with the sale of nutritional supplements are severe. Those restrictions make it difficult to reflect the worldwide scientific community's understanding of the importance of this nutrient and its relationship to certain diseases in the marketplace. I encourage the public to do their own research and to discuss the application to their own health with their medical practitioner.

Calcium is an essential nutrient in our daily diet and is a key factor in a wide range of biological systems within the body. Its role in disease prevention and treatment has been studied, and continues to be studied, by numerous scientists around the world.

A search on the US National Library of Medicine's PubMed system reveals more than 17,000 scientific articles on calcium and its relationship to cancer. In particular, clinical trials have examined the link between calcium consumption and its positive effects on colorectal cancer, one of the most common cancers in Canada (the Canadian Cancer Society estimates that this year 18,000 Canadians will be diagnosed with colorectal cancer and 8,300 will die from it). While the study of calcium continues, its importance is becoming widely recognized even among the more conservative members of the scientific and medical communities. The 2001 "Physicians Desk Reference for Nutritional Supplements" chapter on calcium states that calcium has anti-osteroporotic activity and may also have anticarcinogenic, anti-hypertension and hypocholesterolemic activity.

The problem that Bob Barefoot has with the article "Cancer Scam Alleged" is that many of the statements made were false, and therefore Barefoot believes that the public was deceived. Dr. Barrett, a retired Psychiatrist with no medical license, obviously has a vendetta against Bob Barefoot. Many others currently are suing him for his slanderous attacks. A California court has already ruled that he is biased, and "beyond any credibility" in the area of nutrition. Thus, Dr. Barrett will be handled by the courts. The real problem is the author of the article who allowed this man to spew his warped, and totally unsubstantiated conceptions before the people of Edmonton, my hometown. He allowed Barrett to tell his readers that "there are people who are going to die as a result of what they have been doing" (which is taking coral calcium.) Of course this is false, slanderous and the author, Jeremy Loome, will never be able to give his readers the names of the victims that don't exist, although his readers should insist that he do so. Also, millions of people have been consuming the coral calcium for hundreds of years, and so far, no one has died. When Barefoot asked Loome why he did not inform his readers about Dr. Barrett, his response was that the story was about Bob Barefoot and not Dr. Barrett. When Barefoot objected that his failure to inform his readers would result in a fraudulent story, Loome responded, "so sue me."

Dr. Barrett, who is not a chemist, advises the people of Edmonton to buy calcium carbonate, which he declares is the same as coral calcium. I disagree with the Edmonton Sun's characterization of Drs. Stephen Barrett and Robert Baratz as "medical experts." Robert Baratz operates the National Council Against Health Fraud (NCAHF) out of the back room of his hair removal and ear piercing salon in Braintree,

Massachusetts. I do not believe either the doctor with no license nor the ear piercer are experts on calcium and its relationship to disease. I suspect neither has published peer-reviewed literature based on original research concerning calcium, and I can find no articles by them in the calcium scientific literature. A real expert can see a huge difference between coral calcium and calcium carbonate. Coral calcium has the preferred calcium to magnesium ratio, 2:1, calcium carbonate does not. Coral calcium has about 70 trace nutrients, calcium carbonate does not. Coral calcium has marine microbes to assist in digestion, calcium carbonate does not. Coral calcium, an aragonite, has over 1000 times the surface area of calcium carbonate, calcite. Also, studies done by the Japanese show that most of the calcium form coral calcium is absorbed by the body while very little of the calcium from calcium carbonate is absorbed. Finally, coral calcium has hundreds of years of history with probably millions of testimonials, calcium carbonate does not. Jeremy Loome is doing a real disservice to his readers with his mistaken advice.

Jeremy Loome's claim that doctors advise that the "oxygen link to cancer was disproved more than 60 years ago" was not substantiated, while the man who made the link, Dr. Otto Warburg, won two Nobel prizes because of the oxygen link to cancer. Also, Dr. Baratz's, contention (Council Against Health Care Fraud) that "people are being duped into believing something that has no scientific support at all" is just simply false. Barefoot has hundreds of scientific documents and there are thousands more for Dr. Baratz to read. Also, Dr. Baratz would do well to read Barefoot's books.

Jeremy Loome's claims to what Barefoot said are disputed by Barefoot as being out of context and therefore misleading. Barefoot does take exception, however, to Jeremy Loome's slur of Dr. Carl Reich. Loomes states that Barefoot "failed to mention that Reich was stripped of his Alberta license in 1986." Although Barefoot did not state this, he assumed that any good reporter writing a story should already be aware of the facts. Loome also should have been aware that his fellow reporter, Gary Davies wrote a four page article on Dr. Reich in the Sept/Oct edition of the City Scope magazine where he called Dr. Reich "a man ahead of his time" and "the Father of Preventive Medicine." He also failed to mention that Reich was stripped of his license for declaring that "calcium cures cancer." Several years later, in October 1998, the Journal of the American Medical Association wrote "calcium supplements reverse cancer and make cancer grow back to normal." Since this article, many more have been written so it does appear that Dr. Reich was indeed ahead of his time. He was a great man and a great doctor and Barefoot is very proud to be the co-author of the "Father of Preventive Medicine."

CHAPTER TEN

CALCIUM AND CANCER

Calcium's role in disease prevention and treatment has been studied, and continues to be studied, by numerous Scientists around the world. A search on the US National Library of Medicine's PubMed system reveals mort than 17,000 scientific articles on calcium and its relationship to cancer. In particular, clinical trials have examined the link between calcium consumption and its positive effects on colorectal cancer. While the study of calcium continues, its importance is becoming widely recognized even among the more conservative members of the scientific and medical communities. The 2001 "Physicians Desk Reference for Nutritional Supplements" chapter on calcium states that calcium has anti-osteroporotic activity and may also have anti-carcinogenic, anti-hypertensive and hypocholesterolemic activity.

Could a direct cause and relationship exist between calcium and cancer, as these thousands of scientific publications suggest? Some cancer experts say that there are too many types of cancer for there to be any possible common denominator, and yet these same experts would be shocked in disbelief by the demonstrable relationship between calcium deficiency and the diseases of aging, allergy and stress. There is also a great deal of evidence to show that calcium disorders play a pivotal role in diseases of the young, such as Duchenenne's muscular dystrophy, named for the lack of dystrophin protein in the cells. With muscular dystrophy, both the calcium channels of the cells are open much more of the time, and the calcium ion concentration within the cells is twice as high as normal. This indicates a calcium regulation problem.

Also, allergies have been successfully treated as calcium disorders. With this myriad of human ailments related to calcium disorders, it would seem almost negligent not to discuss the probable integral role that calcium would play in the dreaded disease, *cancer*.

The definition of *"cancer"* according to the dictionary is *"a malignant tumor eating the part it is in, spreading indefinitely and tending to recur when removed."* In more technical terms, *cancer arises when the deoxyribonucleic acid, DNA, is chemically altered, producing mutant cells that multiply without restraint and that produce a family of descendant cells that invade the surrounding tissues with progressive emaciation.* This local invasion can be followed by metastasis, or spread to distant sights by way of lymphatics and the bloodstream, usually making cancer quite lethal. Some cancers can be killed by the use of chemicals (*chemotherapy*), by radiation, or by surgically cutting it out where possible, thereby destroying it *along with the part of the body* in which it resides. Surgery usually leads over time to the spread of (the cancer into other parts of the body (*metastisization*). All must agree that the orthodox approaches are not satisfactory.

As the number of people being saved is growing, so too is the number of people dying from this dreaded disease. Billions of dollars are being spent annually on the search for the *"silver bullet,"* a drug, that will destroy the cancer without killing the patient. But, this is in contradiction to the orthodox stance that there is no one common denominator in cancer for the bullet to be shot at, especially since so many factors have been shown to trigger so many different types of cancer. Despite this, two time Nobel Prize Winner for Medicine, Otto Warburg, believed that the cause of cancer had been well defined which meant that there indeed could be a silver bullet, which he believed would be a combination of nutrients. If the silver bullet is to become a reality, a better understanding of the basic chemistry of cancer would be the best course in leading to the potential common denominator.

Everyone, including the American Cancer Society, agrees that there is a direct relationship between the occurrence of cancer and the foods we eat and the air to which we are exposed. But, that is analogous to saying that life causes death. What is really meant is that there are certain chemicals called "*carcinogens*" that are known to cause cancer when they are exposed in the body under specific conditions. For example, the existence of massive amounts of carcinogens by their sheer numbers can trigger cancer. Or, the addition of a third component, such as specific ultra violet radiation, can trigger cancer. In order to understand the existence of a common denominator, it would first be necessary to more thoroughly understand both the chemical nature of the carcinogens and the chemistry of their entry into the DNA template or mold.

Table #1 US Cancer Deaths
(Source: The American Cancer Society)

Year	Deaths
1970	320,000
1975	365,000
1978	405,000
1985	482,000
1990	514,000

By the 1950's, with cancer striking one out of every four people in North America, *the alkali treatments had long since been forgotten* and radiation was beginning to be used to kill the cancer and, unfortunately, surrounding healthy tissue. By the 1980's, with the incidence of cancer increasing, striking one out of every three people (see Table #1: US Cancer Deaths), chemical therapies (chemotherapies) were being perfected. Today, although there are many survivors, the incidence of cancer is still gaining in momentum and the *orthodox traditions and treatments*, which are obviously *losing the war against cancer*, are firmly entrenched. We are only winning some minor battles. In order to change the course of history, we must gain a more thorough understanding of the chemistry of carcinogens and how they are energized to interact chemically with DNA, incorporating the electron physics involved in the cell membrane.

Table 2: Original Major Nutrients in the Body

Nutrient	Weight %
* Water	39.10
Oxygen	20.30
* Glucose	19.10
* Methane	13.80
* Ammonia	2.90
Calcium	1.60
Iron	1.00
Phosphorous	0.90
Potassium	0.40
Sodium	0.30
Chlorine	0.30
Sulfur	0.25
Magnesium	0.05

Total	**100.00**

* Made up of the following elements

Oxygen	**65.0%**
Carbon	**18.0%**
Hydrogen	**10.0%**
Nitrogen	**2.4%**
	95.4%

Note:
The chemical breakdown of glucose and the chemical combination of oxygen with methane results in production of **34.6 %** more water, making a total of **73.7% water in the human body.**

121

Table 2: Major Nutrients in the Blood (pH 7.3 - 7.5)

Component	Milligrams per 1000cc (ppm)*
Sodium	1400 — 1430
Chloride	1000 — 1040
Triglyceride Fat	950 — 1050
Iron	950 — 1000
Glucose	850 — 1000
LDL Cholesterol	600 — 1300
HDL Cholesterol	450 — 850
Calcium	97 — 106
Total Protein	72 — 75
Potassium	40 — 43
Phosphorus	31 — 35

* ppm stands for parts of nutrients in the blood per million parts of blood.

Before explaining the carcinogenic alteration of DNA, a brief discussion of the *human genetic code* is warranted. To begin with, the human body holds about *ten trillion cells*. Large molecules called proteins determine the structure and function of each cell. A cell nucleus contains *twenty-three pairs* of "*chromosomes*," that control the manufacture of proteins by the cell. A chromosome consists of *two* very long, spirally twisted *strands of DNA*, the chemical that carries genetic information from parents to offspring. DNA is divided into about *one hundred thousand clusters* called "*genes*." A gene determines a human characteristic such as height, eye color, or disease resistance. Genes are composed of *thousands* of "*nucleotides*," the smallest genetic unit. Nucleotides come in *four different shapes* called "*adenine, cytosine, guanine, and thymine*" or "A, C, G and T" respectively, all arranged in pairs along the spiral strands of DNA. About *three billion nucleotides* make up the *human genome*, the blueprint of a human being, and man has only begun to chemically map their significance in the makeup of genes.

Exposure, alone, of the DNA to the carcinogens would be insufficient to create a mutation. Indeed, the body is believed to have several defensive mechanisms to fight off the invasion of carcinogens within the cell. For example, DNA is only able to accept certain specific radicals, and *the carcinogen by itself would not fit into the DNA strand.* Researchers, such as Dr. James P. Whitlock Jr., of Stanford University, knows that carcinogens, such as *dioxin*, can bind with certain soluble intracellular receptors, toxic enzymes, to provide a new complex of *the right shape and size to be capable of binding to specific sequences of nucleotides, causing the DNA template to be bent or angled.* Once so altered, the DNA is capable of incorporating a foreign protein molecule that is not in the genetic code, in place of one of the A, C, G, or T nucleotides. Thus, a *mutant* may be born.

The question therefore arises as to what conditions within the cell are necessary to produce this mutation receptor ? The early work of Nobel Prize winner Otto Warburg, some seventy-five years ago, (*Cause and prevention of Cancer*; Biochem, Zeits, 152: 514-520, 1924), showed clearly that cancer was associated with *anaerobic (deficiency of oxygen) conditions,* resulting in fermentation and a marked drop in the pH of the cell (*Low pH Hyperthermia Cancer Therapy*; Cancer Chemotherapy Pharmocology 4; 137-145, 1980). Moreover, the production of mutation receptors cannot occur with the pH of the cell in the healthy calcium buffered 7.4 to 6.6 range, a range which assures the breakdown of glucose into the A, C, G and T nucleotide radicals that promote healthy DNA synthesis. M. Von Arenne showed that both high and low pH solutions *can quickly kill the cell.* He was also able to show that at a pH slightly above the normal pH of 7.4, the toxic enzymes, which characterize the low pH cells, are neutralized and that the cancer cells will enter a *dormant state*.

Thus the success of the "*caustic solution treatment*" of tumors by the turn-of-the-century doctors could now be explained.

Also, it should be noted that by definition, alkaline solutions are made up of hydroxyl (*oxygen-hydrogen*) radicals and therefore are oxygen rich. In the *absence of oxygen* within the acidic intracellular fluids, the *glucose undergoes fermentation into lactic acid*, causing the pH of the cell to drop even further, thereby *inhibiting the production of A, C, G and T nucleotides* that allow for normal DNA synthesis. This provides the necessary conditions for toxic enzymes to produce radicals that will bond with carcinogens. The complexes they produce will bind with specific sequences of nucleotides in the DNA, causing the template to be altered, thereby setting the scene for the abnormal replication of DNA to trigger cancer.

Thus, in the healthy, calcium buffered, slightly alkaline cell environment, *the conditions required for the propagation of cancer do not exist*. It therefore remains dormant, or dies. Dr. Carl Reich noted that his cancer patients demonstrated. 1) lifestyle defects responsible for deficiency of one or both calcium and vitamin D, 2) symptoms and physical signs of ionic calcium deficiency syndrome, and 3) a greater than normal incidence of these ionic calcium deficiency diseases. Thus, he considered cancer as the ultimate adaptation to ionic calcium deficiency, *"tailor made"* to survive and to thrive in an ionic calcium deficient environment. Dr. Reich found that the cancer in many of his patients seemed to go into remission once their calcium deficiency was rectified, by a change of lifestyle including diet and with mineral and vitamin supplements that raised the pH of their cellular fluids. Their associated ionic calcium deficiency diseases were also suppressed.

Another interesting fact is that cancer is virtually unknown to the *Hopi Indians* of Arizona and the *Hunzas* of Northern Pakistan, so long as they stay in the same environment; this strongly suggests that something they are consuming is protecting them from cancer. The only significant difference is their water supply. The Hopi water is rich in *rubidium and potassium*, and the Hunza water is rich in *cesium and potassium*, making both of the water supplies rich with very *caustically active* metals. Researchers such as Dr. K. Brewer (*The Mechanisms of Carcenogenesis*, 1979, Journal of IAPM, Vol. V, No.2) and Dr. H. Sartori (*Cancer Orwellian or Eutopian*, Life Science Universal Inc., 1985), found that, by not only addressing the calcium deficiency, but by also using these minerals to raise the pH to above the 7.4 range to a pH of 8.5, *the cancer cells would die while the healthy cells would thrive*; thus, once again verifying the observations of both the turn-of-the-century doctors and men like Dr. Reich.

Both Dr. Brewer and Dr. Sartori would treat their cancer patients with the salts of both rubidium and cesium. These salts have large and extremely alkaline metal ions that can enter the cells through the large nutrient channels, but, like the large potassium ions, they have great difficulty in getting out of the cell due to the small ion cell exit channels. Thus, under these oxygen-rich, alkaline conditions, cancer cells die quickly, with no damage to the healthy cells, and therefore no serious side effects. The decomposing dead cells provide the nutrients for the renewed health and normal DNA replication. In his publication, *Cesium Therapy in Cancer Patients*, Sartori describes the two week treatment of 50 last stage, metastisized, terminal cancer patients (13 comatosed), with cesium chloride salts. Ten of the patients had breast cancer, nine had colon cancer, six had prostate cancer, four had pancreas cancer, five had lung cancer, three had liver cancer, three had lymphoma, one had Ewing sarcoma pelvis, one had adeno cancer, and eight had unknown primary cancer. With all 50 patients, conventional treatment had failed and the patients had been sent home to die. All were expected to die within weeks, with the survival rate being less than one in ten million. After 1 to 3 days, the pain disappeared in all of the patients. After 2 weeks,

13 died with autopsies showing no presence of cancer. After 12 months, 12 more had died, but 25, or *an astounding 50% survived*. When compared to the 97% that die when taking conventional chemotherapy, this success had to be considered astounding. Unfortunately, both cries of "*quackery*" and persecution from the medical establishment have driven this caustic cancer therapy research, started by Nobel Prize winner Dr. Otto Warburg, underground.

Dr. Max Gerson was world famous for *curing* supposed incurables, the most famous being *Albert Schweitzer* (**A Cancer Therapy: Results**, 5th Edition, Max Gerson, M.D., Del Mar, CA: Totality Book Publishers, 1958, 1975, 1977). Gerson often used **three caustic potassium salts** to successfully treat his cancer patients: potassium gluconate, acetate and phosphate. He knew that potassium was supposed to be a normal constituent of the cell serum, and should also be found in moderate amounts in blood serum. However, Gerson observed that many of his cancer patients showed *abnormally high levels of this mineral in blood serum*. To the horror of his medical colleagues, he fed these patients large doses of his potassium mixture in juices and found that the potassium level in their blood serum dropped very low as they made fast recoveries. The very alkaline potassium was going back into the cells where it belonged, raising the intracellular pH and thereby *inhibiting the proliferation of the cancer*. Gerson also found that an intravenous treatment of 90% oxygen and 10% ozone injected into the vein, with a very thin needle so that the bubbles of gas were tiny and the gas was quickly absorbed, would attack the malignant tissue on contact. Since the cancer cells are anaerobic, the addition of oxygen is incompatible with, and assists in reversing the production of toxic enzymes thereby disarming cancer's trigger mechanism

Other researchers have recently found that cancerous tumors cultured in a serum deficient in calcium, *will grow*

prolifically, while the same tumor cultured in a serum rich in calcium *remains dormant*. The reason that calcium maintains cell adhesion and that this adhesion has a profound effect on the cancer, preventing it from spreading apart and breaking up. Furthermore, further research has shown that normal cells must be spread out on a solid substrate before they are able to initiate normal DNA synthesis, and that calcium is specifically required for spreading. This calcium induced cell spreading, while encouraging normal DNA synthesis, strongly inhibits abnormal synthesis (**The Role of Calcium in Biological Systems**, Volume 1, pages 157 and 169, CRC Press, 1985).

If all of this calcium is so good at inhibiting cancer, then why is *hypercalcemia* (high calcium in the blood) associated with various types of cancer? Hypercalcemia, which usually occurs in the latter stages of certain cancers with large tumors and metastasis, could be the body's last ditch defense mechanism. This defense is accompanied by *hypophosphatemia* (a low blood serum phosphate) and a *high calcium phosphate renal discharge*. The calcium within the cancerous and very acidic cells (pH as low as 4) will precipitate out as phosphate (Dr. Anghileri, **The Role of Calcium in Biological Systems**, Volume 1, page 46, CRC Press, 1985). To counter this loss in ionic calcium, the cancer cells obtain the calcium from other healthy nearby cells. But, as the cancer becomes massive or widespread, the calcium within is locked up in the phosphate form, and the most available source for the required calcium is the *calcium-rich bones*. When this happens, the blood serum becomes *very high in calcium* while the bones undergo *massive deterioration*. The blood serum is now high in calcium and low in phosphate, as much more phosphate is required for the *now dominant but less efficient sodium ion* to feed nutrients into the inside of the acidic cell, as was the case when the calcium was feeding nutrients into the alkaline cell. Under these conditions, the intestine finds it difficult to absorb digested calcium. The result is the whole calcium cycle system is now totally out of whack. Ironically, despite the very *high serum calcium*, what the system needs to put itself back into balance is more calcium from an external source, as well as sunshine and all of the other nutritious foods, in order to start the individual on the road to recovery. For these and other reasons, it can be demonstrated that many of the unorthodox cancer treatments *may indeed have scientific merit*, and that, when chemically understood, *cancer may be beaten painlessly.*

Thus the preventive medicine approach would be to replenish the depleting stock of ionic calcium through nutrition (see Table 3) and food supplements (see Table 8), thereby removing the need for the body to ravish calcium from the bones. On the other hand, the approach of orthodox medicine would be to find a *drug* to block the calcium from entering the cancerous cell, thereby *treating the effect but not the cause* of the problem, which is ionic calcium deficiency.

Coincidentally, orthodox cancer researchers "have recently recognized a new class of synthetic compounds called carboxy-amide aminoimidazoles (**CAI's**) which, when administered orally (in animals) block the growth of established metastasis by altering the flow of *calcium* into cancer cells (*Cancer Cell Invasion and Metastasis* Lance A. Liotta, **Scientific American** February 1992)." It may be that the CAI's reduce the level of the acidity which promotes both the solubility of bone mineral (*Calcium Homeostasis: Hypercalcemia and Hypocalcemia*, Dr. Gregory R. Mundy, University of Texas) and tumor calcification, as is also the case with the chemical ethanolamine, a very strong alkali which cancer researchers found to also reduce calcium hydrogen phosphate precipitation The Role of Calcium in Biological Systems Volume 1, page 47, CRC Press, 1985). Likewise, nutritious alkaline foods (Table 3) also reduce the level of acidity, but without any toxicity or side effects. Such food also replenishes the dwindling supply of ionic calcium.

Other foods, such as polyunsaturated fats found in corn and other vegetable oils increase the formation of DNA-damaging free radicals (free radicals are "starved" for electrons and therefore thrive in mineral deficient acidic body fluids but are eradicated in mineral sufficient alkali body fluids). Women who eat five grams of these polyunsaturated fats daily *increased their breast-cancer risk by 69 percent*. However, a study released in January 1998, led by Alicja Wolk at the Karolinska Institute in Sweden, which included the participation of the Harvard School of Public Health and was conducted on 61,471 women aged 40 through 76, found that the daily ingestion of at least 10 grams of monounsaturated fat (the kind found in olive and canola oils) - about three-fourths of a tablespoon - *cut the risk of breast cancer in half*. Another study released in November 1997 by the University of Maryland found that by taking huge doses of vitamins (20 times the RDAs of vitamins C and E) before consuming high fat foods like a cheese-burger of fries, the blood-thickening triglycerides are only produced in small amounts. Also the blood vessel expansion remained constant, thereby protecting the body from blood clotting and reducing the risk of heart disease. In addition, a December 1997 study by Matthew Gillman of the Harvard Medical School found that *"raising" the fat in the diet from 26 % to 35 % of total calories resulted in a 30 % reduction in ischemic strokes*.

Unfortunately, as is the case with most degenerative diseases, the orthodox choice is to employ noxious drugs to block the effect rather than nutritious food to cure the cause. Hippocrates, the father of medicine, made his choice clear; *"food is your best medicine and the best foods are the best medicines.*" Hippocrates used garlic and onions to suppress cancerous tumors. It is interesting to note that in the *Journal of the National Cancer Institute* 1989, both U.S. and Chinese scientists reported a study the more people ate garlic and onions, known to contain anti-bacterial, anti-fungal and anti-thrombotic (aggregations of blood platelets) agents, the less likely they were to develop stomach cancer which currently is the most common cause of death among cancer patients on a global scale.

In 1932 Otto Warburg won the Nobel Prize in Medicine for his discovery that cancer was anaerobic: cancer occurs in the absence of free oxygen. As innocuous as this discovery might seem, it is actually a startling and significant finding worthy of a Nobel Prize. What it basically means is that cancer is caused by a lack of free oxygen in the body and therefore, whatever causes this to occur is the cause of all cancers.

It can therefore be demonstrated that, as has been shown with many other diseases, there is indeed a common denominator in all cancers; and as in other diseases *the silver bullet for the treatment of cancer* may turn out to be *"the calcium factor.*"

CHAPTER ELEVEN

THE ANSWER TO CANCER ?

The January 14, 1999 issue of the *Phoenix Republic* wrote in an article entitled *"Calcium Reduces Tumors"* that the *New England Journal of Medicine* reported "adding calcium to the diet can keep you from getting tumors in your large intestine." Then the February, 1999 issue of the *Readers Digest* wrote in an article entitled *"The 'Superstar' Nutrient"* that the *Journal of the American Medical Association* published "when the participants consumption reached 1500 milligrams of calcium a day, cell growth in the colon improved toward normal (this means that the cancer was reversed)." *The Digest* also reported that the Metabolic Bone Center at St. Lukes Hospital believes that "a chronic deficiency of calcium is largely responsible for premenstrual syndrome (PMS)" and that "a lot of women are avoiding the sun and their vitamin D levels may be very low." In the same article, *The Digest* reported, "in 1997 a large federally financed trial found that a diet containing 1200 milligrams of calcium significantly lowered blood pressure in adults." Then the May 3, 1999 edition of *US World News Report* wrote in an article entitled *"Calcium's*

Powerful Mysterious Ways," that, "Researchers are increasingly finding that the humble mineral calcium plays a major role in warding off major illnesses from high blood pressure to colon cancer" and that "You name the disease, and calcium is beginning to have a place there" (David McCarron, a nephrologist at Oregon Health Sciences University). Unfortunately, most doctors have not heard the news that their own journals, major newspapers and magazines are reporting that natural supplements, especially calcium, can cure and prevent disease.

The scientific evidence that calcium is the key to good and long health is overwhelming. Just 20 years ago, any doctor making the claim that calcium supplements could cure cancer would loose his license. Dr. Carl Reich lost his license for making this claim, which the medical authorities of the day branded as *"too simplistic."* Yet today, the doctor's own Journals: *The New England Journal of Medicine, The Journal of the American Medical Association*, and the *American Journal of Clinical Nutrition* are all making the claim that calcium supplements can reverse cancer and that virtually no organ escapes calcium's influence. These journals have been quoted in our popular and respectable newspapers and magazines. We have come a long way, and still have a long way to go. At present, it is almost impossible to find a doctor who is aware of these scientific findings. Therefore, we must get the doctors to read their own Journals and then do an almost impossible task, get the American Medical Association and the Food and Drug Administration to do their jobs and endorse these scientific findings. When this finally occurs, over 90% of disease will be eradicated thereby eliminating massive pain and suffering, and we will be well on our way to *curing America*.

One does not have to be a rocket scientist to read simple articles in reputable newspapers and magazines quoting the doctor's own journals that are all saying that disease can be cured by diet. Also one can simply look at the millions of people around the world that never get sick and say, "Lets do what they do!" Unfortunately, all of their milk of the mountains is consumed as fast as it is produced. However, the Japanese could help cure the world with their "milk of the oceans" known as *coral calcium*, the calcium factor of good health.

CHAPTER TWELVE

CALCIUM AND HEART DISEASE

After all of the discussion in the previous chapters on the *king of the bioelements, calcium*, it will come as no surprise that calcium ions also dominate the health of the heart, with the *king of diseases being heart disease*. The link between these two kings is cell deterioration. Since the general health of the cell is regulated by calcium, any deficiency in calcium causes the cell function to become deregulated and thereby prone to deteriorate. In the heart and arteries this deterioration results in a chain sequence of events that has come to be known as heart disease.

Over one hundred years ago Sidney Ringer's article entitled *"A Future Contribution Regarding the Influence of Different Constituents of the Blood on the Contraction of the Heart"* was published in the **Journal of Physiology**. This work described the fundamental significance of the calcium ion to the maintenance of cardiac contractibility. Although an accidental finding, this work was the important base from which much of the focus on biological calcium originated.

As has been previously described in Chapter 5, because of calcium's most efficient ionization potential, *the heart's electrical muscle contractibility* has been proven by researchers to be due to *calcium ionization*. The most important aspect of heart disease is not a function of the chemistry of the heart muscle, but rather the chemistry of that which passes through it, the blood.

The heart is a hollow muscular organ that maintains the constant circulation of blood by contracting and dilating. When the circulation of blood through one of the coronary arteries (which nourish the heart muscle itself) is restricted or temporarily stopped by restriction and/or blood clotting caused by disease of the wall of this artery, a coronary thrombosis, which causes the death of the heart muscle supplied by the plugged artery, or what is commonly referred to as a *"heart attack,"* occurs. ***Heart disease is the number one killer*** in North America, with ***cancer a close second.***

Heart disease refers to all irregular conditions of the heart, the most predominant of which is the heart attack. This condition usually follows ***angina*** (heart spasms) or heart pain caused by over-exertion of the heart muscle during which the ability of the diseased artery to supply the heart muscle with oxygen was exceeded. This situation is created by a thickening and hardening of the walls of the arteries which diminishes the size of the lumen or opening in the artery. This diseased state of the wall of the artery, known as arteriosclerosis, is usually caused by the gradual buildup of plaque on the walls of the arteries that has been related to several factors of which lack of exercise and faulty nutrition are the most important. Thus the wide variance in the incidence of heart attacks has been related to differences in ***diet and culture***. Economic, occupational and social differences produce variance in stress, diet, exercise, exposure to sunshine and other critical factors that can be related to heart disease.

The obvious question is what is *"plaque"*? It turns out to be a composite of material that builds up over the years. It is composed of collagen, phospholipids, fibrin, triglycerides, muco- polysaccharides, cholesterol, heavy metals, proteins, muscle tissue and debris, ***all bonded together with calcium***. This plaque only builds up in arteries that deliver the blood to the various parts of the body, but not in the much thinner walled veins that return the blood to the heart. If cholesterol is the cause of plaque buildup, as is suggested by the medical community, then why doesn't the same cholesterol in the same blood cause the plaque to build up in the veins? Obviously, **cholesterol is not the cause of plaque buildup** and therefore, the doctors advice that the elderly reduce their cholesterol levels is ill-advised. In addition, the prescription of billions of dollars worth of needless cholesterol reducing drugs each year can only result in potential harm to the health of the public. Cholesterol levels can be lowered safely through balanced nutrition.

Both veins and arteries are lined with the same smooth internal layer that is in contact with the circulating blood. Unlike the vein, however, *the artery has an outer circling muscular layer* that allows for expansion and contraction to regulate the blood pressure maintaining a gradual delivery of blood to the organs as well as an equal distribution of blood nutrients to all parts of the body. As was described in the previous chapter on cancer, a calcium deficient acidic cellular medium can result in cell breakdown. When this inner coat of muscle of the artery breaks down, it is replaced with immobile collagen, probably to protect the artery from bursting, which would result in instantaneous death. This rigidity causes the previously flexible internal layer lining the artery that is in contact with the blood, and the sub-internal layer between it and the muscle coat, to become agitated and to undergo inflammatory degeneration leading to a rupture. The April 1997 issue of the *New England Journal of Medicine, Kilmer McCully* M.D. agrees with this concept by suggesting a radical *"new"* medical theory that *cholesterol* is not the primary *"cause"* of heart disease, but rather, *"inflammation of blood vessel walls is the primary cause* of heart attacks and strokes." The resulting debris, caused by the acidosis degeneration, along with fibrin phospholipids and collagen creates a patch to repair the break. This results in the formation of open negatively charged locations for the positive calcium in the serum to bind. Next, polar stacking, as described in the cell membrane mechanism, occurs; polar (electrically charged oppositely at each end of the molecule) fats begin to stack on the calcium, with cholesterol being only one of many.

At this point a discussion of cholesterol is warranted. It is both only a minor and last stage participant of a process that was instigated by the cellular breakdown of the arterial muscle. As such, deposition of cholesterol, probably to prevent leakage of the acid damaged artery, along with triglycerides and mucopoly- saccharides, is not the instigator of atherosclerosis, as popular misconception would lead you to believe, but only *part of the reparative process* that prevents the body from bleeding to death.

Doctors advise the public to reduce the cholesterol level in the blood by reducing the amount of cholesterol in the diet. Thus the public is warned to reduce the consumption of the two most nutritious foods known, *eggs and butter*, both of which are rich in vitamins, minerals and essential amino acids. However both also contain relatively high quantities of cholesterol. The egg, which contains about 300 milligrams of cholesterol (N.B.: the body manufactures up to *2,000 milligrams* of cholesterol per day) also is the body's main source of *acetylcholine*, an essential neuro-transmitter. Thus we are asked to avoid eggs and risk senility. To make matters worse, we have been asked to substitute cholesterol-rich butter with cholesterol-free margarine. The problem, however, is that margarine contains partially hydrogenated fats known as "*trans-fats*," which actually *promote* increased blood LDL ("bad") cholesterol levels. Nutritionist Margaret A. Flynn, at the University of Missouri, found in an experiment involving 71 faculty members, "basically it made no difference (to the blood cholesterol level) whether they ate margarine or butter." This was probably because, although the butter adds cholesterol to the blood, the *trans -fats* in the margarine induce the body to produce more LDL cholesterol which ends up in the blood. Biochemist Bruce J. Holub at the University of Guelph in Canada states: *"At the very least, one has to ask whether cholesterol-free claims **should be allowed** on high-trans products."* Thus it looks like grandma was right when she said, *"**butter and eggs are good for you**."*

Important facts about cholesterol are that it is *a vital component* of the body, it is found in every cell, it is a component of steroid hormones such as testosterone and estrogen it is used to conduct nerve impulses, and it is present in large quantities in the brain and bile. Additionally, cholesterol is one of the constituents of the skin that is *crucial to the production of sun-on-skin vitamin D*. Finally, but not least important, about 80% of all body cholesterol is not ingested in the diets, but rather, *is manufactured by the body*.

In the blood serum, cholesterol is found *esterified* (made into an organic salt) with fatty acids as a lipid, or fatty acid ester. There are two types of these lipoproteins: high density lipoproteins (HDL) and low density lipoproteins (LDL). The HDL is the good cholesterol, as people who have high levels of it in their blood, actually have less risk of heart disease. When the LDL levels go up in the blood serum, no matter what the hereditary culture factors are, there is a proportional rise in heart disease. Researchers found that eating a diet of trans-fats increased the bad LDL cholesterol level in the blood, while reducing the good HDL cholesterol level (Ronald P. Minsink, Martin B. Katanm *New England Journal of Medicine*, August 1990). Other researchers found *increased heart disease* unless the cholesterol is heat damaged or oxidized. In the **Encyclopedia of Biochemistry**, Dr. W.

Hartroft states *"It still has not been shown **that lowering the cholesterol in the blood (by 20%) will have any protective effect** for the heart and vessels against the development of atheroma or hardening of the arteries, and the onset of serious complications."* Since Dr. Hartroft made this statement, low cholesterol diets have been confirmed in dozens of carefully controlled experiments **not to reduce heart disease**. Thus, cholesterol is only poorly correlated to heart disease.

Then **why is there a popular misconception that cholesterol is bad for you?** The over simplified evidence to back this belief is that cholesterol is found in significant quantities in the arterial plaque. The reason for this has been previously explained as the result of polar stacking, with cholesterol participating as only ingredients of the final nails in the coffin. Since doctors do not really understand how this coffin of plaque is constructed, and the chronology of events in the creation of disease, and since they are pressed by reports of the calcium and cholesterol content of arterial plaque, the recommendation is to avoid the final outcome by avoiding the cholesterol nail. Thus the search for the vital medical factors that could lead to a medical breakthrough, **such as the prevention of calcium deficiency, is ignored or terminated**.

If this logic were to be applied to other diseased parts of the body, then calcium, which is found in excess in the cancerous tumors and in the brain plaque of Alzheimer's and Parkinson's diseases, should also be reduced or eliminated from the diet. But, for the reasons we have previously explained, this would be an equal **disaster to human health**. It should also be noted that Alzheimer's disease is associated with a calcium-aluminum build-up in cortical cerebral arteries, and Parkinson's is associated with a calcium-aluminum-silicon buildup in lenticular cerebral arteries, both of which are the direct result of negative cellular breakdown, or the creation of a negative field in the artery, due to acid buildup within the cell. This condition is then followed by the familiar positive calcium polar stacking mechanism over the open negative field. *Calcium did not cause the problem*, instead, had it been present in the correct amounts in the first place, it would have prevented cellular breakdown by creating the critical 7.4 pH buffered serum to allow proper brain cell function and repair. Correct cytoplasmic calcium concentrations could also have prevented the breakdown, polar stacking and resulting arterial plaque or *"sores"* in patients with hypertension (high blood pressure). The presence of calcium and cholesterol as pallbearers at the cell's funeral does not mean that they were the instigators in the death of the cell and the heart. Rather, the truth is that calcium is the life of the cell, which can eliminate the buildup of the coffin of plaque and thereby render the cholesterol nail harmless to the heart.

Calcium ions also play a central role within the heart muscle itself, as the excitation-contraction coupling and relaxation is accompanied by a rapid redistribution of calcium. With a defective heart, *"as the calcium ion accumulation ability declines so does the ability to carry out contraction and relaxation."* (**The Role of Calcium in Biological Systems**, Volume 1, page 135, CRC Press, 1985).

The British Medical Research Council recently completed a *10 -year study* that looked at the health of *5000 men* aged between 45 and 59. *Only 1 percent* of those who regularly drank more than one-half liter (about one-half U.S. quart) of milk a day suffered heart attacks in the study period, against *10 percent* of those who drank *no milk at all* (a *ten-fold* reduction). Also, drinking more than the one half of a liter further reduced the incidence of heart attack. Dr. Ann Fehily, one of the team of researchers states, *"the association between milk drinking and lower heart attack risk was absolutely clear, and there was no significance about what type of milk: full, semi skimmed or full skimmed."* Thus, the essential ingredient was **calcium**. Also, a 25 year study ending in 1997 by the Finland National Public Health Institute on 4697 cancer-free women aged 15 to 90, concluded that there was *"an overwhelming association between the high consumption of milk and the prevention of breast cancer compared to other factors."* What makes these studies tragic is that they meet all of the prerequisites for scientific authentication that is apparently required by the AMA and yet both studies go unheeded, despite the fact that heeding them could potentially reduce the death rate of heart disease, by ***ten-fold***, thereby saving millions of lives, as well as providing a means for women to prevent cancer. The fortunate drug companies, and the doctors of America, reap hundreds of billions of dollars per year because of this AMA indifference to using milk nutrition to prevent heart disease and also caustic nutrition to prevent cancer. This indifference is also paid for with human suffering as well as hundreds of thousands of lives each year.

    Thus, as has been shown for cancer and other diseases (such as the allergic auto-immune stress diseases, and other diseases usually associated with aging) ***heart disease***, which is the number one killer of man, is also ***caused by cell deterioration*** caused by calcium deficiency. The importance of calcium in the body is now an established and indisputable scientific fact. Calcium is the ***biological*** glue that holds our cells together and provides the crucial conditions for life to flourish. Calcium is crucially involved in hundreds of biological functions. The DNA must be smothered in calcium before it can replicate and repair the body. So, without waiting two decades for the medical profession to catch up, how can we use this knowledge today? Fortunately, Dr. Reich has laid the groundwork. He practiced preventive medicine employing nutritional therapy and was the first doctor to give his patients large quantities of vitamins and minerals. While patients of other doctors were dying from the drugs prescribed, no one ever died from God's nutrients.

Another misinformation myth is that *"**Genes *cause* disease**,"* the implication being that, because you are born with the genes that you have, there is nothing that you can do about the impending disease. But not to worry, because medical research is currently spending billions of dollars working on expensive ways to give you new, and healthy genes. The real tragedy with this situation is this is *the **acidosis** that **causes** degenerative disease, and not the genes.* I'm sure that you're asking, *"If this is true, then what do the genes do?"* The answer is this; *genes are the body's biological computer maps* showing the body which way it can go and can not go. Although they map the body's roadways to disease, they do not make the body go down any particular roadway. To put it in simpler terms, the genes dictate which of the many degenerative diseases to which you will be prone; they do not *cause* the disease. This concept, which is not understood by medicine today, is similar to the misconception that *the sun **causes** skin cancer*, when it is the *mineral deficiency induced **acidosis*** which *causes* the body to become prone to disease, and the genes only pick out which one of the diseases the body will be forced to choose. For some people, their genes are programmed to choose skin cancer.

The problem with propagating this last myth that *"**God's sun is bad for you**,"* is that just the opposite is true. The sun shining on the body's skin does many positive things. One result is the photosynthetic production of the mineral regulator inositol triphosphate, ***INSP-3***, an important biochemical mineral regulator. Another result of the sun shining on the skin is the photosynthesis of ***vitamin D*** in the skin, resulting in increasing the small intestine's capability to absorb mineral nutrients, thereby *reducing the acidosis* known to cause degenerative disease. This includes *all cancers.* As researchers know, the acid in the fluids outside of, and inside of, the human cell can disintegrate the cell wall, allowing toxins and carcinogens to get inside of the cell. Dr. James P. Whitlock Jr., of Stanford University, describes carcinogens, such as dioxin, binding with receptor toxins inside of the cell to form molecules that are just the right shape and size to bind to the DNA's nucleotides. This causes the DNA template (structure) to bend or *mutate* and *a cancer is born*

Thus, the question of whether God's sunshine is good for your health is obviously so important that it should not be the responsibility of those making the claim that *"the sun is good for your health* " to prove the correctness of their claim to the governing medical authorities. The financial burden of further proof should be borne by the establishment. In fact, if the AMA is truly protecting the health of America, it should be responsible for financing the *third party* research to either prove or to disprove any medical claim. The assessment of the results should also be made by a *third party* group that does not have the same prejudice that burdens the current establishment, which is not only *judge and jury*, but also lavishes in the responsibility of being the *prosecutor*, or, in other words, *"three strikes and you're out*.

The question of whether God's nutrients is good for your health, in particular your heart, is also obviously so important that the FDA shoud be forced to determine the validity of the scientific claims. For example, the January 15, 1998 edition of the Arizona Republic ran a story by Richard Know of the Boston Globe titled "Fish Diet May Aid Heart." Eating one serving of fish a week cuts men's risk of sudden cardiac death by half, according to a Harvard University study of nearly 21,000 physicians. The finding has major public health significance because a quartermillion

Americans die suddenly each year from cardiac arrest, most before reaching the hospital. Although great strides have been made in preventing and treating other kinds of heart attacks, sudden cardiac death remains a major medical puzzle. Other research since 1985 has suggested that eating fish protects the heart, but results from the Physicians Health Study, which was released last week, carry weight because they stem from careful study of so many individuals followed for 11 years. Dr. Robert H. Eckel of the University of Colorado, a member of the American heart Association's nutrition committee said that evidence is now strong enough to recommend serving of fish once or twice a week. The benefit of eating fish showed up in a 52 percent reduction in the risk of sudden cardiac death.

Women may be able to reduce their risk of heart disease dramatically by taking three to four times the recommended allowance of two vitamins *folate and B-6* a study suggests. A survey of about 80,000 nurses found that those who consumed far more than the recommended daily allowance were about half as likely to develop heart disease as those who took less than the recommended daily allowance, researchers said in Wednesday's *Journal of the American Medical Association.*

"When huge doses of vitamins C and E were added to the diet, an extraordinary thing happened: Arteries responded to the high-fat meal as though the subjects had eaten a low-fat bowl of cornflakes." Researchers say it appears to bolster scientific 'thinking that antioxidant vitamins can de-crease the heart-disease risk posed by a fatty diet. The 20 subjects who ate the fat-packed McDonald's breakfast had impaired blood vessel function for up to four hours afterwards. But "no such impairment was found on another day when they swallowed 20 times the recommended daily dosage of vitamins C (1200mg) and E (600 IU) immediately before eating the same meal." The research appears in *Journal of the*

American Medical Association, Dr. Gary Plotnick, a professor of Medicine at the University of Maryland Medical Center.

Thus, for the sake of human health, *the burden of proof should be shifted to the well -funded establishment*. The onus should be on the establishment to prove, right or wrong, any claims made, for to fail to do so, will result in the suppression of legitimate medical advancements at a cost of great human suffering. One classical example would be the case of the association of disease to the acidity of the body's fluids. It has been scientifically established that, except for urine and stomach fluids, all of the healthy body's fluids are alkaline. If, as the top cancer researcher said, *"cancer cannot survive in an alkali,"* then cancer cannot survive in the healthy body's alkali fluids. Since the alkalinity of the body's fluids can be maintained by mineral and vitamin nutrients, this means that there is a means currently available to beat cancer, *inexpensive* nutrition, and that the search for an *expensive* manmade chemical drug is the wrong way to go. As this book has shown, cancer is only one of many dreaded diseases that could be beaten by addressing the disease-nutrition issue. The stakes are too high to allow the AMA and the FDA to hide behind their feeble pass-the buck response of *"the burden of proof is on those making the claim."* History has shown that scientific proof that does not conform to the establishment's preconceived concepts is *always rejected* initially; just ask Nobel Prize winners Max Planck, Albert Einstein, and Linus Pauling.

Also, as has been discussed, the FDA has a terrible track record of prematurely approving drugs and then later being forced to take them off the market. These drugs were approved and promoted by the FDA have now been proven to be *"deadly"* to humans. God save us from the FDA.

CHAPTER THIRTEEN

CORAL CALCIUM

The coral calcium from Okinawa contains the perfect biological ratio of calcium to magnesium, 2:1 or 24% calcium and 12% magnesium. It also contains a host of trace metals. Coral calcium is a rich source of iron, containing almost 1,000 ppm. Next to calcium, iron is the most abundant mineral in the human body, one that is crucial for maintaining oxygen. Iron permits effective oxygen transport and storage in muscles and the blood. It is the central component of hemoglobin in the red blood cells. Iron deficiency causes anemia and abnormal fat metabolism. Iron competes with other elements for absorption into the body (competition with magnesium, copper, calcium and zinc). Vitamin C enhances iron absorption and classic consequences of iron deficiency are weakness, fatigue, poor immune function and anemia. The common belief is that *"too much iron can be toxic."* The problem with this is that the words *"too much"* have never been defined. Also, the United Nations Health agency, UNESCO, says that the majority of American women are anemic as a result of iron deficiency. Although the RDA for iron is 18 mg/day of iron, many nutritionists advocate at least 40 mg/day. The full term infant requires 160 mg, and the premature 240 mg during the first year of life. The 240 mg at the average 5% absorption when consumed equals 4800mg/year or 13 mg/day for the first year of life. The RDA for an adult is 18 mg/day. Also, for pregnant women, there is a requirement of 1mg/day in menstruating females. At 5mg/day this is 20mg/day consumption. Pregnancy also increases demand for iron. Expansion of the mother's red blood cell mass requires 400 mg of iron, and the fetus and placenta require an additional 400 mg iron. Blood loss at delivery, including blood loss in the placenta, accounts for another 300 mg iron. The total requirement for a pregnancy, therefore requires about 1100 mg iron. At 5% iron absorption, this works out to a 90 mg/day consumption requirement for a pregnant woman, but the RDA for an adult is only 18 mg/day. Thus, most women in America are being poisoned by iron deficiency.

A crucial factor in human health is that the human body is only capable of absorbing about *800 milligrams of calcium each day*. Unfortunately, calcium is one of the hardest minerals for the body to absorb. Many of the calcium supplements are only in the 2 to 3% absorption range, while the so called *"great"* supplements are about only 15%. The cultures like the Hunzas, who consume over 100,000 mg of calcium each day obviously get their 800 mg absorption, while harmlessly passing the rest through in their urine and excretion. With the Okinawans, because of the rod-like microbes in the coral, discovered by Swedish scientists in the 1990's, it is claimed that the absorption approaches nearly 100%. Therefore, taking 250 mg of calcium in an antacid product, which does severe harm to the elderly by wiping out their crucial stomach acid supplies, usually results in the absorption of 5 mg (2%) calcium by the body over a 20 hour period. Also, there is substantial evidence that much of the nutrients in coral are *absorbed in less than 20 minutes* (the blood chemistry undergoes a drastic change, for the better, in less than 20 minutes). Therefore much of the 250 mg of calcium in the coral can be absorbed by the body in less than 20 minutes, and without destroying the crucial stomach fluids. This is *"dramatically more dramatically faster."* No wonder the coral calcium works so well! In addition, when people have major diseases, the consumption of a triple dose of coral provides the maximum calcium absorption.

Coral calcium was first introduced to Western culture when it was brought to Europe by the Spanish explorers about

500 years ago. They had concluded, as the Japanese scientists of today have concluded, that it was the coral calcium that was responsible for the good health and longevity of the Okinawans. The world's oldest drugstores in Spain, which today are historic monuments, have clay pots on their selves labeled *"Coral Calcium, Okinawa, Japan."* Literature written by doctors of the day told of miraculous cures. By the turn of the 20th Century, the consumption of coral had spread to mainland Japan, where currently there are millions of daily users worldwide. When coral calcium was brought to the Western communities as a *"modern"* dietary supplement in the 1970's, much misunderstanding was propagated by marketing companies. There is a *naive notion* that when coral calcium is added to water it should dissolve completely. I am often asked about this circumstance, but the answer is obvious. If coral were soluble in water completely there would be no coral reefs in the oceans!

The reason why this question is asked often relates to the popular use of coral sand in tea bags which are merely added to water and the water is then consumed. Whilst coral calcium tea bags can import desirable properties to water, such as the transfer of important marine microbes, taking coral calcium in this manner is far less desirable then consuming the whole coral in powder or capsule form. Tea bag coral is less effective, as the user is only benefiting from about 2% of the marine nutrients that dissolve out of the tea bag. The consumer, unless told, is almost unaware that he is consuming coral water with only 2% of the nutrients in the tea bag dissolved. He does not know that to obtain the full benefits of coral calcium, it has to be consumed in its complete format, resulting in the consumption of over 50 times as much mineral nutrients. Also, the marine coral that is totally consumed is rich in the required nutrient, magnesium, as well as richer in all other nutrients.

Fossilized coral that has been washed up onto beaches has lost some of its mineral content by weathering and it may be dried and finely powdered to make a quick change of water pH. In addition, some commercially available coral calcium products have calcium added in hydroxide forms to increase alkalinity. Also, fossilized coral contains less than 1% magnesium, whereas marine coral has about 12% magnesium, which balances the 24% calcium for a perfect biological 2:1 calcium/magnesium ratio. Because of this lack of magnesium in fossilized coral, magnesium compounds are often added, resulting in a substantial dilution of the coral. After studying many types of coral supplements, I have concluded that marine coral, not fossilized coral, taken in complete format is obviously the most ideal way to consume coral calcium for health.

Many commercial companies have promoted coral calcium from Okinawa as though it is all the same material. However, the harvesting of marine bed coral calcium is much more difficult and costly than merely collecting fossilized coral from beach mines. This fossilized coral has undergone thousands, if not millions, of years of erosion, losing most of its magnesium content and much of its trace metal nutrient content. Also, because of the hype generated by coral calcium testimonials, numerous, unscrupulous entrepreneurs are harvesting coral from other locations around the world (this coral does not have the desired microbes), but telling their customers that it comes from Okinawa. Some even go so far as to blend their coral with Okinawan coral so that they can make the claim that it comes from Okinawa.

Despite the deficiencies, both tea bag coral and fossilized coral consumption has led to remarkable health testimonials, although not as many as the consumption of marine coral. This is due to the *"microbe factor"* (explained in detail in the next paragraph). There are some who would believe that the microbes would be destroyed when the coral is heated for dehydration purposes. However, rod-like bacteria can survive poor conditions, conditions, such as severe drought, heat, radiation and various chemicals. They do this by forming structures called **endospores**. A single bacterium will form a small sphere-shaped or oval shaped spore within its cytoplasm. This endospore is protected by a tough outer covering. It remains dormant until favorable conditions reappear, when the spores develop into bacteria cells. In addition there are many other factors that make coral calcium of marine origin more ideal for health. I prefer coral that is used in vegetable capsules or at least capsules that are made to dissolve at the right time to provide the best circumstances for mineral absorption. The practice of breaking capsules and adding the contents to water is unnecessary, except in circumstances where some people cannot readily swallow capsules.

Microbes or bacillus are defined as any genus of rod-shaped bacteria that occur in chains, produce spores and are active only in the presence of oxygen and water. Although some micro-organisms are destroyed in the process of drying, this process is not *per se* lethal to microorganisms. The addition of water can spring them back to life. Living microbes can be found in all living animals and plants. Of course most microbes can live off of plants and food, and are best known for their ability to *"spoil"* the food. Actually **spoiling food is a form of digestion**. Thus spoiled food is pre-digested by the microbes. This is probably the reason that most of the animal kingdom, including humans, have substantial numbers of microbes in their intestines. The strong acid in the stomach can not break down all food, especially complex carbohydrates. However, the microbes in the intestine living off of these foods, do indeed break them down and make them available for absorption by the small intestine. Also, the rod-like shape, allows the microbes to penetrate deep into the *"finger-like villi,"*

5,000,000 lining the intestine, where they can easily be absorbed by:

1) *facilitated diffusion* (glucose combines with a carrier substance which is soluble in the lipid layer of the cell membrane),

2) *osmosis* (the movement of water molecules and dissolved solids through semi-permeable cell membranes from an area of high concentration to an area of low concentration),

3) *filtration* (movement of solvents and dissolved substances across semi-permeable cell membranes by mechanical pressure, usually high pressure to low pressure),

4) *dialysis* (separation of small molecules from large molecules by semi-permeable membrane) and,

5) *pinocytosis* (or "cell drinking" where the liquid nutrient attracted to the surface of the cell membrane is engulfed). As a result, the *"microbes are crucial to life."* Fortunately, most of the hundreds of non-marine microbes found in the human intestine were transferred by the mother. Some animals, like the baby elephant, have to eat their mother's excrement just to get the needed microbes.

The liver, pancreas, and intestine, all secrete fluids to assist the absorption of nutrients. Each day the liver secretes *almost a quart* of yellow, brownish, or olive-green liquid called bile. It has a pH of 7.6 to 8.6 and consists of water, bile salts, bile acids, a number of lipids, and two pigments called biliverdin and bilirubin. When red blood cells are broken down, iron, globin and bilirubin are released. The iron and globin are recycled, but some of the bilirubin excreted into the bile ducts. Bilirubin is eventually broken down in the intestines, and its breakdown products give feces their color. Other substances found in bile aid in the digestion of fats by emulsifying them and are required for their absorption. Each day the pancreas produces about *a quart and a half* of a clear colorless liquid called pancreatic juice, which consists mostly of water, some salts, sodium bicarbonate and enzymes. The sodium bicarbonate gives the pancreatic juice an alkaline pH (7.1 to 8.2) that helps neutralize stomach acids and stops the action of pepsin from the stomach and creates the proper environment for enzymes in the small intestine. The enzymes in the pancreatic juice include a carbohydrate-digesting enzyme, several protein digesting enzymes, the only active fat digesting enzyme, and a nucleic acid-digesting enzyme. The intestine itself produces up to *three quarts* of intestinal juice. It is a clear fluid with an alkaline pH of 7.6. It contains water, mucus, and enzymes that complete the digestion of carbohydrates, proteins and nucleic acid. Thus the liver, pancreas and intestinal juices are crucial in the digestive process which help to liberate the nutrients. Bacteria also plays a crucial role in the digestive process as well as in the absorption process.

The genera of bacteria that are found in the intestinal tract are: Bacteroides (22 species, non-sporing rods), Clostidium (61 species, heat resistant spore-forming rods), Citrobacter (2 species, lactose fermenting rods), Enterobacter (2 rods, ferment glucose and lactose), Escherichia (one specie, rods), Lactobacillus (27 species, non-sporing rods employed in the production of fermented milks), Proteus (5 species, aerobic rods that hydrolyze urea), Pseudomonas, 29 species, most important bacteria in spoilage of meats, poultry, eggs and sea foods), Salmonella (1800 species that ferment sugars and glucose), Shigella (4 species, aerobic, like pollution), Staphylococcus (3 species, coagulate blood, also common in nasal cavities) and Streptococcus (21 species).

Salt greater than 1% can cross the cell membranes of most bacterium by osmosis, which results in growth inhibition and possibly death of the microbes. Everyone is also familiar with the preservation of meat by *"salting,"* which kills or inhibits the bacteria. Thus large quantities of salt in the intestinal tract, which occur when large quantities of nutrients have been digested (hydrochloric acid from the stomach reacting with the sodium bicarbonate from the pancreas produces salt in the duodenum), can kill the microbes, thereby inhibiting nutrient absorption by the body, especially when large amounts of nutrients have been ingested.

On the contrary, *"marine microbes,"* such as those found in coral calcium by the Swedish, thrive in high salt environments. Also, because of their original salty marine environment, as well as their calcium magnesium and mineral environment, the marine microbes have no difficulty assisting the body to absorb high quantities of these minerals, especially when the intestine is saline, resulting from the consumption of large amounts of mineral nutrients. These same salts, however, incapacitate the natural microbes in the intestinal tract, thereby inhibiting nutrient absorption. Thus, the coral marine microbes resolve this problem, dramatically increasing the absorption of the nutrients by the body.

Those people using a small sachet teabag that allows only a tiny amount of coral to dissolve in the liquid in which they are placed, and those using fossilized coral, still get some benefits from the marine microbes, hence the testimonials. Also, these testimonies emanating from the small intake of nutrients is nothing short of astounding. The reason for this success is that when the teabag or the fossilized coral is placed in a liquid, the microbes come to life and are consumed when the liquid is drank. These microbes can then latch on to nutrients already in the duodenum and pull them into the body resulting in health benefits. Consumption of marine coral, on the other hand, allows the *"total nutrient content of the coral"* to be consumed as well, and therefore provides far greater health benefits, leading to more testimonials. The bottom line is that all coral from Okinawa has fantastic health benefits, but the *marine coral is far superior.*

Coral is also very much like human bone and the body does not reject it, and it is conducive to allowing new bone growth. In Germany, surgeons will pack the cracks and holes in the broken bones of the elderly with a coral paste made from coral calcium and water. Within 3 weeks the coral is displaced with new bone growth. James Tobin in the Detroit News writes that *"because of a gift from the sea, coral calcium, Christian Growth is swimming again.'* The coral rests snuggly inside the femur (thigh bone) of his right leg, just above the knee. It fills a hole the size of a large marble, replacing a benign tumor that was making it harder and harder for Chris, 14, to play the sports he loves. If you use a powerful microscope to compare the coral to Chris' bone, you could not tell the difference. Chris is one of the first people in Metro Detroit to have a bone repaired with sea coral and is *doing everything,"* said his doctor, Ronald Irwin, an orthopedic oncologist affiliated with the Beaumint Hospital, Royal Oak. *It looks good,"* Irwin said, *"he'll ski this year !"*

In the May issue of the New England Journal of Medicine, 2001, there was an article about the *"bionic thumb."* Doctor Charles Vacanti at the University of Massachusetts re-created a thumb for Paul Murcia who had lost his thumb in a machine accident. First a small sample on bone from the patient's arm bone was cultured to multiply. Then, a sea coral scaffold was sculpted into the shape of the missing thumb bone and implanted into Murcia's thumb. The patient's own bone cells, grown in the lab, were then injected onto the scaffold. The bone cells grew a blood supply and the coral scaffold slowly melted away leaving a new living thumb bone. The doctors predict that eventually all that will be left will be a thumb bone with healthy bone cells and no coral. 28 months after the surgery the patient is able to use his thumb relatively normally and the doctors say that the experiment in tissue engineering using the coral is working.

All testimonials are considered as hearsay and are inadmissible to most scientists. However, when testimonials begin flooding out of countries all over the world, by shear number, they themselves become scientific fact, and scientific fact cannot be ignored by any scientist. Although coral has only been in America for a few years, already the testimonies are flooding in. The next chapter will provide a few examples.

CHAPTER FOURTEEN

TESTIMONIALS

Unfortunately, the world's leading authorities in health all scoff at the notion of testimonials. They can give you dozens of reasons why testimonials are invalid, and although this may be true when only a few testimonials are involved, when the numbers of testimonials reach the sky, then by their sheer numbers, the existence of such testimonials should become scientific facts. Also, if you personally are one of those giving testimonials, then you must be offended by the experts who declare your opinion to be insignificant. Personally, I have experienced that after I have given talks to any group on coral calcium, over half will acknowledge a testimonial within one month. As I have talked to tens of thousands, this becomes a significant figure. And when added to the fact that hundreds if not millions of people have taken coral calcium over its 600 year history, the number must be in the millions. Thus, no reasonable expert could dismiss this phenomenon. I therefore believe that I should share some testimonials with you, and let you decide of their validity for yourself:

TESTIMONIES:

1. Cancer June 27, 2003, a P.E.T. scan revealed a silver dollar size tumor in the lower lobe of my right lung (soft tissue), enlarged lymph nodes behind my breast bone. It was diagnosed by a lung specialist as mesothelioma from exposure to asbestos many years ago in my work. Treatment recommended ...none, incurable. Having nothing to lose, on July 3, I started on your coral calcium program with sunshine. Today, August 18, I reported to the hospital for a C.A.T. scan and needle biopsy.

Surprise-surprise-surprise, as Gomer Pyle used to say, the tumor was so small, like a pencil eraser, the doctor decided that there was no need for a biopsy.

Wallace Green, Sacramento, California.

2.   Locked Elbow My name is Derrick Lamb. Although, not with the high profile of Michael J. Fox, my work as a film animator has been honored with numerous international prizes, including an Academy Award Oscar for the 1980 film "Every Child" and I have also won the British Academy Award. Damage to my right elbow in childhood was seriously affecting my ability to draw and animate, which is my love and livelihood. I was experiencing swelling and pain with my right elbow locked in a 35 degree angle. I had to use my left arm exclusively for day to day activities. I looked for help in some of our prestigious Boston hospitals and clinics. Specialists ruled out surgery as too risky for nerve damage. I was offered Ibuprofen and arthritis medication which was totally ineffective. It was coral calcium that got me back to the drawing board (quite literally). I began using your coral calcium and can honestly say that six months later I am drawing as well as ever. My elbow is strong and has almost straightened itself. I have no pain and go to the gym and swim daily. Finally, I admire your passion to share your knowledge and understanding with so many.

Derk Lamb, Cambridge MA.

3.   Psoriasis   Bob, an interim report on my psoriasis and melanoma on my face. Both are diminishing at the same rate and are within two weeks of a complete cure. I had decreased my dosage to 3 capsules a day from 6 in about May and they started getting worse, so I have been taking 6 coral daily since and both are almost gone. The internet shows that there is no known cure for psoriasis but they did not try the simple Barefoot cure and probably won't for some time to come as it would mean no money for the drug companies.

Jack McCallum, Sunday, August 24, 2003

4.   Non-Hodgkins Lymphoma   Both my father and I had cancer. I was diagnosed with Non-Hodgkins Lymphoma a year ago and my father was diagnosed three weeks before me with Multiple Myloma. He was looking at knee surgery before we both started taking your coral calcium. Dad was so impressed that he carries your phone number and web site on a card so he can share your info with anyone who will listen. My dad and I both had cancer and I want to thank you for a product that I believe made the difference.

Stacy Pfamenstiel, Victoria, Kansas

5.   Multiple Scerosis   I began taking the Coral Calcium Supreme in the middle of September, 2002. I have secondary progressive multiple sclerosis and had gone through chemo treatments for three years being told for the second time that I was a paraplegic. I became determined to walk, first with a walker and then a cane. After taking Coral Calcium Supreme for ten days, my balance became much improved. On Christmas Eve my family was at my parents house and I went to their back bathroom and then walked through the house as they were ready to open gifts. I sat down and everyone shouted wanting to know where my cane was. I had walked without a cane and did not even realize it. I now use nothing to walk, but in public I take my cane for protective measure. Coral Calcium Supreme has definitely made a huge difference in my life, as I have not walked this well since 1994. As I was taking no medication, the Coral Calcium Supreme was the only viable explanation.

Lisa H., Ohio, August 26, 2003

6. Pain I started on coral over a month ago. I have breast cancer. It has been two years since I went through the cut and burn. Now I am on Arimidex for the next five years. I told my doctor about the horrible bone pain and he is telling me that it is arthritis. I DON'T THINK SO! One of the side effects to the estrogen in the drug is bone pain. Of course the doctor won't listen. The first day that I took your coral, I felt something. And now, I have such energy, I cannot believe it! Although the pain is not totally gone, I can open a ketchup bottle, open orange juice bottles, pump gas into my car, step on the brake of my car, and every little thing that we don't think about, I am doing much better. Last year was living hell. Now, with coral calcium, I can get up each day and not want to die. Thanks Bob.

Debbie from Texas, June 19, 2003

7. Acid Reflux I have been using coral calcium for about five months. I have to tell you from the bottom of my heart that this is the best product on the planet! I no longer suffer from acid reflux, my feet and legs have no more pain, and my skin looks so good that my wife says that I look 10 years younger. I feel like I did when I was 20 years old, and I am not ashamed to tell you that I am 50 and feel like I have been given a new lease on life. Thank you Bob Barefoot for great work and thank God for a perfect nutrient.

Blake Myers, Nehalem, Oregon June 26, 2003

8. Arthritis and Diabetes I started taking Coral Calcium Supreme about six months ago. At that time I was unable to walk up steps, even the three that were in front of my house. My right knee had arthritis and it was so bad that it crunched with every step. I could not bear weight on that leg. My husband had diabetes so we decided to start taking coral calcium together.

Well, to tell you the truth, it was two weeks later and I came up the steps holding on the rail but I could bear weight on my leg. My husbands blood sugar started coming down and within two weeks was 120 after eating. Within a month my husband was out shoveling snow for 5 hours and his blood sugar didn't drop. Soon I could come up the steps without holding on to the rail. My husband had foot pain that they said was diabetic neuropathy that would never go away. His pain disappeared. My persistent headaches are gone and I have not had a migraine since I started taking coral calcium. All of my husbands diabetic symptoms are gone. I want to thank you, Bob Barefoot, for saving us from the doctors. I can hardly wait to see what happens over the next 6 months. Saying thank you is not enough. I will be a coral calcium customer for the rest of my life.

Ginny H, Florida, June 28, 2003

9.   Prostate Cancer   On October 2000 I was diagnosed with prostate cancer. Although I was told I needed immediate surgery my insurance did not kick in until January 2001. I wore a catheter for 4 months and in January was operated on. My PSA at that time was 4.0 but went up the first year to 6.0 Then, by March 2003 my PSA was 9.8. The only thing left was chemotherapy, but I refused. At that time, my wife read every word that you wrote in your books, The Calcium Factor and Death By Diet. She stuck with your program and made me do it too. On June 10, 2003 I took another PSA test and today the doctor announced to me that my PSA was 0.5. **I THANK MY GOD. I THANK MY WIFE.** And last but not least, **MY BEST FRIEND ROBERT BAREFOOT.** God bless you!!!

Charles David Loucks, San Antonio, Florida, June 17, 2003

10.   Aching Muscles   I am 60 years old and my brother is 58. I used to have to rock back and forth to get up off the couch because of aching muscles. My brother had the same problem. My wife's legs ached so bad that she thought that she would soon need a wheel chair. When I drove my truck, I always got out bent over and it would take considerable time to straighten out. Then came Coral Calcium Supreme. After a few days I got up from the couch without rocking and so did my brother. Half way across the room he stopped, turned back with a shocked look on his face. My wife's legs no longer hurt. I just want to thank you for a great product that actually works.

Jerry B., Irvington, Alabama, August 17, 2003

10.   Stress   I suffer from anxiety and I have been under a lot of stress lately. The number one thing that bugged me was that everyone used to tell me I was pale all of the time. The first day I took your coral calcium I felt a little light headed. I was clued in afterwards that it was the increase in oxygen levels in my blood. I am no longer pale. I have less muscle twitching and my anxiety is under control, but not completely as I have only been taking coral calcium for two weeks.

Darrel B. Saint John, New Brunswick, Canada, Sept. 4, 2003

11.   Respiratory Infections   I am a 51 year old female who has worked 20 years as a school custodian. We use a lot of chemicals and for the past 11 years I was at the doctors office with upper respiratory infections. I was always tired and run down. I started taking your coral after seeing you on your infomercial and it wasn't long before I noticed a change, Not only did I feel better but I went through the whole winter without the flu or a cold. When I went for my physical my doctor told me that I needed a bone density scan. The results were that of a 30 year old. Despite my protests, my doctor told me that coral had nothing to do with it. But that's ok, because I know how my health has changed. God bless you Bob Barefoot.

Pat Moore, LCMS, Sept. 11, 2003

12.   Acid Reflux   I have used Bob Barefoot's coral calcium for a little over 3 months. Within days of starting on this product my acid reflux was gone. I also have lymphodema, a circulatory problem that causes swelling in my feet and ankles. The swelling has decreased and at times my feet almost look normal. Recently I noticed that my back and neck, for which I regularly see a chiropractor, have given me no problems. I will take coral calcium forever.

Lauren S., Ohio, July 17, 2003

13.   Bladder Cancer   My dad was one day away from bladder removal and being outfitted with a plastic bag. He was not sure he would go through with the surgery. It was hopeless. Then, that night we were blessed to see Bob Barefoot on TV and we just knew that we had a way to go. From December 28th, 2002 to January 29, 2003 Dad went on coral calcium and the Barefoot program. Dad had a biopsy and there was no malignancy found. We cannot thank you all enough Bob Barefoot.

Bob Sabrina and Kathy Garganese, Las Vegas, Nevada

14.   High Blood Pressure   I am a Black American and as most Black Americans know our race suffers the worst ravages of high blood pressure, diabetes, cancer, stroke, heart disease and a number of other degenerative diseases. I myself was a sufferer of high blood pressure and diabetes. After almost two months of taking Barefoot's coral calcium my pressure and sugar levels are normal again and I am off all medications.

Regardless of what the nay sayers or your critics say, when it comes to helping the 30 million Blacks in America obtain good health, your dream of "Curing America" starting with Black America first, is one that I believe, that even Dr. Martin Luther King himself would have applauded.

Jake Jordon, Washingon, D.C., August 2002

15.   Chronic Fatigue Syndrome   I developed Epstein Bar Virus, which I nearly died from and now I have chronic fatigue syndrome, which my insurance does not cover. I caught you on television talking about coral calcium and now I sleep eight hours every night. My lifestyle has improved so very much that I just want to say, "Thank you from the bottom of my heart."

Catricia A., April 26, 2003

16.   Neck Pain   In February 1997 I was in a four-wheeling accident. Since then I have had severe neck and back pain causing stressful days and sleepless nights. I have been taking your Coral Calcium Supreme for 3 months now and my neck and back pain is gone. I sleep all night and feel very rested in the morning. Mr. Barefoot, I am 38 years old and have 5 children. My family and I thank you from the bottom of our hearts for your coral calcium Supreme.

Lynda Monteith, Goshen, New York, April 8, 2003

17.   Arthritis   After seeing you on television and hearing your story about coral calcium I bought your books and a supply of coral calcium. After only three weeks on coral calcium I have eliminated 99% of the pain associated with an arthritic knee and shoulder bone spurs. I walk naturally again, as for a year I required a cane to walk. The only thing that I have done differently since reading your book is to switch to

Coral Calcium. My energy level is higher and I look forward to seeing my health improve even further.

Kenneth R Davis, Nashville, TN, March 29, 2002.

18.   Osteoporosis   I am 51 years old and have been diagnosed with osteoporosis of the lower lumbar spine. Being a post- meno-pausal female, I have refused the conventional HRT treatment, and have started taking coral calcium. Within three days I have had two age spots on my face disappear, and am experiencing an energy boost I haven't felt for sometime now.

Sharon W. Priester, March 7, 2002

19.   Pain   Twenty years ago my wife had three brain surgeries. She takes a lot of pain medication daily including four Tylenol's. After being on coral calcium for less than a week, she takes one a day occasionally. Myself, I have noticed that my chronic muscle aching has been reduced. Also, the first night after I started taking coral calcium I slept better than I remember sleeping since I was a 29 years old and I live in Decatur, Ohio. I am athletic and consider myself to be in good health. A few months ago my neck began to child. This coral calcium looks like it's the answer to some secret prayers.

Larry Wall, Houghton, MI, March 12, 2002.

20.   Malignant Cancer   Hello, my name is Conrad Sims, I experienced soreness and swelling. I tried to ignore it, but it began to become painful. It was not long before the swelling was the size of a golf ball and my co-workers demanded that I see a doctor. It was diagnosed as *malignant cancer* and the doctor told me that it had to be removed surgically. He said there was no other way. I did not have health insurance for the surgery and I was terrified. A friend suggested I try coral calcium. I thought, "what's a little calcium going to do for me?" I was desperate so I started taking the coral and within a week the pain had subsided. After two weeks the size of the tumor was dramatically reduced, and after four weeks it appeared to be gone. I am back to my old self and feeling great.

God bless coral calcium, Conrad Sim. (March, 2001)

21. Diabetes and Bells Palsy My name is Sue Ann Miller and I live in Akron, Ohio. I had been suffering for years with several diseases: *diabetes, Bells Palsy, carpel tunnel syndrome*. I also have had hip knee and elbow replacements. I lived on drugs and was in constant pain. I could barely walk and could not climb stairs. Then my sister went to a talk by Mr. Barefoot and brought me some coral calcium. I was in such pain and was so desperate that I would try anything. In just a few weeks the pain went away. A few weeks later and I returned to full mobility as my swelling went down and my hands straightened out. A few weeks more and I could bend over, touch my toes and run up stairs. I have gotten my life back. The coral was magic and I thank God for the coral and Bob Barefoot.

I love you all, Sue Ann Miller, Ohio

22. Chronic Fatigue Syndrome My name is Donna Crow and I am struggling to recover from *Chronic Fatigue Syndrome* which struck me severely 12 years ago. One of the problems with CFS victims, as I am sure you know, is that we have problems absorbing and/or using minerals. As a result we often have insomnia, heart palpitations and multitudes of intestinal problems.

A friend told me about coral calcium. She sent me a tape by Dr. Robert Barefoot. I was skeptical because someone else had sent me coral calcium that came in little tea bags and I had tried it with no noticeable benefit. But I value this friend's nutritional advise and out of honor for our friendship I listened to the tape. It was so educational. It opened up, for me, a whole new understanding of the need for calcium in the body. I loved the information and became determined to try some.

I got my first bottle and opened a cap and dumped it in my mouth since I seem to absorb better when I do that and within two minutes I felt the most amazing things in my body. Peace would be the best word to describe it. And from that day on I never have had the stress in my chest I had, had for 12 years prior. And my digestion is wonderful now; no acid reflux anymore. And I have no heart palpitations at all.

This product is more wonderful to me than I can say. Unless you have had constant heart stress and other calcium/magnesium related problems long term, you cannot imagine how wonderful it is to go through a day without those problems. It is like getting out of prison.

I have all my friends and family on this stuff and they all love it for various reasons. That is the beauty of getting your mineral needs met. Your body will use them to do the unique repairs that you need. The body is so smart. If you give it the tools to work with it will literally work wonders for you.
Thank you for a product that has been like a miracle for me.

Donna Crow, Newport, Oregon

23. Fibromyalgia Hi to everyone, just wanted to let you all know that I've been using the Coral Calcium, and it is definitely helping me. I am especially excited over the fact that I am sleeping better. My usual night activity is *frequent urination*, getting up 6 to 8 times in a 8 hour period to use the bathroom, plus I wake up in pain all through the night. Since the very first night, I slept at least 4 hours straight before I had to relieve my bladder, then I took another calcium (not sure if it was necessary at that point) and slept like a baby another 4 hours. It's wonderful. This happens every night now. I have had such a sleep deficit for so long. Now some more good news: I have less pain. Oh Thank God! I have *Fibromyalgia*, and after years of disability due to such horrible, constant pain, a wheel chair, and a walker, I have hope of getting better, and I'm not so fatigued. To have any less pain is a miracle, and such a Blessing. Now if I can start exercising and lose weight I will be so forever grateful to this product, and to Donna. Exercising makes Fibromyalgia worse, plus I have a back problem, a foot problem, and very weak legs. But somehow I know I'm going to keep getting better. THANKS to Donna for sharing this information with me. I encourage you all to try it also. I've taken other calcium product, but never achieved these good results.

Bless you all,   Joanie O.

24.   Hypertension   My name is Allen Jensen and I have battled *high blood pressure* for years and have been diagnosed with diabetes for three years. Medication has helped me more or less keep both "in check," but has done nothing to lower either the blood pressure or my blood sugar level. Then, in October 1997, I was diagnosed with Guillaine-Barre Syndrome, a neurological disorder in which the nerves are destroyed by a: glitch" in the body's immune system. I lost a great deal of strength and dexterity in my hands, arms and legs. My active lifestyle of riding horses and a 30 year career as a telephone installer/repair technician ended with no choice but to take early disability retirement. In mid-May, 2000, I began taking coral calcium. Blood work showed a drastic improvement from tests in November 1999. My triglycerides improved from 1074 to 510, cholesterol from 380 to 210, and my blood sugar from 284 to 168. My doctor told me to "Keep doing whatever you're doing." With daily use of the coral calcium I am confident that I will eventually be able to discontinue all of my medications. Coral calcium has virtually given me back the life

I was beginning to believe I would not be able to enjoy again.

Allen Jenson, Breckenridge, Texas.

25. Arthritic Dog With nothing to loose, we started giving our *crippled arthritic dog*, Bandit, 2 coral calcium capsules every day, figuring that if an average person takes 6/day to fight serious illness, then Bandit, at about 43 pounds should take 2. She takes her capsules in peanut butter! That was July 1, 2000. Within just a day or two, she was eating again and walking out into the backyard and "using the facilities." Within a week she was walking normally. In 2 weeks she would actually "trot" out to the back yard, get on and off the couch, and come upstairs. By the end of 3 weeks she was actually playing "wrestling" with our 4-year-old dog, something she had not done in 2 years. Our veterinarian saw her and asked what we had done to create the "miracle." He bought some coral and said that he would be experimenting on some of his patients. By August, Bandit was like a new dog. She'll actually run now!

Bob Zacher, Memphis, Tennessee

26. Arthritic Cat My name is Lisa Macintire and my *18 year old cat*, "Tootsie," who weighs nine pounds started *limping* about 2 years ago and became very stiff-legged. She couldn't jump on things like the washer where she eats. She obviously had arthritis and it was getting worse. About 2 months ago I started giving her 2 capsules of coral calcium every day, and in less than 2 weeks, she stopped limping. I kept giving her 1 capsule each day after that. In less than a month she started jumping and climbing all over the furniture. A check-up by the Vet showed her blood work, urine, etc. revealed no ill effects. The Vet's words were, "She's in perfect shape." The only side effect Tootsie suffered was "feeling GREAT." This coral calcium is truly a miracle.

Lisa Macintire, Memphis, Tennessee

27. Multiple Sclerosis   I was diagnosed with *Multiple Sclerosis* in 1978, and along with the disease came excruciating pain. In 1986 a pump was surgically installed in my abdomen, which put morphine into my spinal fluid 24 hour a day, and brought me modest relief. Last year, after 9 times in the hospital and 8 surgeries someone introduced me to colloidal minerals, which began to turn my life around. When I heard about *Coral Calcium* I thought, *"How is a calcium product going to help me? "* Well, I tried it June 24th, and it didn't take me long to realize that this was not the "run of the mill" calcium. About the first of July, I realized that I had no pain. For the first time in 19 years I had no pain and I could work 12 hours a day without stopping to lie down.

Earl Bailley, PhD, Doctor of Divinity, Ohio.

28. Arthritis   Hi, my name is Dorothy Boyer and I will be 80 years old in June 2001. I have had problems at night time with my legs. They get a nervous feeling and I have to get up and stomp around the room to get it to stop and then retire again. It is quite tiring to have to do this every night. My daughter has tried to help me with many kinds of calcium and magnesium products, some were quite expensive and none gave relief. Then she found Dr. Robert Barefoot's coral calcium and said, "Try this." And the very first night I slept through the night without any leg problems. That was several months ago and I haven't had any nighttime leg problems since starting the coral calcium. Also I am very happy because I feel like I can think again. I have been very active mentally all my life and just in the last year I started to have trouble concentrating and staying focused. After just a few days on this coral calcium I felt like I could think again. I am very happy about that.

The biggest thing though is that I have a congestive enlarged heart and it doesn't take much for me to get a really rapid heart beat. Just putting on a blouse in the morning would cause my heart to race and I would have to sit on the side of the bed and just calmly breathe until it passed. From the first day I took coral calcium I have not had that again and that is the thing I am most happy about. It was very scary and it is nice to not be afraid every day.

Sincerely, Dorothy Boyer, Newport, Oregon

29.   Joint Pain   Your book did wonders for me. I had reached the point that *joint pain* was a part of my everyday life. Then, six weeks on coral calcium and I had become virtually pain free. Now, one year later, I feel better than I have in eight or nine years. Now my only problem is making my family and friends believe that being healthy can be so easy.

Rick Whedbee, Covington, Georgia

30.   Heel Spurs   My husband Mark had *painful heel spurs.* He was advised to have surgery. He began taking coral calcium, 6 per day, and within two months he almost was pain-free. Within three months, all of the pain was gone and the doctors have advised that he no longer needs surgery. Coral was a miracle as Mark's job has him working on his feet all day long.

Betty Gosda, Illinois

31.   Prostate Cancer   My name is Patty and my husband was recently diagnosed with *prostate cancer*. My husband is 69 years old, 6'6," and works 12 to 14 hours every day from 5am to 5pm and later. Rather than expose himself to the horror of conventional treatment, he began taking coral calcium. After three weeks he had more x-rays and no cancer was found. Three weeks later, he went for a second opinion and had more extensive x-rays and once again, no cancer was found. God bless

Coral Calcium.
Patty, Ponca City, Oklahoma

32. Lung Cancer First of all, I want to start off by telling you about my brother. Mr. Barefoot, you have spoken with my father several times about him. He has *lung cancer*. When it was detected, he had four lesions on his lung, one was the size of a peach seed. My Dad convinced my brother to take coral calcium. After 6 weeks when they ran another scan, 3 of the lesions were immeasurable, the big one had shrunk 60%. AMAZING!

Jeff Townsend, Kentucky

33. Hodgkins Disease Your website and research has truly been a blessing in my recovery of Hodgkins Disease.

Denise Horick

34. Pain Just want to take a moment to thank you for all your help. What coral calcium has done for me over a brief period, is nothing short of profound. I can't remember any time in the last 29 years that I wasn't *in substantial pain*... that is until now. I have tried every pain remedy the orthodox medical community has in their arsenal, including narcotics, steroids, and anti-inflammatories, just to name a few. Most of them did a great job of messing with my head, a feeling I literally hate, but did very little for the pain. I know almost nothing about the science behind this majestic mineral, coral calcium, I only know that it works. I have more energy, more range of motion, and less pain than I ever thought possible ! I know that there was a time in my life that I was pain free, I just couldn't remember how it felt until now. There are no words I can think of to adequately explain how much better I feel or what it means to me. Thank you so very much!

Best Regards, Gary T. Schilling

35. Emphysema I heard about your program from a lady who attended your meeting in Twin Falls this summer. My husband has a *rare genetic disorder called Alpha I Antitripsin*, which is genetic emphysema that develops because the liver is not functioning properly, and therefore, the lungs do not function properly either. He has been under a doctor's care for 9 years. After leaning about your recommendations to help heal disease, my husband began taking the vitamins and the coral calcium and has been on the program for 7 weeks. He let go of his drugs and monthly prolastin infusion program. He is now very careful about what he eats. He feels better and better every day and has just let go of his inhaler. He has seen great improvement. I would love to speak to you and share this miracle unfolding before our very eyes. You are wonderful...thank you for your research and efforts.

Mary Wiggins

36. Melanoma I thank you for the confidence that you built for me. After being diagnosed with *melanoma* with no real hope for treatment if it were to reoccur, I felt devastated. My surgery was done at the Mayo Hospital in Rochester which is supposed to be "world renowned for its advancements in medicine," but that can't mean advancements in reference to the treatment of cancer! I now feel a sense of security for which I thank you. In a world of chaos and pain due to surgery, I felt that I was "drowning" in a sense. Thank-you, thank-you, thank-you, from the bottom of my heart and the hearts of my precious family in Minnesota. I have given your information to anyone who has felt the perils of ill health and you are indeed held in high admiration for your work and devotion to healing mankind!! YES for CORAL CALCIUM!!!

Marcy in Minnesota

37.   Pain   I can't believe how different I feel after taking coral calcium. I lived with ***constant pain in my heel*** for months. I could not jog because I could just barely walk. After taking coral calcium for two months, the pain is gone. I am back jogging. I would not have done this if had not been for you.

Thank you very much, Russ Tomin

38.   Arthritis   When one has been active all their life, it is impossible to understand the pain one suffers when the body is ravished by ***Rheumatoid Arthritis***. Knowing that it was important to stay active, I enrolled in a fitness class.. One of the activities involved lifting weights (20 pounds) with my legs. Due to the weakened condition of my legs, I tore a vital part of my knee. This sent me to the doctor and to physical therapy. When the pain did not go away, the doctor realized that the Rheumatoid Arthritis had taken over. I had been diagnosed 37 years prior with lymph edema which had caused fluid buildup in my legs. There was no known cure. The fluid must constantly be pumped out of my legs. This caused further damage and I no longer could have the fluid pumped out. I was in exacerbated pain now. Then I learned about coral calcium. Within two weeks I began to notice an appreciable decline in the arthritic pain. Within three months I became pain-free and I am off my walker. Also the swelling had gone down in my mouth and I could use my dentures once again. Even my barber commented on how thick my hair had gotten. I am now "72 years young" after only 3 months on coral calcium. I can't wait to see what 3 years on coral calcium will accomplish. All I can say is, God bless all those who have made nutritional discoveries, especially coral calcium.

Willette Barbee, Plano, Texas

39.   **Leukemia**   The "Cancer Answer." The first week of march 2001, my step-father was diagnosed with *Leukemia*. They wanted to start chemotherapy right away. He asked for a 21 day delay so he could start a nutritional program with coral calcium In addition, Bob Barefoot recommended vitamin D and other minerals. On April 3, 2001 he went back to the doctors to run further tests on his condition. The doctors were amazed and totally baffled. They told him for reasons unexplained he doesn't need chemotherapy and that everything checked out normal. Hey folks, I thought Bob Barefoot had a screw loose when he claimed "coral calcium" could cure cancer. Turns out, he was right!

Jane and Sharon Gerding, Baker, LA

40.   **Bone Spur**   My name is Susan Hedrik, age 49. I worked in a furniture factory carrying, stretching and cutting large rolls of cloth until it almost destroyed my body. I've had *back surgery* and suffered from a *painful bone spur* on my right thumb which two doctors told me would have to be removed by surgery. I also suffer from *arthritis* in my left leg. I was introduced to coral calcium and began taking it on January 27, 2001, and after 4 weeks **"MY BONE SPUR WAS GONE!!!"** I now can walk without a limp from the arthritis and no longer have to begin my mornings with a heating pad on my neck. For me, coral calcium is a "MIRACLE!"

Susan Hedrick, IR from Lincolnton, NC

41.   **Arthritis**   I have a 14 year and 6 month Dachshund named "Andrea" suffering from *arthritis in her hindquarters*. She couldn't walk without falling over. She was unable to jump on a bed or the couch, even with the help of a foot stool. I purchased coral calcium for Andrea and after 5 days she was becoming more active. After 8 days she was jumping on the

173

couch, begging for treats and running and playing. Andrea not only returned to normal activity, she also lost six pounds. Coral calcium also helped her teeth. Since she only has half of her teeth, I used to break her dog biscuit in half so she could chew it. Now, she chomps it down whole. As for myself, I have chronic arthritis in my lower spine. After seeing what coral calcium did for Andrea, I began using coral calcium myself. After 4 days I no longer had to take my prescription drug "Relafen," which costs over $3.00 per pill (I was taking 2/day). I now am a firm believer in coral calcium as I have personally witnessed what it can do.

Jack Polhill, Lincolnton, NC

42. Osteoporosis   I would like to confirm that the use of coral calcium has been beneficial to my health. My *knee replacements* are deferred and my golf swing has improved. I'll be 74 this summer and I trust this sophomoric feeling is not a second child-hood.

Eugene T. Hall, Calgary, Canada

43. Fibromyalgia I am an osteopathic physician practicing osteopathic manipulation in the cranial field in south central PA. I have a patient who has suffered from severe *fibromyalgia* for the past several years. Recently she started taking coral calcium. This patient has improved dramatically. She has more flexibility and motion in her muscles and joints than she has in several years and she is nearly pain-free on many days. She has been able to discontinue a multitude of other medication, including chronic pain pills. The information in your books and tapes corresponds well to the science, the practical, the safe, the reasonable. I thank you for the time you have expended educating us.

Marianne Herr-Paul, D.O.

174

44. Cholesterol My mother, who has been on coral calcium for the past two months, paid a visit to her doctor to have her *cholesterol* re-tested. Her cholesterol had dropped 204 points and the doctor was amazed! She is now a believer in coral calcium. I thank God for you finding this product that is changing people's lives and giving their health back.

Cindy Metzger

45. Breast Cancer My cousin Shirley had been diagnosed in May with *breast cancer and colon cancer*. She was scheduled for a double mastectomy and was also going to have her colon removed. You advised her to take the coral calcium and other nutrients and by July the breast cancer was gone and the colon cancer had shrunk. (Note: The October 1, 1998 issue of *Annuls of Internal Medicine* printed a Harvard study of 89,000 women that found daily multivitamins reduced the risk of colon cancer by as much as 75%). Her doctors, needless to say, are absolutely amazed. I can't thank you enough for helping my cousin, Shirley, as she means everything to me.

Patti Hernandez, Oklahoma City, Oklahoma

46. Prostate Cancer I am 62 years old and have always enjoyed good health. In July 1997 I was diagnosed with *prostate cancer*. The diagnosis was confirmed with a biopsy and an ultra-sound. Two of six biopsies were positive with cancer. My doctors strongly urged me to take hormones and have my prostate removed. I thought about it but looked for alternative remedies. For six months I boiled Chinese herbs and did Qui Gong exercises and thought that this kept the cancer in abeyance. But in the spring of 1998 a second biopsy turned out to be similar to the first. "As a result of reading **The Calcium**

Factor I received excellent treatment and eventually cured myself of prostate cancer. A third biopsy in July 1998 showed only one positive but reduced active cancer. I continued to take coral calcium and other supplements. A fourth biopsy in January 1999 showed that where the tumors had been, there was now only benign prostatic tissue. I had beaten the cancer. As a result I would strongly recommend that anyone suffering from cancer or similar debilitating diseases, should study Barefoot's book **The Calcium Factor** and take responsibility for their own health. I have yet to find anyone who has written such well-reasoned and scientifically based material. I have been taking coral calcium for 3 years and it has saved my life.

David G McLean, Chairman of the Board, Canadian National Railways

47. Prostate Cancer In October 1996 I was diagnosed with *prostate cancer.* The diagnosis was confirmed by biopsy. In October of that year I started following Robert Barefoot's coral calcium regime. In July 1997 I had another prostate biopsy in which no evidence of malignancy was found. The regime outlined in the book **The Calcium Factor** improves the immune system to where the body can heal itself, without intrusive measures like surgery, chemotherapy or radiation.

S. Ross Johnson, Retired President of Prudential Insurance Company of America

48.   Good Health   "I am a physician, President and Executive Medical Director of Health Insight, S..B.S. and Health Advocate Inc., in the State of Michigan. I have extensive credentials and honors that reach the White House and Heads of States in other countries. Mr. Robert Barefoot has worked over the past 20 years with many medical doctors and scientists across the United States and in other countries doing Ortho-molecular Research on various diseases. The information has been culminated in the book, **The Calcium Factor,** which has been used technically as Bibles of Nutrition. Many people I know have thanked Mr. Barefoot for *both saving their lives and returning them to good health*. Mr. Barefoot is an amazing and extraordinary man who is on a 'Great Mission' for all mankind. I thank God for Robert Barefoot and thank God for coral calcium.

Liska M. Cooper, M.D., Detroit, Michigan

49. Silicone Implants "Mr. Barefoot has been, and continues to be, an advocate for health and natural healing through nutrition and knowledge. He has championed the cause of well over 440,000 American women and children who have been exposed to the *toxic effects of silicone implanted devices*. Mr. Barefoot, one of the rare silica chemists in the world, has delivered a message of hope to these suffering individuals, who didn't have any hope before, but are now arming themselves with the book **The Calcium Factor** and are spreading the word, especially about the miracle nutrient, coral calcium. His work with hundreds of scientists and medical doctors, researching diet, has elevated him to one of the top speakers on nutrition in the nation."

Jill M. Wood, President Idaho Breast Implant Information Group, Boise Idaho.

50. Prostate Cancer I graduated from Harvard University in 1942 (BSc Chemistry) and worked as a Research Director and in corporate management, and have been awarded two patents. Mr. Barefoot has been highly influential in my survival of *prostate cancer*, with which I was diagnosed in the fall of 1991.

a library of literature on calcium in the body. For the average reader who just wants to be informed about something of consequence to his health, he can feel assured by the sheer number of emphatic statements quoted from these men of science, that *calcium is the crucial factor in good health*. For example, another quote is, "The past five years has seen an *explosion of knowledge* concerning the properties and functions of calcium ion channels," by J. C. Venter and D. Tiggle, from the book **Structure and Physiology of the Slow Inward Calcium Channel**, 1987, Alan R. Liss, Inc. And lastly, physicians can be assured that the peaked health consciousness of the public today along with the computerized capability for communications will not allow the establishment to keep them from using this information to help their patients.

Another reason the medical profession should want to read, interpret and adopt this important information is the fact that *the vitamins and minerals are both so inexpensive and available*, and that the *pH test,* spitting on a pennie's worth of pH paper, a pH of less than 6.5 indicates calcium deficiency is also so inexpensive and simple. Unfortunately for the physicians, the general public can readily attend to their own health. In addition, the pH test is so graphic that it leaves little doubt to both the sick and the healthy as to the long term state of their health. After reading the references from all the men of science about the importance of calcium, and then realizing that *the pH test is indirectly a calcium test*, everyone will *"want to be blue"* (pH of 7.5), just like their *"healthy friends and animals. "* Also, men of medicine should put their own economic fears aside and leap at the chance to beat cancer, heart disease and all of the other debilitating diseases of man, and go down in history as doing it in their lifetime.

The bottom line is that thousands of scientists are discovering just how crucial calcium is to human health. Their studies are offering some exciting opportunities to cure the diseases that the medical establishment believe are incurable. Thus, for sure, if we listen to the men of medicine and continue waiting for a white drug chemical, no disease will be cured. The best example is cancer, which was at 3% at the turn of the 20th Century and now, at the turn of the 21st Century is at 39%. At the current rate of increase it will reach 100% by the end of this century. Or, we could examine, review and evaluate the work done by our best scientists who say there is hope. Ironically, two time Nobel Prize winner Otto Warburg told Americans that "there is no disease that we know more about the cause and the cure, than cancer." Thus, if the FDA and AMA are truly responsible to the people and for the people they will immediately commence the evaluation of biological calcium.

Not only will using the medicinal knowledge of biological calcium help us dramatically improve the quality of life, but it will also result in a *dramatic drop in the burgeoning costs of medical treatment*. The two big killers, heart disease that strikes one out of every two people, and cancer that strikes one out of every three people, could be eradicated, and put in the same category as polio and diphtheria, being extremely rare. The now popular surgical gall bladder removal could become a rare occurrence. It is interesting to note that although Western medicine considers the gall bladder to serve no useful function, Mother Nature uses it to store the alkaline bile, pH 7.1 to pH 8.6, from the pancreas and liver. If too much of this bile is consumed by the blood (due to mineral deficiency), the gall bile becomes less alkaline (or more acidic) resulting in the precipitation of painful gallstones. (**Your Health, Your Choice**, by Dr. M. Ted Mortter Jr., Fell Publishers Inc., 1990.) Kidney stones, which are created in a similar way, due to mineral deficiency, could also become a rare occurrence. The crippling diseases of aging could be minimized. Up to *one third of all elderly men and wome*n will accidentally fracture

These stories are always full of passion and pain. However, although these stories involve only a handful of people, there were more than 106,000 people who died in 1999, from adverse reaction to drugs, and 50,000 people who were killed last year with anesthetics, and 350,000 people who were killed last year by mistake with drugs. When comparing these half million people to the handful of herbal supplement stories, the campaign to degradate the supplement industry becomes trivial. Although it is true that the drug industry has numerous successes, it is also true that the nutrient industry has numerous successes. The difference is that the nutrient industry does not have to kill hundreds of thousands of people to accomplish these successes. If there is to be fairness in the Press, then there should be articles on "Bad Medicine in the Drug Industry." Also, instead of using passion to bypass truth, the media should talk about the half million victims that the drug industry kills every year. Also, fairness would demand that there be a few articles on the successes of the nutrient industry.

The common complaint that food supplements have not undergone the same scientific scrutiny that drugs have, is unfair for two reasons. First, both the FDA and the drug industry refuse to carry out tests on products that they cannot patent and therefore profit from. Since vitamins, minerals and herbs are all natural substances, they cannot be patented. If the nutrient industry were forced to carry out these expensive tests by themselves, prices would skyrocket. The FDA, which has been given both the man date and the money to protect the public, instead chooses to protect the drug industry. The ultimate result would likely be the retirement of most drugs. Even with herbs, which are drug supplements, the FDA refuses to fulfill its mandate to protect the public. The second reason for the unfairness is the fact that no one has ever been killed by God's vitamins and minerals, unless given in such staggering large doses that the same amount of anything would result in death. If the FDA and drug industry had put as much money into testing food supplements as it has into its propaganda campaign to discredit the food supplement industry, then most supplements could have undergone the scientific scrutiny that the FDA claims is missing. However, had this been done, the green light for supplements that would have resulted, would also have convinced most Americans to switch from drugs. Meanwhile the FDA spends our money trying to convince Americans that God's nutrients *"may be toxic."* This is both hypocritical and ludicrous.

This problem is further complicated with prescription drug abuse rivaling illicit drug abuse. "Since millions of prescription pills enter the illicit drug market every year, some see a double standard in drug enforcement because of grants of leniency towards doctors (75% of physicians convicted by the courts of prescription drug crime kept their license) and their rich clientele who abuse drugs," Dan Weckel, *"Prescription Fraud: Abusing the System,"* Los Angeles Times, August 18, 1996. To compound this further, of the 20 billion dollars that the government spends on its war on drugs, only 80 million dollars goes to the DEA to investigate prescription drug offenses. That's less than 1% of the budget, and this despite the fact that prescription drugs make up 44% of the illegal drug trade.

Thus doctors prosper selling *"drugstore heroin,"* readily made available by the drug industry, while most of those caught get to keep their licenses. And through all of this, where are the supposed protectors of American health, the FDA/AMA coalition ? They are busy doing two things. First they are busy trying to tell the American public that God does not know what he is doing as His vitamins and minerals *"may be toxic."* Second, they are busy trying to convince the American public that Congress made a mistake when it passed the "Dietary

Supplement Health Education Act." Logically, it is quite obvious that the American public does not need protection from God and Congress, but it is equally obvious that the American public does need protection from the FDA/AMA cartel.

Tragically, FDA stands for the Food and Drug Administration which spends almost all of its time and money on drugs, while rarely concerning itself with food unless it's a nutrient deemed to be competing with drugs. In addition, every year the FDA puts out a list of toxic drugs, that were determined to be killing the public, which it had just approved in previous years. And, unfortunately for the unsuspecting public, the drugs that the FDA does approve are all processed through unregulated, licensed drug wholesalers, many of whom have no knowledge of pharmaceuticals. On December 22, 2002, 60 Minutes, CBS News, reported in a show called "Bad Medicine" that, "It takes little more than an air conditioner and a refrigerator to become a licensed wholesaler of drugs and that there is no need for a biochemistry degree or any knowledge of pharmaceuticals." It also contended that these wholesalers, because the drugs can't be traced, often make more money by turning one batch of drugs into four. 60 Minutes complained that this is a common occurrence and that the FDA's position is that "It has no legal obligation to tell people it has sold drugs to that there is something wrong with those drugs." Thus, the FDA, whose mandate it is to protect the American public from harm caused by food or drugs, has failed miserably in living up to its mandate and its leaders should be forced to answer to Congress.

Fortunately, good health is both simply and inexpensively attainable from the knowledge expounded in this book, *Let's Cure Humanity*. The goal of good health for the masses will not be easy, as the *undercover dictatorship* referred to in 1776 by *Dr. Benjamin Rush,* America's first Surgeon General and the only American doctor to sign the

Declaration of Independence, is now well entrenched in the power structure and has a vested interest in continuing *to oppose* preventive medicine. Thus, the freedom *to choose* and the freedom *to practice* the medicine of your choice must be *put back into* the American Constitution. Dr. Benjamin Rush tried strenuously, but failed, to have *"medical freedom"* enshrined in the Constitution. He stated *"The constitution of this Republic should make special provisions for Medical Freedom. To restrict the art of healing to one class of men and deny equal privileges to others will constitute the Bastille of medical science. All such laws are un-American and despotic.*

For over 20 years now, Bob Barefoot has watched as thousands of people used nutrition to cure themselves. His co-author of his book *The Calcium Factor*, Dr. Carl Reich M.D. had demonstrated how he had for over 30 years used nutrition to cure his patients from a host of diseases. Many others that Barefoot watched cure themselves, were friends and family. This meant that if love prevails, the message must be spread, despite the perils and attacks of the FDA, FTC and AMA. When Barefoot held his first grandson in his arms, he raised him up to the sky over his head and swore to God that this child would never have to undergo the ravishes of degenerative diseases. He has done the same for his other four grandchildren, all who have become the *"coral calcium kids."* Although Barefoot can sigh relief for his loved ones, his heart aches for the other children of the world. He knows that if we take action and get the doctors prescribing nutrient therapy, then most diseases that are ravishing mankind can quickly be eradicated. He believes since Otto Warburg gave his warning that millions of Americans will die needlessly (over 20,000,000 have died to date), because the medical establishment refuses to endorse the claim that cancer can be cured, that millions more will have to die unless the FTC, FDA and AMA begin to listen to reason. He therefore advertises his dream for all who will listen.

transporter mediating intestinal calcium absorption. *J Biol Chem* 1999;274:22739-22746.

3. Zhuang L, Peng JB, Tou L, Takanaga H, Adam RM, Hediger MA, Freeman MR. Calcium-selective ion channel, CaT1, is apically localized in gastrointestinal tract epithelia and is aberrantly expressed in human malignancies. *Lab Invest* 2002;82:1755-1764.

4. Fleet JC, Wood RJ. Specific $1,25(OH)_2D_3$-mediated regulation of transcellular csalcium transport in Caco-2 cells. *Am J Physiol* 1999;276:G958-G964.

5. Barger-Lux MJ, Heaney RP, Recker RR. Time course of calcium absorption in humans: Evidence for a colonic component. *Calcif Tissue Int* 1989;44:308-311.

6. Cashman K. Prebiotics and calcium bioavailability. *Curr Issues Intest Microbiol* 2003;4:21-32.

7. Ireland P, Fordtran JS. Effect of dietary calcium and age on jejunal calcium absorption in humans studied by intestinal perfusion. *J Clin Invest* 1973;52:2672-2681.

8. Gallagher JC, Riggs BL, DeLuca HF. Effect of estrogen on calcium absorption and serum vitamin D metabolites in postmenopausal osteoporosis. *J Clin Endocrinol Metab* 1980;51:1359-1364.

9. Heaney RP, Saville PD, Recker RR. Calcium absorption as a function of calcium intake. *J Lab Clin Med* 1975;85:881-890.

10. Heaney RP, Recker RR, Stegman MR, Moy AJ. Calcium absorption in women: Relationships to calcium intake, estrogen status, and age. *J Bone Min Res* 1989;4:469-475.

11. Heaney RP, Weaver CM, Fitzsimmons ML. Influence of calcium load on absorption fraction. *J Bone Min Res* 1990;5:1135-1138.

12. Abrams SA, Wen J, Stuff JE. Absorption of calcium, zinc and iron from breast milk by five-to seven-month-old infants. *Pediatr Res* 1996;39:384-390.

13. Heaney RP. Effect of calcium on skeletal development, bone loss, and risk of fractures. Am J Med. 1991 Nov 25;91(5B):23S-28S.

14. Bullamore JR, Wilkinson R, Gallagher JC, Nordin BEC, Marshall DH. Effects of age on calcium absorption. *Lancet* 1970;ii:535-537.

15. Wolf RL, Cauley JA, Baker CE, Ferrell RE, Charron M, Caggiula AW, Salamone LM, Heaney RP, Kuller LH. Factors associated with calcium absorption efficiency in pre- and perimenopausal women. *Am J Clin Nutr.* 2000;72:466-471.

16. Pattanaungkul S, Riggs BL, Yergey AL, Vieira NE, O'Fallon WM, Khosla S. Relationship of intestinal calcium absorption to 1,25-dihydroxyvitamin D [1,25(OH)2D] levels in young *versus* elderly women: Evidence for age-related intestinal resistance to 1,25(OH)2D action. *J Clin Endocrinol Metab* 2000;85:4023-4027.

17. Abrams SA, Silber TJ, Esteban NV, Vieira NE, Stuff JE, Meyers R, Majd M, Yergey AL. Mineral balance and bone turnover in adolescents with anorexia nervosa. *J Pediatr* 1993;123:326-331.

18. Abrams SA, O'Brien KO, Stuff JE. Changes in calcium kinetics associated with menarche. *J Clin Endocrinol Metab* 1996;81:2017-2020.

19. Farmer ME, White LR, Brody JA, Bailey KR. Race and sex differences in hip fracture incidence. *Am J Public Health* 1984;74:1374-1380.

20. Kellie SE, Brody JA. Sex-specific and race-specific hip fracture rates. *Am J Pub Health* 1990;80:326-328.

21. Dawson-Hughes B, Harris S, Kramich C, Dallal G, Rasmussen HM. Calcium retention and hormone levels in black and white women on high- and low-calcium diets. *J Bone Min Res* 1993;8:779-787.

22. Drinkwater B, Bruemner B, Chestnut C. Menstrual history as a determinant of current bone density in young athletes. *JAMA* 1990;263:545-548.
23. Marcus R, Cann C, Madvig P, Minkoff J, Goddard M, Bayer M, Martin M, Gaudiani L, Haskell W, Genant H. Menstrual function and bone mass in elite women distance runners. Endocrine and metabolic features. *Ann Intern Med* 1985;102:158-163.
24. Berkelhammer CH, Wood RJ, Sitrin MD. Acetate and hypercalciuria during total parenteral nutrition. *Am J Clin Nutr* 1988;48:1482-1489.
25. Sebastian A, Harris ST, Ottaway JH, Todd KM, Morris RC Jr. Improved mineral balance and skeletal metabolism in postmenopausal women treated with potassium bicarbonate. *N Engl J Med* 1994;330:1776-1781.
26. Bell NH, Yergey AL, Vieira NE, Oexmann MJ, Shary JR. Demonstration of a difference in urinary calcium, not calcium absorption, in black and white adolescents. *J Bone Min Res* 1993;8:1111-1115.
27. Spencer H, Kramer L, Lensiak M, DeBartolo M, Norris C, Osis D. Calcium requirements in humans. Report of original data and a review. *Clin Orthop Related Res* 1984;184:270-280.
28. Jackman LA, Millane SS, Martin BR, Wood OB, McCabe GP, Peacock M, Weaver CM. Calcium retention in relation to calcium intake and postmenarcheal age in adolescent females. *Am J Clin Nutr* 1997;66:327-333.
29. Institute of Medicine. Calcium. In: *Dietary Reference Intakes for Calcium, Phosphorus, Magnesium, Vitamin D, and Fluoride.* National Academy Press, Washington, DC, 1997, chapter IV.
30. Miller K, Waye JD. Colorectal polyps in the elderly: What should be done? *Drugs Aging* 2002;19:393-404.
31. American Cancer Society. *Cancer Facts and Figures 2002.* (44 pages) http://www.cancer.org.
32. Turini ME, DuBois RN. Primary prevention: Phytoprevention and chemoprevention of colorectal cancer. *Hematol Oncol Clin North Am* 2002;16:811-840.
33. Potter JD. Nutrition and colorectal cancer. *Cancer Causes Control* 1996;7:127-146.
34. Marilley D, Vonlanthen S, Gioria A, Schwaller B. Calretinin and calretinin-22k increase resistance toward sodium butyrate-induced differentiation in CaCo-2 colon adenocarcinoma cells. *Exp Cell Res* 2001;268:93-103.
35. Gordon JI, Schmidt GH, Roth KA. Studies of intestinal stem cells using normal, chimeric and transgenic mice. *FASEB J* 1992;6:3039-3050.
36. Eastwood GL. A review of gastrointestinal epithelial renewal and its relevance to the development of adenocarcinomas of the gastrointestinal tract. *J Clin Gastroenterol* 1995; 21(Suppl. 1): S 1-S 1 1 .
37. Schmidt GH, Wilkinson MM, Ponder BA. Cell migration pathway in the intestinal epithelium: An in situ marker system using mouse aggregation chimeras. *Cell* 1985;40:425-429.
38. Wright NA, Irwin M. The kinetics of villus cell populations in the mouse small intestine. I. Normal villi: The steady state requirement. *Cell Tissue Kinet* 1982;15:595-609.
39. Whitfield JF, Bird RP, Chakravarthy BR, Isaacs RJ, Morley P. Calcium – Cell cycle regulator, differentiator, killer, chemopreventor, and maybe, tumor promoter. *J Cell Biochem Suppl* 1995;22:74-91.
40. Kerr JFR, Wyllie AH, Currie AR. Apoptosis: A basic biological phenomenon with wide-ranging implications in tissue kinetics. *Br J Cancer* 1972;26:239-257.
41. Arends MJ, Wyllie AH. Apoptosis: Mechanisms and roles in pathology. *Int*

79. McLellan EA, Bird RP. Aberrant crypts: Potential preneoplastic lesions in the murine colon. *Cancer Res* 1988;48:6187-6192.

80. Bird RP. Observations and quantification of aberrant crypts in the murine colon treated with a colon carcinogen: Preliminary findings. *Cancer Lett* 1987;37:147-151.

81. Correa P. Epidemiology of polyps and cancer. *Major Prob Pathol* 1978;10:126-152.

82. Hill MJ. Etiology of the adenoma-carcinoma sequence. *Major Prob Pathol* 1978;10:153-162.

83. Kendall CW, Janezic SA, Friday D, Venket Rao A. Dietary cholesterol enhances preneoplastic aberrant crypt formation and alters cell proliferation in the murine colon treated with azoxymethane. *Nutr Cancer* 1992;17:107-114.

84. Magnuson BA, Carr I, Bird RP. Ability of aberrant crypt characteristics to predict colonic tumour incidence in rats fed cholic acid. *Cancer Res* 1993;53:4499-4504.

85. Pretlow TP, Barrow BJ, Ashton WS, O'Riordan MA, Pretlow TG, Jurcisek JA, StellatoTA. Aberrant crypts: Putative preneoplastic foci in human colonic mucosa. *Cancer Res* 1991;51:1564-1567.

86. Pretlow TP, O'Riordan MA, Somich GA, Amini SB, Pretlow TG. Aberrant crypts correlate with tumour incidence in F344 rats treated with azoxymethane and phytate. *Carcinogenesis* 1992;13:1509-1512.

87. Rao CV, Desai D, Simi B, Kulkarni N, Amin S, Reddy BS. Inhibitory effect of caffeic acid esters on azoxymethane-induced biochemical changes and aberrant crypt foci formation in rat colon. *Cancer Res* 1993;53:4182-4188.

88. Shivapurkar N, Tang ZC, Frost A, Alabaster O. Inhibition of progression of aberrant crypt foci and colon tumour development by vitamin E and carotene in rats on a high-risk diet. *Cancer Lett* 1995;91:125-132.

89. Zarkovic M, Qin X, Nakatsuru Y, Oda H, Nakamura T, Shamsuddin AM, Ishikawa T. Tumour promotion by fecapentaene-12 in a rat colon carcinogenesis model. *Carcinogenesis* 1993;14:1261-1264.

90. Höpfner M, Lemmer K, Jansen A, Hanski C, Riecken E-O, Gavish M, Mann B, Buhr H, Glassmeier G, Scherübl H. Expression of functional P2-purinergic receptors in primary cells cultures of human colorectal carcinoma cells. *Biochem Biophys Res Commun* 1998;251:811-817.

91. Höpfner M, Maaser K, Barthel B, von Lampe B, Hanski C, Riecken E-O, Zeitz M, Scherubl H. Growth inhibition and apoptosis induced by P2Y2 receptors in human colorectal carcinoma cells: Involvement of intracellular calcium and cyclic adenosine monophosphate. *Int J Colorectal Dis* 2001;16:154-166.

92. Harden TK, Boyer JL, Nicholas RA. P2-purinergic receptors: Subtype-associated signaling responses and structure. *Annu Rev Pharmacol Toxicol* 1995;35:541-579.

93. Lustig KD, Conklin BR, Herzmark P, Taussig R, Bourne HR. Type II adenylylcyclase integrates coincident signals from G_s, Gi and G_q. *J Biol Chem* 1993;268:13900-13905.

94. Farese RV. Calcium as an intracellular mediator of hormone action: Intracellular phospholipid signaling systems. *Am J Med Sci* 1988;296:223:230.

95. Whitfield JF, Boynton AL, Macmanus JP, Sikorska M, Tsang BK. The regulation of cell proliferation by calcium and cyclic AMP. *Mol Cell Biochem* 1979;27:155-179.

96. Weiss H, Amberger A, Widschwendter M, Margreiter R, Ofner D, Dietl P. Inhibition of store-operated calcium entry contributes to the anti-proliferative effect of non-steroidal anti-inflammatory drugs in human colon cancer cells. *IntJ Cancer* 2001;92:877-882.

97. Korczak B, Whale C, Kerbel RS. Possible involvement of Ca^{2+} mobilization and protein kinase C activation in the induction of spontaneous metastasis by mouse mammary adenocarcinoma. *Cancer Res* 1989;49:2597-2560.

98. Liu B, Renaud C, Nelson KK, Chen YQ, Bazaz R, Kowynia J, Timar J, Diglio CA, Honn KV. Protein kinase C inhibitor calphostin C reduces B 16 amelanotic melanoma cell adhesion to endothelium and lung colonization. *Int J Cancer* 1992;52:147-152.

99. Amstad PA, Krupitza G, Cerutti PA. Mechanism of c-*fos* induction by active oxygen. *Cancer Res* 1992;52:3952-3960.

100. Kelloff GJ, Crowell JA, Steele VE, Lubet RA, Boone CW, Malone WA, Hawk ET, Lieberman R, Lawrence JA, Kopelovich L, Ali I, Viner JL, Sigman CC. Progress in cancer chemoprevention. *Ann N Y Acad Sci* 1999;889:1-13.

101. Fischer SM, Lee ML, Maldve RE, Morris RJ, Trono D, Burrow DL, Butler AP, Pavone A, Warren B. Association of protein kinase C activation with induction of ornithine decarboxylase in murine but not human keratinocytes cultures. *Mol Carcinog* 1993;7:228-237.

102. Klein IK, Ritland SR, Burgart LJ, Ziesmer SC, Roche PC, Gendler SJ, Karnes WE Jr. Adenoma-specific alterations of protein kinase C isozyme expression in *APCmin* mice. *Cancer Res* 2000;60:2077-2080.

103. Stauble B, Boscoboinik D, Tasinato A, Azzi A. Modulation of activator protein-1 (AP-1) transcription factor and protein kinase C by hydrogen peroxide and ?-tocopherol in vascular smooth muscle cells. *Eur J Biochem* 1994;226:393-402.

104. Russell DH. Ornithine decarboxylase: A key regulatory enzyme in normal and neoplastic growth. *Drug Metab Rev* 1981;16:1-88.

105. Janne J, Poso H, Raina A. Polyamines in rapid growth and cancer. *Biochem Biophys Acta* 1978;473:241-293.

106. Williams-Ashman HG, Canellakis ZN. Polyamines in mammalian biology and medicine. *Perspect Biol Med* 1979;2:421-453.

107. Pegg AE. Polyamine metabolism and its importance in neoplastic growth and a target for chemotherapy. *Cancer Res* 1988;48:759-774.

108. Luk GD, Baylin SB. Ornithine decarboxylase as a biologic marker in familial colonic polyposis. *N Engl J Med* 1984;311:80-83.

109. Love RR, Verma AK, Surawicz TS, Morrissey JF. Absence of effect of supplemental oral calcium on ornithine decarboxylase (ODC) activity in colonic mucosae of healthy individuals with a family history of colorectal cancer. J Surg Oncol. 1990 Feb;43(2):79-82.

110. Hibshoosh H, Johnson M, Weistein IB. Effects of overexpression of ornithine decarboxylase (ODC) on growth control and oncogene-induced cell transformation. *Oncogene* 1991;6:739-743.

111. Ishizuka J, Bold RJ, Townsend CM Jr, Thompson JC. Role of calcium in the regulation of ornithine decarboxylase enzyme activity in mouse colon cancer cells. *Cancer Invest* 1995;13:181- 187.

112. Steele VE, Moon RC, Lubet RA, Grubbs CJ, Reddy BS, Wargovich M, McCormick DL, Pereira MA, Crowell JA, Bagheri D, Sigman CC, Boone CW, Kelloff GJ. Preclinical efficacy evaluation of potential chemopreventive agents in animal carcinogenesis models: Methods and results from the NCI Chemoprevention Drug Development Program. *J Cell Biochem Suppl* 1994;20:32-54.

113. Jarvis WD, Turner AJ, Povirk LF, Taylor RS, Grant S. Induction of apoptotic DNA fragmentation and cell death in HL-60 human promyelocytic leukemia cells by pharmacological inhibitors of protein kinase C. *Cancer Res* 1994;54:1707-1714.

114. Whelan RD, Parker PJ. Loss of protein kinase C function induces a proapoptotic response. *Oncogene* 1998;16:1939-1944.

115. Hannun YA. Functions of ceramide in coordinating cellular responses to stress. *Science* 1996;274:1855-1859.

116. Haimovitz-Friedman A, Kolesnick RN, Fuks Z. Ceramide signaling in apoptosis. *Br Med Bull* 1997;53:539-553.

117. Bradham C, Quian T, Streetz K, Trautwein C, Brenner DA, Lemasters JJ. The mitochondrial permeability transition is required for tumor necrosis factor mediated apoptosis and cytochrome *c* release. *Mol Cell Biol* 1998;18:6353-6364.

118. Chinnaiyan AM. The apoptosome: Heart and soul of the cell death machine. *Neoplasia* 1999;1:5-15.

119. Kluck RM, Bossy-Wetzel E, Green DR, Newmeyer DD. The release of cytochrome c from mitochondria: A primary site of Bcl-2 regulation of apoptosis. *Science* 1997;275:1132-1136.

120. Kallay E, Bajna E, Wrba F, Kriwanek S, Peterlik M, Cross HS. Dietary calcium and growth modulation of human colon cancer cells: Role of the extracellular calcium-sensing receptor. *Cancer Detect Prev* 2000;24:127-136.

121. Cross HS, Pavelka M, Slavik J, Peterlik M. Growth control of human colon cancer cells by vitamin D and calcium in vitro. *J Natl Cancer Inst* 1992;84:1355-1357.

122. Lamprecht SA, Lipkin M. Chemoprevention of colon cancer by calcium, vitamin D and folate: Molecular mechanisms. *Nat Rev Cancer* 2003;3:601-614.

123. Morotomi M, Guillem JG, Weinstein IB. Production of diacylglycerol, an activator of protein kinase C, by human intestinal microflora. *Cancer Res* 1990;50:3595-3599.

124. Morotomi M, LoGerfo P, Weinstein IB. Fecal excretion, uptake and metabolism by colon mucosa of diacylglycerol in rats. *Biochem Biophys Res Commun* 1991;181:1028-1034.

125. Friedman E, Isaksson P, Rafter J, Marian B, Winawer S, Newmark H. Fecal diglycerides as selective endogenous mitogens for premalignant and malignant human colonic epithelial cells. *Cancer Res* 1989;49:544-548.

126. Craven PA, Pfanstiel J, DeRubertis, FR. Role of activation of protein kinase C in the stimulation of colonic epithelial proliferation and reactive oxygen formation by bile acids. *J Clin Invest* 1987;79:532-541.

127. Weinstein IB. Cancer prevention: Recent progress and future opportunities. *Cancer Res* 1991;51:5080-5085.

128. Atillasoy E, Fein B, Weinstein IB, Holt PR. Fecal diacylglycerol concentrations and calcium supplementation. *Cancer Epidemiol Biomarkers Prev* 1995;4:795-796.

129. Steinbach G, Lupton J, Reddy BS, Kral JG, Holt PR. Effect of calcium supplementation on rectal epithelial hyperproliferation in intestinal bypass subjects. *Gastroenterology* 1994;106:1162-1167.

130. Holt PR, Moss SF, Whelan R, Guss J, Gilman J, Lipkin M. Fecal and rectal mucosal diacylglycerol concentrations and epithelial proliferative kinetics. *Cancer Epidemiol Biomarkers Prev* 1996;5:937-940.

131. Tangpricha V, Flanagan JN, Whitlatch LW, Tseng CC, Chen TC, Holt PR, Lipkin MS, Holick MF. 25-hydroxyvitamin D-1?-hydroxylase in normal and malignant colon tissue. *Lancet* 2001;357:1673-1674.

132. Cross HS, Bareis P, Hofer H, Bischof MG, Bajna E, Kriwanek S, Bonner E, Peterlik M. 25-Hydroxyvitamin D3-1? hydroxylase and vitamin D receptor gene expression in human colonic mucosa is elevated during early cancerogenesis. *Steroids* 2001;66:287-292.

133. Zehnder D, Bland R, Williams MC, McNinch RW, Howie AJ, Stewart PM, Hewison M. Extrarenal expression of 25-hydroxyvitamin D3-1? hydroxylase. *J Clin Endocrinol Metab* 2001;86:888-894.

134. Baron JA, Beach M, Mandel JS, van Stolk RU, Haile RW, Sandler RS, Rothstein R, Summers RW, Snover DC, Beck GJ, Frankl H, Bond JH, Greenberg ER. Calcium supplements and colorectal adenomas. Calcium Polyp Prevention Study Group. *N Engl J Med* 1999;340:101-107.

135. Brenner BM, Russell N, Albrecht S, Davies RJ. The effect of dietary vitamin D3 on the intracellular calcium gradient in mammalian colonic crypts. *Cancer Lett* 1998;127:43-53.

136. Holt PR, Arber N, Halmos B, Forde K, Kissileff H, McGlynn KA, Moss SF, Kurihara N, Fan K, Yang K, Lipkin M. Colonic epithelial cell proliferation decreases with increasing levels of serum 25-hydroxy vitamin D. *Cancer Epidemiol Biomarkers Prev* 2002;11:113-119.

137. Holt PR, Atillasoy EO, Gilman J, Guss J, Moss SF, Newmark H, Fan K, Yang K, Lipkin M. Modulation of abnormal colonic epithelial cell proliferation and differentiation by low-fat dairy foods. A randomized controlled trial. *JAMA* 1998;280:1074-1079.

138. Lointier P, Wargovich MJ, Saez S, Levin B, Wildrick DM, Boman BM. The role of vitamin D3 in the proliferation of a human colon cancer cell line *in vitro*. *Anticancer Res* 1987;7:817-821.

139. Giuliano AR, Franceschi RT, Wood RJ. Characterization of the vitamin D receptor from the Caco-2 human colon carcinoma cell line: Effect of cellular differentiation. *Arch Biochem Biophys* 1990;285:261-269.

140. Harper KD, Iozzo RV, Haddad JG. Receptors for and bioresponses to 1,25-dihydroxyvitamin D in a human colon carcinoma cell line (HT-29). *Metabolism* 1989;38:1062-1069.

141. Suda T, Shinki T, Takashashi N. The role of vitamin D in bone and intestinal cell differentiation. *Annu Rev Nutr* 1990;10:195-211.

142. Tanaka Y, Bush KK, Eguchi T, Ikekawa N, Taguchi T, Kobayashi Y, Higgins PJ. Effects of 1,25-dihydroxyvitamin D3 and its analogs on butyrate-induced differentiation of HT029 human colonic carcinoma cells and on the reversal of the differentiated phenotype. *Arch Biochem Biophys* 1990;276:415-423.

143. Eisman JA, Barkla DH, Tutton PJM. Suppression of *in vivo* growth of human cancer solid tumor xenografts by 1,25-dihydroxyvitamin D3. *Cancer Res* 1987;47:21-25.

144. Brehier A, Thomasset M. Human colon cell line HT-29: Characterization of 1,25-dihydroxyvitamin D3 receptor and induction of differentiation by the hormone. *J Steroid Biochem* 1988;29:265-270.

145. Lointier P, Meggouh F, Dechelotte P, Pezet D, Ferrier C, Chipponi J, Saez S. 1,25-dihydroxyvitamin D3 receptors and human colon adenocarcinoma. *Br J Surg* 1991;78:435-439.

146. Lointier P, Meggouh F, Pezet D, Dapoigny M, Dieng PND, Saez S, Chipponi J. Specific receptor for 1,25-dihydroxyvitamin D3 (1,25-DR) and human colorectal carcinogenesis. *Anticancer Res* 1989;9:1921-1924.

147. Meggouh F, Lointier P, Saez S. Sex steroid and 1,25-dihydroxyvitamin D3 receptors in human colorectal adenocarcinoma and normal mucosa. *Cancer Res* 1991;51:1227-1233.

148. Danes BS, De Angelis P, Traganos F, Melamed MR. Heritable colon cancer: Influence of increased calcium concentration on increased in vitro tetraploidy (IVT). *Med Hypotheses* 1991;36:69- 72.

149. Danes BS. Effect of increased calcium concentration on *in vitro* growth of human colonic mucosal lines. *Dis Colon Rectum* 1991;34:552-556.

150. Buset M, Lipkin M, Winawer S, Swaroop S, Friedman E. Inhibition of human colonic epithelial cell proliferation in vivo and in vitro by calcium. *Cancer Res* 1986;46:5426-5430.

151. Friedman E, Lipkin M, Winawer S, Buset M, Newmark H. Heterogeneity in the response of familial polyposis epithelial cells and adenomas to increasing levels of calcium in vitro. *Cancer* 1989;63:2486-2491.

152. Buras RR, Shabahang M, Davoodi F, Schumaker LM, Cullen KJ, Byers S, Nauta RJ, Evans SRT. The effect of extracellular calcium on colonocytes: Evidence for differential responsiveness based upon degree of cell differentiation. *Cell Prolif* 1995;28:245-262.

153. Cross HS, Hulla W, Tong W-M, Peterlik M. Growth regulation of human colon adenocarcinoma-derived cells by calcium, vitamin D and epidermal growth factor. *J Nutr* 1995;125:2004S-2008S.

154. Wargovich MJ. Calcium and colon cancer. *J Am Coll Nutr* 1988;7:295-300.

155. Kelloff GJ, Crowell JA, Boone CW, Steele VE, Lubet RA, Greenwald P, Alberts DS, Covey JM, Doody LA, Knapp GG, Nayfield S, Parkinson DR, Prasad VK, Prorok PC, Sausville EA, Sigman CC. Clinical development plan: Calcium. Chemoprevention Branch and Agent Development Committee. National Cancer Institute. *J Cell Biochem Suppl* 1994;20:86-109.

156. Eshleman JR, Markowitz SD. Microsatellite instability in inherited and sporadic neoplasms. *Curr Opin Oncol* 1995;7:83-89.

157. Thibodeau SN, Bren G, Schaid D. Microsatellite instability in cancer of the proximal colon. *Science* 1993;260:816-819.

158. Tsao JL, Dudley S, Kwok B, Nickel AE, Laird PW, Siegmund KD, Liskay RM, Shibata D. Diet, cancer and aging in DNA mismatch repair deficient mice. *Carcinogenesis* 2002;23:1807-1810.

159. Aaltonen LA, Peltomaki P, Leach FS, Sistonen P, Pylkkanen L, Mecklin J-P, Jarvinen H, Powell SM, Jen J, Hamilton SR, Petersen GM, Kinzler KW, Vogelstein B, de la Chapelle A. Clues to the pathogenesis of familial colorectal cancer. *Science* 1993;260:812-816.

160. Marra G, Boland CR. Hereditary nonpolyposis colorectal cancer: The syndrome, the genes, and historical perspectives. *J Natl Cancer Inst* 1995;87:1114-1125.

161. Peltomaki P, Vasen HF. Mutations predisposing to hereditary nonpolyposis colorectal cancer: Database and results of a collaborative study. The International Collaborative Group on Hereditary Nonpolyposis Colorectal Cancer. *Gastroenterolog* 1997;113:1146-1158.

162. Van Aken E, De Wever O, Correia da Rocha AS, Mareel M. Defective E-cadherin/catenin complexes in human cancer. *Virchows Arch* 2001;439:725-751.

163. Ilyas M, Tomlinson IPM. The interactions of APC, E-cadherin and catenin in tumour development and progression. *J Pathol* 1997;182:128-137.

164. Chakrabarty S, Radjendirane V, Appelman H, Varani J. Extracellular calcium and calcium sensing receptor function in human colon carcinomas: promotion of E-cadherin expression and suppression of beta-catenin/TCF activation. *Cancer Res* 2003;63:67-71.

165. Kallay E, Bonner E, Wrba F, Thakker RV, Peterlik M, Cross HS. Molecular and functional characterization of the extracellular calcium-sensing receptor in human colon cancer cells. *Oncol Res* 2003;13:551-559.

166. Chattopadhyay N, Yamaguchi T, Brown EM. Ca^{2+} receptor from brain to gut: Common stimulus, diverse actions. *Trends Endocrinol Metab* 1998;9:354-359.

167. Sheinin Y, Kallay E, Wrba F, Kriwanek S, Peterlik M, Cross HS. Immunocytochemical localization of the extracellular calcium-sensing receptor

in normal and malignant human large intestinal mucosa. *J Histochem Cytochem* 2000;48:595-602.

168. Gama L, Baxendale - Cox LM, Breitwieser GE. Ca^{2+}- sensing receptors in intestinal epithelium. *Am J Physiol Cell Physiol* 1997;273:1168-1175.

169. De Luca F, Baron J. Molecular biology and clinical importance of the Ca^{2+}-sensing receptor. *Curr Opin Pediatr* 1998;10:435-440.

170. Takeichi M. Cadherin cell adhesion receptors as a morphogenetic regulator. *Science* 1991;251:1451-1455.

171. Bostick RM, Potter JD, Fosdick L, Grambsch P, Lampe JW, Wood JR, Louis TA, Ganz R, Grandits G. Calcium and colorectal epithelial cell proliferation: A preliminary randomized, double-blinded, placebo-controlled clinical trial. *J Natl Cancer Inst* 1993;85:132-141.

172. Newmark HL, Lipkin M. Calcium, vitamin D, and colon cancer. Cancer Res. 1992 Apr 1;52(7 Suppl):2067s-2070s.

173. Wargovich MJ, Baer AR. Basic and clinical investigations of dietary calcium in the prevention of colorectal cancer. *Prev Med* 1989;18:672-679.

174. Rozen P. An evaluation of rectal epithelial proliferation measurement as biomarker of risk for colorectal neoplasia and response in intervention studies. *Eur J Cancer Prev* 1992;1:215-224.

175. Speer G, Cseh K, Mucsi K, Takacs I, Dworak O, Winkler G, Szody R, Tisler A, Lakatos P. Calcium-sensing receptor A986S polymorphism in human rectal cancer. *Int J Colorectal Dis* 2002;17:20-24.

176. Berx G, Staes K, van Hengel J, Molemans F, Bussemakers MJ, van Bokhoven A, van Roy F. Cloning and characterization of the human invasion suppressor gene E-cadherin (CDH1). *Genomics* 1995;26:281-289.

177. Graff JR, Herman JG, Lapidus RG, Chopra H, Xu R, Jarrard DF, Isaacs WB, Pitha PM, Davidson NE, Baylin SB. E-cadherin expression is silenced by DNA hypermethylation in human breast and prostate carcinomas. *Cancer Res* 1995;55:5195-5199.

178. Hennig G, Behrens J, Truss M, Frisch S, Reichmann E, Birchmeier W. Progression of carcinoma cells is associated with alterations in chromatin structure and factor binding at the E-cadherin promoter in vivo. *Oncogene* 1995;11:475-484.

179. Dorudi S, Sheffield JP, Poulson R, Northover JM, Hart IR. E-cadherin expression in colorectal cancer: An immunochemical and *in situ* hybridization study. *Am J Pathol* 1993;142:981-986.

180. Azarschab P, Porschen R, Gregor M, Blin N, Holzmann K. Epigenetic control of the E-cadherin gene (CDH1) by CpG methylation in colectomy samples of patients with ulcerative colitis. *Genes Chromosomes Cancer* 2002;35:121-126.

181. Bedi A, Pasricha PJ, Akhtar AJ, Barber JP, Bedi GC, Giardello FM, Zehnbauer BA, Hamilton SR, Jones RJ. Inhibition of apoptosis during development of colorectal cancer. *Cancer Res* 1995;55:1811-1816.

182. Boland CR. The biology of colorectal cancer: Implications for pretreatment and follow-up management. *Cancer* 1993;71:4180-4186.

183. Fearon ER. Molecular genetic studies of the adenoma-carcinoma sequence. *Adv Intern Med* 1994;39:123-147.

184. Rustgi AK. Molecular genetics and colorectal cancer. *Gastroenterology* 1993;104:1223-1225.

185. Greenwald P, Kelloff GJ, Boone CW, McDonald SS. Genetic and cellular changes in colorectal cancer: Proposed targets of chemopreventive agents. *Cancer Epidemiol Biomarkers Prev* 1995;4:691-702.

186. Slattery ML, Schaffer D, Edwards SL, Ma K-N, Potter JD. Are dietary factors involved in DNA methylation associated with colon cancer? *Nutr Cancer*

1997;28:52-62.

187. Rosty C, Ueki T, Argani P, Jansen M, Yeo CJ, Cameron JL, Hruban RH, Goggins M. Overexpression of S100A4 in pancreatic ductal adenocarcinomas is associated with poor differentiation and DNA hypomethylation. *Am J Pathol* 2002;160:45-50.

188. Bronckart Y, Decaestecker C, Nagy N, Harper L, Schafer BW, Salmon I, Pochet R, Kiss R, Heizman CW. Development and progression of malignancy in human colon tissues are correlated with expression of specific Ca^2+-binding S100 proteins. *Histol Histopathol* 2001;16:707-712.

189. Stulik J, Osterreicher J, Koupilova K, Knizek, Macela A, Bures J, Jandik P, Langr F, Dedic K, Jungblut PR. The analysis of S100A9 and S100A8 expression in matched sets of macroscopically normal colon mucosa and colorectal carcinoma: The S100A9 and S100A8 positive cells underlie and invade tumor mass. *Electrophoresis* 1999;20:1047-1054.

190. Kristinsson J, Armbruster CH, Ugstad M, Kriwanek S, Nygaard K, Ton H, Fuglerud P. Fecal excretion of calprotectin in colorectal cancer. Relationship to tumor characteristics. *Scand J Gastroenterol* 2001;36:202-207.

191. Takenaga K, Nakanishi H, Wada K, Suzuki M, Matsuzaki O, Matsuura A, Endo H. Increased expression of S100A4, a metastasis-associated gene, in human colorectal adenocarcinomas. *Clin Cancer Res* 1997;3:2309-2316.

192. Stulik J, Osterreicher J, Koupilova K, Knizek J, Bures J, Jandik P, Langr F, Dedic K, Schafer BW, Heizmann CW. Differential expression of the Ca^{2+} binding S100A6 protein in normal, preneoplastic and neoplastic colon mucosa. *Eur J Cancer* 2000;36:1050-1059.

193. Barraclough R. Calcium-binding protein S100A4 in health and disease. *Biochim Biophys Acta* 1998;1448:190-199.

194. Komatsu K, Andoh A, Ishiguro S, Suzuki N, Hunai H, Kobune-Fujiwara Y, Kameyama M, Miyoshi J, Akedo H, Nakamura H. Increased expression of S100A6 (Calcyclin), a calcium-binding protein of the S100 family, in human colorectal adenocarcinomas. *Clin Cancer Res* 2000;6:172-177.

195. Summerton CB, Longlands MG, Wiener K, Shreeve DR. Faecal calprotectin: A marker of inflammation throughout the intestinal tract. *Eur J Gastroenterol Hepatol* 2002;14:841-845.

196. Gongoll S, Peters G, Mengel M, Piso P, Klempnauer J, Kreipe H, von Wasielewski R. Prognostic significance of calcium-binding protein S100A4 in colorectal cancer. *Gastroenterology* 2002;123:1478-1484.

197. Steinbach G, Heymsfield S, Olansen NE, Tighe A, Holt PR. Effect of caloric restriction on colonic proliferation in obese persons: Implications for colon cancer prevention. *Cancer Res* 1994;54:1194-1197.

198. Cats A, Kleibeuker JH, van der Meer R, Kuipers F, Sluiter WJ, Hardonk MJ, Oremus ET, Mulder NH, de Vries EG. Randomized, double-blinded, placebo-controlled intervention study with supplemental calcium in families with hereditary nonpolyposis colorectal cancer. *J Natl Cancer Inst* 1995;87:598-603.

199. Chadwick VS, Gaginella TS, Carlson GL, Debognie JC, Phillips SF, Hofmann AF. Effect of molecular structure on bile acid-induced alterations in absorptive function, permeability and morphology in the perfused rabbit colon. *J Lab Clin Med* 1979;94:661-674.

200. Deschner EE, Cohen BI, Raicht RF. Acute and chronic effect of dietary cholic acid on colonic epithelial cell proliferation. *Digestion* 1981;21:290-296.

201. Deschner EE, Raicht RF. Influence of bile on kinetic behavior of colonic epithelial cells of the rat. *Digestion* 1981;19:322-327.

202. Koga S, Kaibara N, Takeda R. Effect of bile acids on 1,2-dimethylhydrazine-

induced colon cancer in rats. *Cancer* 1982;50:543-547.

203. Cohen BI, Raicht RF. Effects of bile acids on colon carcinogenesis in rats treated with carcinogens. *Cancer Res* 1981;41:3759-3760.

204. Cruse JP, Lewin MR, Clark CG. The effects of cholic acid and bile salt binding agents on 1,2-dimehylhydrazine induced colon carcinogenesis in the rat. *Carcinogenesis* 1981;2:439-443.

205. Reddy BS, Narisawa T, Weisburger JH, Wynder EL. Effect of sodium deoxycholate on colon adenocarcinomas in germ free rats. *J Natl Cancer Inst* 1976;56:441-442.

206. Wargovich MJ. Phytic acid, a major calcium chelator from fiber-rich cereals stimulates colonic cellular proliferation (abstract). *Gastroenterology* 1986;90:1684.

207. Rafter JJ, Eng VWS, Furrer R, Bruce WR. Effects of calcium and pH on the mucosal damage produced by deoxycholic acid in the rat colon. *Gut* 1986;27:1320-1329.

208. Reddy BS, Watanabe K. Effect of cholesterol metabolism and promoting effect of lithocolic acid on colon carcinogenesis in germ-free and conventional F344 rats. *Cancer Res* 1979;39:1521-1524.

209. Glauert HP, Bennik MB. Influence of diet or intrarectal bile acid injections on colon epithelial cell proliferation in rats previously injected with 1,2-dimethylhydrazine. *J Nutr* 1983;113:475-482.

210. Sakaguchi M, Hiramatsu Y, Takada H, Yamamura M, Hioki K, Saito K, Yamamoto M. Effect of dietary unsaturated and saturated fats on azoxymethane-induced colon carcinogenesis in rats. *Cancer Res* 1984;44:1472-1477.

211. Bull AW, Nigro ND, Golembieski WA, Crissman JD, Marnett LJ. In vivo stimulation of DNA synthesis and induction of ornithine decarboxylase in rat colon by fatty acid hydroperoxides, autoxidation products of unsaturated fatty acids. *Cancer Res* 1984;44:4924-4928.

212. Silverman SJ, Andrews AW. Bile acids: Co-mutagenic activity in the Salmonella-mammalian-microsome mutagenicity test (Brief communication). *J Natl Cancer Inst* 1977;59:1557-1559.

213. Richards TC. Changes in crypt cell populations of mouse colon during recovery from treatment with 1,2-dimethylhydrazine. *J Natl Cancer Inst* 1981;66:907-912.

214. Cohen BI, Raicht RF, Deschner EE, Takahashi M, Sarwal AN, Fazzini E. Effect of cholic acid feeding on *N*-methyl-*N*-nitrosourea induced colon tumors and cell kinetics in rats. *J Natl Cancer Inst* 1980;64:573-578.

215. Nagengast FM, Grubben MJAL, van Munster IP. Role of bile acids in colorectal carcinogenesis. *Eur J Cancer* 1995;31A:1067-1070.

216. Lapre JA, de Vries HT, van der Meer R. Dietary calcium phosphate inhibits cytotoxicity of fecal water. *Am J Physiol* 1991;261:G907-G912.

217. Newmark HL, Lupton JR. Determinants and consequences of colonic luminal pH: Implications for colon cancer. *Nutr Cancer* 1990;14:161-173.

218. Reddy BS. Dietary fat and colon cancer: Animal model studies. *Lipids* 1992;27:807-813.

219. Kanazawa K, Konishi F, Mitsuoka T, Terada A, Itoh K, Narushima S, Kumemura M, Kimura H. Factors influencing the development of sigmoid colon cancer. Bacteriologic and biochemical studies. *Cancer* 1996;77(8 Suppl):1701-1706.

220. Samelson SL, Nelson RL, Nyhus LM. The protective effect of fecal pH on experimental colon carcinogenesis. *J R Soc Med* 1985;78:230-233. 221. Appleton GV, Bristol JB, Williamson RC. Increased dietary calcium and small

bowel resection have opposite effects on colonic cell turnover. *Br J Surg* 1986;73:1018-1021.

222. Appleton GV, Davies PW, Bristol JB, Williamson RC. Inhibition of intestinal carcinogenesis by dietary supplementation with calcium. *Br J Surg.* 1987;74:523-525.

223. Beaty MM, Lee EY, Glauert HP. Influence of dietary calcium and vitamin D on colon epithelial cell proliferation and 1,2-dimethylhydrazine-induced colon carcinogenesis in rats fed high fat diets. *J Nutr* 1993;123:144-152.

224. Pence BC, Buddingh F. Inhibition of dietary fat-promoted colon carcinogenesis in rats by supplemental calcium or vitamin D3. *Carcinogenesis* 1988;9:187-190.

225. Pereira MA, Barnes LH, Rassman VL, Kelloff GV, Steele VE. Use of azoxymethane-induced foci of aberrant crypts in rat colon to identify potential cancer chemopreventive agents. *Carcinogenesis* 1994;15:1049-1054.

226. Vinas-Salas J, Biendicho-Palau P, Pinol-Felis C, Miguelsanz-Garcia S, Perez-Holanda S. Calcium inhibits colon carcinogenesis in an experimental model in the rat. *Eur J Cancer* 1998;34:1941-1945.

227. Wang A, Yoshimi N, Tanaka T, Mori H. The inhibitory effect of magnesium hydroxide on the bile acid-induced cell proliferation of colon epithelium in rats in comparison to the action of calcium lactate. *Carcinogenesis* 1994;15:2661-2663.

228. Wargovich MJ, Stephens LC, Gray K. Effect of two "human" nutrient density levels of calcium on the promotional phase of colon tumorigenesis in the F344 rat (abstract). *Proc Am Assoc Cancer Res* 1989;30:196.

229. Stern HS, Gregoire RC, Kashtan H, Stadler J, Bruce RW. Long-term effects of dietary calcium on risk markers for colon cancer in patients with familial polyposis. *Surgery* 1990;108:528-533.

230. Van Faassen A, Hazen MJ, van den Brandt PA, van den Bogaard AE, Hermus RJ, Janknegt RA. Bile acids and pH values in total feces and in fecal water from habitually omnivorous and vegetarian subjects. *Am J Clin Nutr* 1993;58:917-922.

231. Gregoire RC, Stern HS, Yeung KS, Stadler J, Langley S, Furrer R, Bruce WR. Effect of calcium supplementation on mucosal cell proliferation in high risk patients for colon cancer. *Gut* 1989;30:376-382.

232. Govers MJAP, Termont DSML, Lapre JA, Kleibeuker JH, Vonk RJ, Van der Meer R. Calcium in milk products precipitates intestinal fatty acids and secondary bile acids and thus inhibits colonic cytotoxicity in humans. *Cancer Res* 1996;56:3270-3275.

233. Behling AR, Greger JL. Mineral metabolism of aging female rats fed various commercially available calcium supplements of yogurt. *Pharmacol Res* 1988;5:501-505.

234. Adell-Carceller R, Segarra-Soria M, Gibert-Jerez J, Salvador Sanchis JL, Lazaro-Santander R, Escrig-Sos J, Ruiz-Castillo J. Inhibitory effect of calcium on carcinogenesis at the site of colonic anastomosis: An experimental study. *Dis Colon Rectum* 1997;40:1376-1381.

235. Arlow FL, Walczak SM, Luk GD, Majumdar AP. Attenuation of azoxymethane-induced colonic mucosal ornithine decarboxylase and tyrosine kinase activity by calcium in rats. *Cancer Res* 1989;49:5884-5888.

236. Barsoum GH, Thompson H, Neoptolemos JP, Keighley MR. Dietary calcium does not reduce experimental colorectal carcinogenesis after small bowel resection despite reducing cellular proliferation. *Gut* 1992;33:1515-1520.

237. Behling AR, Kaup SM, Greger JL. Changes in intestinal function of rats initiated with DMH and fed varying levels of butterfat, calcium, and magnesium. *Nutr Cancer* 1990;13:189-199.

238. Hambly RJ, Rumney CJ, Cunninghame M, Fletcher JM, Rijken PJ, Rowland IR. Influence of diets containing high and low risk factors for colon cancer on early stages of carcinogenesis in human flora-associated (HFA) rats. *Carcinogenesis* 1997;18:1535-1539.

239. Li H, Kramer PM, Lubet RA, Steele VE, Kelloff GJ, Pereira MA. Effect of calcium on azoxymethane-induced aberrant crypt foci and cell proliferation in the colon of rats. *Cancer Lett* 1998;124:39-46.

240. Liu Z, Tomotake H, Wan G, Watanabe H, Kato N. Combined effect of dietary calcium and iron on colonic aberrant crypt foci, cell proliferation and apoptosis, and fecal bile acids in 1,2-dimethylhydrazine-treated rats. *Oncol Rep* 2001;8:893-897.

241. Molck A-M, Poulsen M, Meyer O. The combination of 1alpha,25(OH2)-vitamin D3, calcium and acetylsalicylic acid affects azoxymethane-induced aberrant crypt foci and colorectal tumours in rats. *Cancer Lett* 2002;186:19-28.

242. Nelson RL, Tanure JC, Andrianopoulos G. The effect of dietary milk and calcium on experimental colorectal carcinogenesis. *Dis Colon Rectum* 1987;30:947-949.

243. Sitrin MD, Halline AG, Abrahams C, Brasitus TA. Dietary calcium and vitamin D modulate 1,2-dimethylhydrazine-induced colonic carcinogenesis in the rat. *Cancer Res* 1991;51:5608-5613.

244. Thiagarajan DG, Bennink MR, Bourquin LD, Kavas FA. Prevention of precancerous colonic lesions in rats by soy flakes, soy flour, genistein, and calcium. *Am J Clin Nutr* 1998;68(6 Suppl):1394S-1399S.

245. Behling AR, Kaup SM, Choquette LL, Greger JL. Lipid absorption and intestinal tumor incidence in rats fed on varying levels of calcium and butterfat. *Br J Nutr* 1990;64:505-513.

246. Llor X, Jacoby RF, Teng B-B, Davidson NO, Sitrin MD, Brasitus TA. K-*ras* mutations in 1,2-dimethylhydrazine-induced colonic tumors: Effects of supplemental dietary calcium and vitamin D deficiency. *Cancer Res* 1991;51:4305-4309.

247. Skrypec DJ, Bursey RG. Effect of dietary calcium on azoxymethane-induced intestinal carcinogenesis in male F 344 rats fed high fat diets (abstract). *FASEB* 1988;2:A857.

248. Cats A, Mulder NH, de Vries EG, Oremus ET, Kreumer WM, Kleibeuker JH. Calcium phosphate: An alternative calcium compound for dietary prevention of colon cancer? A study on intestinal and faecal parameters in healthy volunteers. *Eur J Cancer Prev* 1993;2:409-415.

249. Van der Meer R, Termont DS, De Vries HT. Differential effects of calcium ions and calcium phosphate on cytotoxicity of bile acids. *Am J Physiol* 1991;260:G142-G147.

250. Govers MJAP, Van der Meer R. Effects of dietary calcium and phosphate on the intestinal interactions between calcium, phosphate, fatty acids, and bile acids. *Gut* 1993;34:365-370.

251. Lapre JA, De Vries HT, Koeman JH, Van der Meer R. The antiproliferative effect of dietary calcium on colonic epithelium is mediated by luminal surfactants and dependent on the type of dietary fat. *Cancer Res* 1993;53:784-789.

252. Newmark HL, Wargovich MJ, Bruce WR. Colon cancer and dietary fat, phosphate, and calcium: A hypothesis. *J Natl Cancer Inst* 1984;72:1323-1325.

253. Van der Meer R, Kleibeuker JH, Lapre JA. Calcium phosphate, bile acids and colorectal cancer. *Eur J Cancer Prev* 1991;1(Suppl 2):55-62.

254. Van der Meer R, Lapre JA, Govers MJ, Kleibeuker JH. Mechanisms of the intestinal effects of dietary fats and milk products on colon carcinogenesis.

Cancer Lett 1997;114:75-83.
255. Wargovich MJ, Allnutt D, Palmer C, Anaya P, Stephens LC. Inhibition of the promotional phase of azoxymethane-induced colon carcinogenesis in the F344 rat by calcium lactate: Effect of simulating two human nutrient density levels. *Cancer Lett* 1990;53:17-25.
256. Welberg JW, Kleibeuker JH, Van der Meer R, Kuipers F, Cats A, Van Rijsbergen H, Termont DS, Boersma-van Ek W, Vonk RJ, Mulder NH, de Vries EGE. Effects of oral calcium supplementation on intestinal bile acids and cytolytic activity of fecal water in patients with adenomatous polyps of the colon. *Eur J Clin Invest* 1993;23:63-68.
257. Lapre JA, de Vries HT, Termont DSML, Kleibeuker JH, de Vries EGE, van der Meer R. Mechanism of the protective effect of supplemental dietary calcium on cytolytic activity of fecal water. *Cencer Res* 1993;53:248-253.
258. Van der Meer R, Welberg JW, Kuipers F, Kleibeuker JH, Mulder NH, Termont DSML, Vonk RJ, de Vries HT, de Vries EGE. Effects of supplemental dietary calcium on the intestinal association of calcium phosphate and bile acids. *Gastroenterology* 1990;99:1653-1659.
259. Pence BC, Dunn DM, Zhao C, Patel V, Hunter S, Landers M. Protective effects of calcium from nonfat dried milk against colon carcinogenesis in rats. *Nutr Cancer* 1996;25:35-45.
260. Appleton GV, Owen RW, Williamson RC. The effect of dietary calcium supplementation on intestinal lipid metabolism. *J Steroid Biochem Mol Biol* 1992;42:383-387.
261. Appleton GV, Owen RW, Wheeler EE, Challacombe DN, Williamson RC. Effect of dietary calcium on the colonic luminal environment. *Gut* 1991;32:1374-1377.
262. Lapre JA, De Vries HT, Van der Meer R. Cytotoxicity of fecal water is dependent on the type of dietary fat and is reduced by supplemental calcium phosphate in rats. *J Nutr* 1993;123:578-585.
263. Suzuki K, Suzuki K, Mitsuoka T. Effect of low-fat, high-fat, and fiber-supplemented high-fat diets on colon cancer risk factors in feces of healthy subjects. *Nutr Cancer* 1992;18:63-71.
264. Haenszel W, Correa P, Cuella C. Social class differences among patients with large bowel cancer in Cali, Columbia. *J Natl Cancer Inst* 1975;54:1031-1035.
265. Hill MJ, Drasar BS, Aries V, Crowther JS, Hawksworth G, Williams REO. Bacteria and aetiology of cancer of the large bowel. *Lancet* 1971;i:95-100.
266. Hill MJ. Steroid nuclear dehydrogenation and colon cancer. *Am J Clin Nutr* 1974;27:1475-1480.
267. Jensen OM, MacLennan R, Wahrendorf J. Diet, bowel function, fecal characteristics, and large bowel cancer in Denmark and Finland. *Nutr Cancer* 1982;4:5-19.
268. Mower HF, Ray RM, Shoff R, Stemmermann GN, Nomura A, Glober GA, Kamiyama S, Shimada A, Yamakawa H. Fecal bile acids in two Japanese populations with different colon cancer risks. *Cancer Res* 1979;39:328-331.
269. Reddy BS, Hedges AR, Laakso K, Wynder EL. Metabolic epidemiology of large bowel cancer: Fecal bulk and constituents of high-risk North American and low-risk Finnish populations. *Cancer* 1978;42:2832-2838.
270. Turjman N, Goodman GT, Jacgar B, Nair PP. Diet, nutrition intake, and metabolism in populations at high and low risk for colon cancer: Metabolism of bile acids. *Am J Clin Nutr* 1984;40:937-941.
271. Alberts DS, Ritenbaugh C, Story JA, Aickin M, Rees-McGee S, Buller MK, Atwood J, Phelps J, Ramanujam PS, Bellapravalu S, Patel J, Bextinger L, Clark L. Randomized, double-blinded, placebo-controlled study of effect of wheat

bran fiber and calcium on fecal bile acids in patients with resected adenomatous colon polyps. *J Natl Cancer Inst* 1996;88:81-92.

272. Lupton JR, Steinbach G, Chang WC, O'Brien BC, Wiese S, Stoltzfus CL, Glober GA, Wargovich MJ, McPherson RS, Winn RJ. Calcium supplementation modifies the relative amounts of bile acids in bile and affects key aspects of human colon physiology. *J Nutr* 1996;126:1421-1428.

273. Alder RJ, McKeown-Eyssen G, Bright-See E. Randomized trial of the effect of calcium supplementation on fecal risk factors for colorectal cancer. *Am J Epidemiol* 1993;138:804-814.

274. Lipkin M, Newmark H. Effect of added dietary calcium on colonic epithelial-cell proliferation in subjects at high risk for familial colonic cancer. *N Engl J Med* 1985;313:1381-1384.

275. Van Gorkom BA, van der Meer R, Karrenbeld A, van der Sluis T, Zwart N, Termont DS, Boersma-van Ek W, de Vries EG, Kleibeuker JH. Calcium affects biomarkers of colon carcinogenesis after right hemicolectomy. *Eur J Clin Invest* 2002;32:693-699.

276. Welberg JW, Monkelbaan JF, de Vries EG, Muskiet FA, Cats A, Oremus ET, Boersma-van Ek W, van Rijsbergen H, van der Meer R, Mulder NH, Kleibeuker JH. Effects of supplemental dietary calcium on quantitative and qualitative fecal fat excretion in man. *Ann Nutr Metab* 1994;38:185-191.

277. Little J, Owen RW, Fernandez F, Hawtin PG, Hill MJ, Logan RF, Thompson MH, Hardcastle JD. Asymptomatic colorectal neoplasia and fecal characteristics: A case-control study of subjects participating in the Nottingham fecal occult blood screening trial. *Dis Colon Rectum* 2002;45:1233-1241.

278. Geltner-Allinger U, Brismar B, Reinholt FP, Andersson G, Rafter JJ. Soluble fecal acidic lipids and colorectal epithelial cell proliferation in normal subjects and in patients with colon cancer. *Scand J Gastroenterol* 1991;26:1069-1074.

279. Hofstad B, Vatn MH, Andersen SN, Owen RW, Larsen S, Osnes M. The relationship between faecal bile acid profile with or without supplementation with calcium and antioxidants on recurrence and growth of colorectal polyps. *Eur J Cancer Prev* 1998;7:287-294.

280. Van Munster IP, Tangerman A, de Haan AF, Nagengast FM. A new method for the determination of the cytotoxicity of bile acids and aqueous phase of stool: The effect of calcium. *Eur J Clin Invest* 1993;23:773-777.

281. Glinghammar B, Venturi M, Rowland IR, Rafter JJ. Shift from a dairy product-rich to a dairy product-free diet: Influence on cytotoxicity and genotoxicity of fecal water - potential risk factors for colon cancer. *Am J Clin Nutr* 1997;66:1277-1282.

282. Pence BC. Role of calcium in colon cancer prevention: Experimental and clinical studies. *Mutat Res* 1993;290:87-95.

283. Richter F, Newmark HL, Richter A, Leung D, Lipkin M. Inhibition of Western-diet induced hyperproliferation and hyperplasia in mouse colon by two sources of calcium. *Carcinogenesis* 1995;16:2685-2689.

284. Rozen P, Liberman V, Lubin F, Angel S, Owen R, Trostler N, Shkolnik T, Kritchevsky D. A new dietary model to study colorectal carcinogenesis: Experimental design, food preparation, and experimental findings. *Nutr Cancer* 1996;25:79-100.

285. Nobre-Leitao C, Chaves P, Fidalgo P, Cravo M, Gouveia-Oliveira A, Ferra MA, Mira FC. Calcium regulation of colonic crypt cell kinetics: Evidence for a direct effect in mice. *Gastroenterology* 1995;109:498-504.

286. Belleli A, Shany S, Levy J, Guberman R, Lamprecht SA. A protective role of

1,25-dihydroxyvitamin D3 in chemically induced rat colon carcinogenesis. *Carcinogenesis* 1992;13:2293-2298.

287. Barthold SW, Beck D. Modification of early dimethylhydrazine carcinogenesis by colonic mucosa hyperplasia. *Cancer Res* 1980;40:4451-4455.

288. Yu B, Wu J, Zhou X. [Interference of selenium germanium and calcium in carcinogenesis of colon cancer.] *Zhonghua Wai Ke Za Zhi* 1995;33:167-169.

289. Ahnen J. Are animal models of colon cancer relevant to human diseases? *Dig Dis Sci* 1985;30:103S-106S.

290. Chang WWL. Histogenesis of colon cancer in experimental animals. *Scand J Gastroenterol* 1984;19(Suppl. 104):27-43.

291. Ranhotra GS, Gelroth JA, Glaser BK, Schoening P, Brown SE. Cellulose and calcium lower the incidence of chemically-induced colon tumors in rats. *Plant Foods Hum Nutr* 1999;54:295-303.

292. Potten CS, Loeffler M. Stem cells: Attributes, cycles, spirals, pitfalls and uncertainties. Lessons for and from the crypt. *Development* 1990;110:1001-1020.

293. Comer PF, Clark TD, Glauert HP. Effect of dietary vitamin D3 (cholecalciferol) on colon carcinogenesis induced by 1,2-dimethylhydrazine in male Fischer 344 rats. *Nutr Cancer* 1993;19:113-124.

294. Tao L, Kramer PM, Wang W, Yang S, Lubet RA, Steele VE, Pereira MA. Altered expression of *c-myc*, p16 and p27 in rat colon tumors and its reversal by short-term treatment with chemopreventive agents. *Carcinogenesis* 2002;23:1447-1454.

295. Pence BC, Dunn DM, Zhao C, Landers M, Wargovich MJ. Chemopreventive effects of calcium but not aspirin supplementation in cholic acid-promoted colon carcinogenesis: Correlation with intermediate endpoints. *Carcinogenesis* 1995;16:757-765.

296. Wargovich MJ, Jimenez A, McKee K, Steele VE, Velasco M, Woods J, Price R, Gray K, Kelloff GJ. Efficacy of potential chemopreventive agents on rat colon aberrant crypt formation and progression. *Carcinogenesis* 2000;21:1149-1155.

297. Wargovich MJ, Chen CD, Jimenez A, Steele VE, Velasco M, Stephens LC, Price R, Gray K, Kelloff GJ. Aberrant crypts as a biomarker for colon cancer: Evaluation of potential chemopreventive agents in the rat. *Cancer Epidemiol Biomarkers Prev* 1996;5:355-360.

298. Belbraouet S, Felden F, Pelletier X, Gastin I, Lambert D, Floquet J, Gueant JL, Debry G. Dietary calcium salts as protective agents and laminin P1 as a biochemical marker in chemically induced colon carcinogenesis in rats. *Cancer Detect Prev* 1996;20:294-299.

299. McSherry CK, Cohen BI, Bokkenheuser VD, Mosbach EH, Winter J, Matoba N, Scholes J. Effects of calcium and bile acid feeding on colon tumors in the rat. *Cancer Res* 1989;49:6039-6043.

300. Quilliot D, Belbraouet S, Pelletier X, Gueant JL, Floquet J, Debry G. Influence of a high-calcium carbonate diet on the incidence of experimental colon cancer in rats. *Nutr Cancer* 1999;34:213-219.

301. Reshef R, Rozen P, Fireman Z, Fine N, Barzilai M, Shasha SM, Shkolnik T. Effect of a calcium-enriched diet on the colonic epithelial hyperproliferation induced by *N*-methyl-*N'*-nitro-*N*-nitroso-guanidine in rats on a low calcium and fat diet. *Cancer Res* 1990;50:1764-1767.

302. Weisburger JH, Rivenson A, Hard GC, Zang E, Nagao M, Sugimura T. Role of fat and calcium in cancer causation by food mutagens, heterocyclic amines. *Proc Soc Exp Biol Med* 1994;205:347-352.

303. Bird RP. Effect of dietary components on the pathobiology of colonic epithelium: Possible relationship with colon tumorigenesis. *Lipids* 1986;21:289-291.

304. Sesink AL, Termont DS, Kleibeuker JH, Van der Meer R. Red meat and colon cancer: Dietary haem-induced colonic cytotoxicity and epithelial hyperproliferation are inhibited by calcium. *Carcinogenesis* 2001;22:1653-1659.

305. Nundy S, Malamud D, Obeertrop H, Sczerban J, Malt RA. Onset of cell proliferation in the shortened gut: Colonic hyperplasia after ileal resection. *Gastroenterology* 1977;72:263-266.

306. Williamson RCN, Bauer FLR, Ross JS, Malt RA. Proximal enterectomy stimulates distal hyperplasia more than bypass or pancreato-biliary diversion. *Gastroenterology* 1978;74:16-23.

307. Rainey JB, Davies PW, Williamson RCN. Relative effects of ileal resection and bypass on intestinal adaptation and carcinogenesis. *Br J Surg* 1984;71:197-202.

308. Scudamore CH, Freeman HJ. Effects of small bowel transection, or bypass in 1,2-dimethylhydrazine induced rat intestinal neoplasia. *Gastroenterology* 1983;84:725-731.

309. Williamson RCN, Bauer FLR, Terpstra OT, Ross JS, Malt RA. Contrasting effects of subtotal enteric bypass, enterectomy, and colectomy on azoxymethane-induced intestinal carcinogenesis. *Cancer Res* 1980;40:538-543.

310. Bristol JB, Wells M, Williamson RCN. Adaptation to jejunoileal bypass promotes experimental colorectal carcinogenesis. *Br J Surg* 1984;71:123-126.

311. Terpstra OT, Dahl EP, Williamson RCN, Ross JS, Malt RA. Colostomy closure promotes cell proliferation and dimethylhydrazine-induced carcinogenesis in rat distal colon. *Gastroenterology* 1981;81:475-480.

312. Williamson RCN, Bauer FLR, Ross JS, Watkins JB, Malt RA. Enhanced colonic carcinogenesis with azoxymethane in rat after pancreatobiliary diversion in mid small bowel. *Gastroenterology* 1979;76:1386-1392.

313. Rainey JB, Maeda M, Williamson RCN. The tropic effect of intrarectal deoxycholate on rat colorectum is unaffected by oral metronidazole. *Cell Tissue Kinet* 1986;19:485-490.

314. Williamson RCN, Rainey JB. The relationship between intestinal hyperplasia and carcinogenesis. *Scand J Gastroenterol* 1984;19(Suppl. 104):57-76.

315. Harte PJ, Steele G Jr, Rayner AA, Munroe AE, King VP, Wilson RE. Effect of major small bowel resection on dimethylhydrazine-induced bowel carcinogenesis. *J Surg Oncol* 198 1; 18:87-93.

316. Williamson RCN, Bauer FLR, Oscarson JEA, Ross JS, Malt RA. Promotion of azoxymethane-induced colonic neoplasia by resection of the proximal small bowel. *Cancer Res* 1978;38:3212-3217.

317. Lipkin M. Biomarkers of increased susceptibility to gastrointestinal cancer: New applications to studies of cancer prevention in human subjects. *Cancer Res* 1988;48:235-245.

318. Wargovich MJ, Lointier PH. Calcium and vitamin D modulate mouse colon epithelial proliferation and growth characteristics of a human colon tumor cell line. *Can J Physiol Pharmacol* 1987;65:472-477.

319. Penman ID, Liang QL, Bode J, Eastwood MA, Arends MJ. Dietary calcium supplementation increases apoptosis in the distal murine colonic epithelium. *J Clin Pathol* 2000;53:302-307.

320. Hambly RJ, Saunders M, Rijken PJ, Rowland IR. Influence of dietary components associated with high or low risk of colon cancer on apoptosis in the rat colon. *Food Chem Toxicol* 2002;40:801-808.

321. Preston-Martin S, Pike MC, Ross RK, Jones PA, Henderson BE. Increased cell division as a cause of human cancer. *Cancer Res* 1990;50:7415-7421.

322. Ames BN, Gold LS, Willett WC. The causes and prevention of cancer. *PNAS USA* 1995;92:5258-5265.

323. Lipkin M, Blattner WE, Fraumeni JF Jr, Lynch HT, Deschner E, Winawer S.

Tritiated thymidine ($\emptyset_p$, $\emptyset h$) labeling distribution as a marker for hereditary predisposition to colon cancer. *Cancer Res* 1983;43:1899-1904.

324. Ponz de Leon M, Roncucci L, Di Donato P, Tassi L, Smerieri O, Grazia M, Malagoli AG, De Maria D, Antonioli A, Chahin N, Perini M, Rigo G, Barberini G, Manenti A, Biasco G, Barbara L. Pattern of epithelial cell proliferation in colorectal mucosa of normal subjects and of patients with adenomatous polyps or cancer of the large bowel. *Cancer Res* 1988;48:4121-4126.

325. Scalmati A, Lipkin M. Intermediate biomarkers of increased risk for colorectal cancer: Comparison of different methods of analysis and modifications by chemopreventive interventions. *J Cell Biochem Suppl* 1992;16G:65-71.

326. Palmieri GMA. Dietary calcium and colonic cancer (letter). *N Engl J Med* 1986;314:1388.

327. Anti M, Marra G, Armelao F, Percesepe A, Ficarelli R, Ricciuto GM, Valenti A, Rapaccini GL, de Vitis I, D'Agostino G, Brighi S, Vecchio FM. Rectal epithelial cell proliferation patterns as predictors of adenomatous colorectal polyp recurrence. *Gut* 1993;34:525-530.

328. Bleiberg H, Buyse M, Galand P. Cell kinetic indicators of premalignant stages of colorectal cancer. *Cancer* 1985;56:124-129.

329. Lipkin M, Blattner WA, Gardner EJ, Burt RW, Lynch H, Deschner E, Winawer S, Fraumeni JF Jr. Classification and risk assessment of individuals with familial polyposis, Gardner's syndrome and familial non-polyposis colon cancer from [³H]thymidine labeling patterns in colonic epithelial cells. *Cancer Res* 1984;44:4201-4207.

330. Lipkin M, Enker WE, Winawer SJ. Tritiated-thymidine labeling of rectal epithelial cells in "non-prep" biopsies of individuals at increased risk for colonic neoplasia. *Cancer Lett* 1987;37:153-161.

331. Lipkin M, Uehara K, Winawer S, Sanchez A, Bauer C, Phillips R, Lynch HT, Blattner WA, Fraumeni JF Jr. Seventh-Day Adventist vegetarians have quiescent proliferative activity in colonic mucosa. *Cancer Lett* 1985;26:139-144.

332. Paganelli GM, Biasco G, Santucci R, Brandi G, Lalli AA, Miglioli M, Barbara L. Rectal cell proliferation and colorectal cancer risk level in patients with nonfamilial adenomatous polyps of the large bowel. *Cancer* 1991;68:2451-2454.

333. Risio M, Lipkin M, Candelaresi G, Bertone A, Coverlizza S, Rossini FP. Correlations between rectal mucosa cell proliferation and the clinical and pathological features of nonfamilial neoplasia of the large intestine. *Cancer Res* 1991;51:1917-1921.

334. Rooney PS, Clarke PA, Gifford KA, Hardcastle JD, Armitage NC. Identification of high and low risk groups of colorectal cancer using rectal mucosal crypt cell production rate (CCPR). *Br J Cancer* 1993;68:172-175.

335. Scalmati A, Roncucci L, Ghidini G, Biasco G, Ponz de Leon M. Epithelial cell kinetics in the remaining colorectal mucosa after surgery for cancer of the large bowel. *Cancer Res* 1990;50:7937-7941.

336. Stadler J, Yeung KS, Furrer R, Marcon N, Himal HS, Bruce WR. Proliferative activity of rectal mucosa and soluble fecal bile acids in patients with normal colons and in patients with colonic polyps or cancer. *Cancer Lett* 1988;38:315-320.

337. Terpstra OT, van Blankenstein M, Dees J, Eilers GAM. Abnormal pattern of cell proliferation in the entire colonic mucosa of patients with colon adenoma or cancer. *Gastroenterology* 1987;92:704-708.

338. Welberg JW, de Vries EG, Hardonk MJ, Mulder NH, Harms G, Grond J, Zwart N, Koudstaal J, de Ley L, Kleibeuker JH. Proliferation rate of colonic mucosa

in normal subjects and patients with colonic neoplasms: A refined immunohistochemical method. *J Clin Pathol* 1990;43:453-456.

339. Barsoum GH, Hendrickse C, Winslet MC, Youngs D, Donovan IA, Neoptolemos JP, Keighley MR. Reduction of mucosal crypt cell proliferation in patients with colorectal adenomatous polyps by dietary calcium supplementation. *Br J Surg* 1992;79:581-583.

340. Deschner EE, Lewis DM, Lipkin M. *In vitro* study of human rectal epithelial cells. 1. Atypical zone of H^3 thymidine incorporation in mucosa of multiple polyposis. *J Clin Invest* 1963;42:1922-1928.

341. Riddell RH. Dysplasia and cancer in ulcerative colitis: A soluble problem? *Scand J Gastroenterol* 1984;19 (Suppl. 104):137-149.

342. Biasco G, Lipkin M, Minarini A, Higgins P, Miglioli M, Barbara L. Proliferative and antigenic properties of rectal cells in patients with chronic ulcerative colitis. *Cancer Res* 1984;44:5450-5454.

343. Bleiberg H, Mainguet P, Galand P, Chretien J, Dupont-Mairesse M. Cell renewal in the human rectum: *In vitro* autoradiographic study on active ulcerative colitis. *Gastroenterology* 1970;58:851-855.

344. Deschner EE, Winawer SJ, Katz S, Katzka I, Kahn E. Proliferation defects in ulcerative colitis patients. *Cancer Invest* 1983;1:41-47.

345. Gerdes H, Gillin JS, Zimbalist E, Urmacher C, Lipkin M, Winawer SJ. Expansion of the epithelial proliferative compartment and frequency of adenomatous polyps in the colon correlate with strength of family history of colorectal cancer. *Cancer Res* 1993;53:279-282.

346. Paganelli GM, Santucci R, Biasco G, Miglioli M, Barbara L. Effect of sex and age on rectal cell renewal in humans. *Cancer Lett* 1990;53:117-121.

347. Roncucci L, Ponz de Leon M, Scalmati A, Malgoli G, Pratissoli S, Perini M, Chalin NJ. The influence of age on colonic epithelial cell proliferation. *Cancer* 1988;62:2373-2377.

348. Risio M, Coverlizza M, Ferrari A, Candelaresi G, Rossini F. Immunohistochemical study of epithelial cell proliferation in hyperplastic polyps, adenomas, and adenocarcinomas of the large bowel. *Gastroenterology* 1988;94:899-906.

349. Anti M, Marra G, Armelao F, Bartoli GM, Ficarelli R, Percesepe A, de Vitis I, Maria G, Sofo L, Rapaccini GL, Gentiloni N, Piccioni E, Miggiano G. Effect of ₆-3 fatty acids on rectal mucosal cell proliferation in subjects at risk for colon cancer. *Gastroenterology* 1992;103:883-891.

350. Biasco G, Zannoni U, Paganelli GM, Santucci R, Gionchetti P, Rivolta G, Miniero R, Pironi L, Calabrese C, Di Febo G, Miglioli M. Folic acid supplementation and cell kinetics of rectal mucosa in patients with ulcerative colitis. *Cancer Epidemiol Biomarkers Prev* 1997;6:469-471.

351. Cascinu S, Del Ferro E, Grianti C, Foglietti GP, Olivieri Q, Bartolucci M, Saba V, Lungarotti F, Catalano G. Hyperproliferative status of the epithelium in the remaining colorectal mucosa after surgery for cancer of the large bowel: Its implications in the prediction of adenomatous polyps recurrence. *GI Cancer* 1995;1:119-122.

352. Nakamura S, Kino I, Baba S. Nuclear DNA content of isolated crypts of background colonic mucosa from patients with familial adenomatous polyposis and sporadic colorectal cancer. *Gut* 1993;34:1240-1244.

353. Wargovich MJ, Harris C, Chen D, Palmer C, Steele VE, Kelloff GJ. Growth kinetics and chemoprevention of aberrant crypts in the rat colon. *J Cell Biochem* 1992;(Suppl. 16G):51-54.

354. Potten CS, Kellett M, Roberts SA, Rew DA, Wilson GD. Measurement of *in vivo* proliferation in human colorectal mucosa using bromodeoxyuridine. *Gut*

385. McCullough ML, Robertson AS, Rodriguez C, Jacobs EJ, Chao A, Carolyn J, Calle EE, Willett WC, Thun MJ. Calcium, vitamin D, dairy products, and risk of colorectal cancer in the cancer prevention study II nutrition cohort (United States). *Cancer Causes Control* 2003;14:1-12.

386. Terry P, Baron JA, Bergkvist L, Holmberg L, Wolk A. Dietary calcium and vitamin D intake and risk of colorectal cancer: A prospective cohort study in women. *Nutr Cancer* 2002;43:39-46.

387. Zheng W, Anderson KE, Kushi LH, Sellers TA, Greenstein J, Hong CP, Cerhan JR, Bostick RM, Folsom AR. A prospective cohort study of intake of calcium, vitamin D, and other micronutrients in relation to incidence of rectal cancer among postmenopausal women. *Cancer Epidemiol Biomarkers Prev* 1998;7:221-225.

388. Kato I, Akhmedkhanov A, Koenig K, Toniolo PG, Shore RE, Riboli E. Prospective study of diet and female colorectal cancer: The New York University Women's Health Study. *Nutr Cancer* 1997;28:276-281.

389. Garland C, Shekelle RB, Barrett-Connor E, Criqui MH, Rossof AH, Paul O. Dietary vitamin D and calcium and risk of colorectal cancer: A 19-year prospective study in men. *Lancet* 1985;1:307-309.

390. Bostick RM, Potter JD, Sellers TA, McKenzie DR, Kushi LH, Folsom AR. Relation of calcium, vitamin D, and dairy food intake to incidence of colon cancer among older women. The Iowa Women's Health Study. *Am J Epidemiol* 1993;137:1302-1317.

391. Sellers TA, Bazyk AE, Bostick RM, Kushi LH, Olson JE, Anderson KE, Lazovich D, Folsom AR. Diet and risk of colon cancer in a large prospective study of older women: An analysis stratified on family history (Iowa, United States). *Cancer Causes Control* 1998;9:357-367.

392. Faivre J, Boutron MC, Senesse P, Couillault C, Belighiti C, Meny B. Environmental and familial risk factors in relation to the colorectal adenoma—carcinoma sequence: Results of a case-control study in Burgundy (France). *Eur J Cancer Prev* 1997;6:127-131.

393. Wu K, Willett WC, Fuchs CS, Colditz GA, Giovannucci EL. Calcium intake and risk of colon cancer in women and men. *J Natl Cancer Inst* 2002;94:437-446.

394. Newmark HL, Shiff SJ. Re: Calcium intake and risk of colon cancer in women and men (letter). *J Natl Cancer Inst* 2003;95:169.

395. Almendingen K, Trygg K, Larsen S, Hofstad B, Vatn MH. Dietary factors and colorectal polyps: A case-control study. *Eur J Cancer Prev* 1995;4:239-246.

396. Nakaji S, Shimoyama T, Wada S, Sugawara K, Tokunaga S, MacAuley D, Baxter D. No preventive effect of dietary fiber against colon cancer in the Japanese population: A cross-sectional analysis. *Nutr Cancer* 2003;45:156-159.

397. Arbman G, Axelson O, Ericsson-Begodzki AB, Fredriksson M, Nilsson E, Sjodahl R. Cereal fiber, calcium, and colorectal cancer. *Cancer* 1992;69:2042-2048.

398. Marcus PM, Newcomb PA. The association of calcium and vitamin D, and colon and rectal cancer in Wisconsin women. *Int J Epidemiol* 1998;27:788-793.

399. Yang G. [Relationship between colorectal cancer and ten inorganic elements.] *Zhonghua Yu Fang Yi Xue Za Zhi* 1993;27:282-285.

400. Yang G, Gao Y-T, Ji B-T. [A case-control study on colorectal cancer and dietary fiber and calcium of various sources.] *Zhonghua Yu Fang Yi Xue Za Zhi* 1994;28:195-198.

401. Slattery ML, Edwards SL, Boucher KM, Anderson K, Caan BJ. Lifestyle and colon cancer: an assessment of factors associated with risk. *Am J Epidemiol* 1999;150:869-877.

402. Kearney J, Giovannucci E, Rimm EB, Ascherio A, Stampfer MJ, Colditz GA, Wing A, Kampman E, Willett WC. Calcium, vitamin D, and dairy foods and the occurrence of colon cancer in men. *Am J Epidemiol* 1996;143:907-917.

403. Kampman E, Giovannucci E, van 't Veer P, Rimm E, Stampfer MJ, Colditz GA, Kok FJ, Willett WC. Calcium, vitamin D, dairy foods, and the occurrence of colorectal adenomas among men and women in two prospective studies. *Am J Epidemiol* 1994;139:16-29.

404. De Stefani E, Mendilaharsu M, Deneo-Pellegrini H, Ronco A. Influence of dietary levels of fat, cholesterol, and calcium on colorectal cancer. *Nutr Cancer* 1997;29:83-89.

405. Ferraroni M, La Vecchia C, D'Avanzo B, Negri E, Franceschi S, Decarli A. Selected micronutrient intake and the risk of colorectal cancer. *Br J Cancer* 1994;70:1150-1155.

406. Peters RK, Pike MC, Garabrant D, Mack TM. Diet and colon cancer in Los Angeles County, California. *Cancer Causes Control* 1992;3:457-473.

407. Satia-Abouta J, Galanko JA, Martin CF, Potter JD, Ammerman A, Sandler RS. Associations of micronutrients with colon cancer risk in African Americans and whites: Results from the North Carolina Colon Cancer Study. *Cancer Epidemiol Biomarkers Prev* 2003;12:747-754.

408. Kune S, Kune GA, Watson LF. Case-control study of dietary etiological factors: The Melbourne Colorectal Cancer Study. *Nutr Cancer* 1987;9:21-42.

409. Slattery ML, Potter JD, Sorenson AW. Age and risk factors for colon cancer (United States and Australia): Are there implications for understanding differences in case-control and cohort studies? *Cancer Causes Control* 1994;5:557-563.

410. Yang C-Y, Chiu H-F, Chiu J-F, Tsai S-S, Cheng M-F. Calcium and magnesium in drinking water and risk of death from colon cancer. *Jpn J Cancer Res* 1997;88:928-933.

411. Yang C-Y, Chiu H-F. Calcium and magnesium in drinking water and risk of death from rectal cancer. *Int J Cancer* 1998;77:528-532.

412. Yang C-Y, Hung C-F. Colon cancer mortality and total hardness levels in Taiwan's drinking water. *Arch Environ Contam Toxicol* 1998;35:148-151.

413. Yang C-Y, Tsai S-S, Lai T-C, Hung C-F, Chiu H-F. Rectal cancer mortality and total hardness levels in Taiwan's drinking water. *Environ Res* 1999;80:311-316.

414. Slattery ML, Sorenson AW, Ford MH. Dietary calcium intake as a mitigating factor in colon cancer. *Am J Epidemiol* 1988;128:504-514.

415. Martinez ME, Marshall JR, Sampliner R, Wilkinson J, Alberts DS. Calcium, vitamin D, and risk of adenoma recurrence (United States). *Cancer Causes Control* 2002;13:213-220.

416. Slattery ML, Caan BJ, Potter JD, Berry TD, Coates A, Duncan D, Edwards SL. Dietary energy sources and colon cancer risk. *Am J Epidemiol* 1997;145:199-210.

417. Martinez ME, McPherson RS, Levin B, Glober GA. A case-control study of dietary intake and other lifestyle risk factors for hyperplastic polyps. *Gastroenterology* 1997;113:423-429.

418. Whelan RL, Horvath KD, Gleason NR, Forde KA, Treat MD, Teitelbaum SL, Bertram A, Neugut AI. Vitamin and calcium supplement use is associated with decreased adenoma recurrence in patients with a previous history of neoplasia. *Dis Colon Rectum* 1999;42:212-217.

419. Levi F, Pasche C, Lucchini F, La Vecchia C. Selected micronutrients and colorectal cancer: A case-control study from the canton of Vaud, Switzerland. *Eur J Cancer* 2000;36:2115-2119.

420. Whittemore AS, Wu-Williams AH, Lee M, Shu Z, Gallagher RP, Deng-ao J,

Lun Z, Xianghui W, Kun C, Jung D, Teh C-Z, Chengde L, Yao XJ, Paffenbarger RS, Henderson BE. Diet, physical activity, and colorectal cancer among Chinese in North America and China. *JNCI* 1990;82:915-926.

421. Kampman E, Slattery ML, Caan B, Potter JD. Calcium, vitamin D, sunshine exposure, dairy products and colon cancer risk (United States). *Cancer Causes Control* 2000;11:459-466.

422. La Vecchia C, Braga C, Negri E, Franceschi S, Russo A, Conti E, Falcini F, Giacosa A, Montella M, Decarli A. Intake of selected micronutrients and risk of colorectal cancer. *Int J Cancer* 1997;73:525-530.

423. Govosdis B, Triantafillidis JK, Chrisochou H, Kalogerakos S, Perdicouris P. Effect of calcium intake on the incidence of sporadic colorectal polyps (letter). *Am J Gastroenterol* 1994;89:952-953.

424. White E, Shannon JS, Patterson RE. Relationship between vitamin and calcium supplement use and colon cancer. *Cancer Epidemiol Biomarkers Prev* 1997;6:769-774.

425. Wong H-L, Seow A, Arakawa K, Lee H-P, Yu MC, Ingles SA. Vitamin D receptor start codon polymorphism and colorectal cancer risk: Effect modification by dietary calcium and fat in Singapore Chinese. *Carcinogenesis* 2003;24:1091-1095.

426. Boyapati SM, Bostick RM, McGlynn KA, Fina MF, Roufail WM, Geisinger KR, Wargovich M, Coker A, Hebert JR. Calcium, vitamin D, and risk for colorectal adenoma: Dependency on vitamin D receptor BsmI polymorphism and nonsteroidal anti-inflammatory drug use? *Cancer Epidemiol Biomarkers Prev* 2003;12:631-637.

427. Ma J, Giovannucci E, Pollak M, Chan JM, Gaziano JM, Willett W, Stampfer MJ. Milk intake, circulating levels of insulin-like growth factor-I, and risk of colorectal cancer in men. *J Natl Cancer Inst* 2001;93:1330-1336.

428. Martinez ME, Giovannucci EL, Colditz GA, Stampfer MJ, Hunter DJ, Speizer FE, Wing A, Willett WC. Calcium, vitamin D, and the occurrence of colorectal cancer among women. *J Natl Cancer Inst* 1996;88:1375-1382.

429. Kampman E, Goldbohm RA, van den Brandt PA, van 't Veer P. Fermented dairy products, calcium, and colorectal cancer in The Netherlands Cohort Study. *Cancer Res* 1994;54:3186-3190.

430. Gaard M, Tretli S, Loken EB. Dietary factors and risk of colon cancer: A prospective study of 50,535 young Norwegian men and women. *Eur J Cancer Prev* 1996;5:445-454.

431. Slob ICM, Lambregts JLMC, Schuit AJ, Kok FJ. Calcium intake and 28-year gastro-intestinal cancer mortality in Dutch civil servants. *Int J Cancer* 1993;54:20-25.

432. Hyman J, Baron JA, Dain BJ, Sandler RS, Haile RW, Mandel JS, Mott LA, Greenberg ER. Dietary and supplemental calcium and the recurrence of colorectal adenomas. *Cancer Epidemiol Biomarkers Prev* 1998;7:291-295.

433. Stemmermann GN, Nomura A, Chyou P-H. The influence of dairy and nondairy calcium on subsite large-bowel cancer risk. *Dis Colon Rectum* 1990;33:190-194.

434. Willett WC, Stampfer MJ, Colditz GA, Rosner BA, Speizer FE. Relation of meat, fat and fiber intake to the risk of colon cancer in a prospective study among women. *N Engl J Med* 1990;323:1664-1672.

435. Jarvinen R, Knekt P, Hakulinen T, Aromaa A. Prospective study on milk products, calcium and cancers of the colon and rectum. *Eur J Clin Nutr* 2001;55:1000-1007.

436. Malila N, Virtanen M, Pietinen P, Virtamo J, Albanes D, Hartman AM, Heinonen OP. A comparison of prospective and retrospective assessments of

diet in a study of colorectal cancer. *Nutr Cancer* 1998;32:146-153.

437. Heilbrun LK, Hankin JH, Nomura AM, Stemmermann GN. Colon cancer and dietary fat, phosphorus, and calcium in Hawaiian-Japanese men. *Am J Clin Nutr* 1986;43:306-309.

438. Morimoto LM, Newcomb PA, Ulrich CM, Bostick RM, Lais CJ, Potter JD. Risk factors for hyperplastic and adenomatous polyps: Evidence for malignant potential? *Cancer Epidemiol Biomarkers Prev* 2002;11:1012-1018.

439. Negri E, La Vecchia C, D'Avanzo B, Franceschi S. Calcium, dairy products, and colorectal cancer. *Nutr Cancer* 1990;13:255-262.

440. Pritchard RS, Baron JA, Gerhardsson de Verdier M. Dietary calcium, vitamin D, and the risk of colorectal cancer in Stockholm, Sweden. *Cancer Epidemiol Biomarkers Prev* 1996;5:897-900.

441. Levine AJ, Harper JM, Ervin CM, Chen YH, Harmon E, Xue S, Lee ER, Frankel HD, Haile RW. Serum 25-hydroxyvitamin D, dietary calcium intake, and distal colorectal adenoma risk. *Nutr Cancer* 2001;39:35-41.

442. Meyer F, White E. Alcohol and nutrients in relation to colon cancer in middle-aged adults. *Am J Epidemiol* 1993;138:225-236.

443. Martinez ME, McPherson RS, Annegers JF, Levin B. Association of diet and colorectal adenomatous polyps: Dietary fiber, calcium, and total fat. *Epidemiology* 1996;7:264-268.

444. Tseng M, Murray SC, Kupper LL, Sandler RS. Micronutrients and the risk of colorectal adenomas. *Am J Epidemiol* 1996;144:1005-1014.

445. Lee HP, Gourley L, Duffy SW, Esteve J, Lee J, Day NE. Colorectal cancer and diet in an Asian population: A case-control study among Singapore Chinese. *Int J Cancer* 1989;43:1007-1016.

446. Tuyns AJ, Haelterman M, Kaaks R. Colorectal cancer and the intake of nutrients: Oligosaccharides are a risk factor, fats are not: A case-control study in Belgium. *Nutr Cancer* 1987;10:181-196.

447. Freudenheim JL, Graham S, Marshall JR, Haughey BP, Wilkinson G. A case-control study of diet and rectal cancer in western New York. *Am J Epidemiol* 1990;131:612-624.

448. Graham S, Marshall J, Haughey B, Mittelman A, Swanson M, Zielezny M, Byers T, Wilkinson G, West D. Dietary epidemiology of cancer of the colon in western New York. *Am J Epidemiol* 1988;128:490-503.

449. Macquart-Moulin G, Riboli E, Cornee J, Charnay B, Berthezene P, Day N. Case-control study on colorectal cancer and diet in Marseilles. *Int J Cancer* 1986;38:183-191.

450. Benito E, Cabeza E, Moreno V, Obrador A, Bosch FX. Diet and colorectal adenomas: A case-control study in Majorca. *Int J Cancer* 1993;55:213-219.

451. Peters U, McGlynn KA, Chatterjee N, Gunter E, Garcia-Closas M, Rothman N, Sinha R. Vitamin D, calcium, and vitamin D receptor polymorphism in colorectal adenomas. *Cancer Epidemiol Biomarkers Prev* 2001;10:1267-1274.

452. Macquart-Moulin G, Riboli E, Cornee J, Kaaks R, Berthezene P. Colorectal polyps and diet: A case-control study in Marseilles. *Int J Cancer* 1987;40:179-188.

453. Neugut AI, Horvath K, Whelan RL, Terry MB, Garbowski GC, Bertram A, Forde KA, Treat MR, Waye J. The effect of calcium and vitamin supplements on the incidence and recurrence of colorectal adenomatous polyps. *Cancer* 1996;78:723-728.

454. Ghadirian P, Lacroix A, Maisonneuve P, Perret C, Potvin C, Gravel D, Bernard D, Boyle P. Nutritional factors and colon carcinoma: A case-control study involving French Canadians in Montreal, Quebec, Canada. *Cancer* 1997;80:858-864.

455. Kampman E, van 't Veer P, Hiddink GJ, van Aken-Schneijder P, Kok FJ,

Hermus RJ. Fermented dairy products, dietary calcium and colon cancer: A case-control study in The Netherlands. *Int J Cancer* 1994;59:170-176.

456. Benito E, Stiggelbout A, Bosch FX, Obrador A, Kaldor J, Mulet M, Munoz N. Nutritional factors in colorectal cancer risk: A case-control study in Majorca. *Int J Cancer* 1991;49:161-167.

457. Zaridze D, Filipchenko V, Kustov V, Serdyuk V, Duffy S. Diet and colorectal cancer: Results of two case-control studies in Russia. *Eur J Cancer* 1993;29A:112-115.

458. Breuer-Katschinski B, Nemes K, Marr A, Rump B, Leiendecker B, Breuer N, Goebell H. Colorectal adenomas and diet: a case-control study. Colorectal Adenoma Study Group. *Dig Dis Sci* 2001;46:86-95

459. Boutron M-C, Faivre J, Marteau P, Couillault C, Senesse P, Quipourt V. Calcium, phosphorus, vitamin D, dairy products and colorectal carcinogenesis: A French case—control study. *Br J Cancer* 1996;74:145-151.

460. Peleg II, Lubin MF, Cotsonis GA, Clark WS, Wilcox CM. Long-term use of nonsteroidal antiinflammatory drugs and other chemopreventors and risk of subsequent colorectal neoplasia. *Dig Dis Sci* 1996;41:1319-1326.

461. Bonithon-Kopp C, Kronborg O, Giacosa A, Rath U, Faivre J. Calcium and fibre supplementation in prevention of colorectal adenoma recurrence: A randomised intervention trial. European Cancer Prevention Organisation Study Group. *Lancet* 2000;356:1300-1306.

462. Slattery ML, Potter JD. Physical activity and colon cancer: Confounding or interaction? *Med Sci Sports Exerc* 2002;34:913-919.

463. Wu AH, Paganini-Hill A, Ross RK, Henderson BE. Alcohol, physical activity and other risk factors for colorectal cancer: A prospective study. *Br J Cancer* 1987;55:687-694.

464. Bergsma-Kadijk JA, van 't Veer P, Kampman E, Burema J. Calcium does not protect against colorectal neoplasia. *Epidemiology* 1996;7:590-597.

465. Wargovich MJ, Lynch PM, Levin B. Modulating effects of calcium in animal models of colon carcinogenesis and short-term studies in subjects at increased risk for colon cancer. *Am J Clin Nutr* 1991;54(1 Suppl.):202S-205S.

466. Sandler RS. Epidemiology and risk factors for colorectal cancer. *Gastroenterol Clin North Am* 1996;25:717-735.

467. Garland CF, Garland FC, Gorham ED. Calcium and vitamin D. Their potential roles in colon and breast cancer prevention. *Ann N Y Acad Sci* 1999;889:107-119.

468. Martinez ME, Willett WC. Calcium, vitamin D, and colorectal cancer: A review of the epidemiologic evidence. *Cancer Epidemiol Biomarkers Prev* 1998;7:163-168.

469. Pignone M, Levin B. Recent developments in colorectal cancer screening and prevention. *Am Fam Physician* 2002;66:297-302.

470. Gatof D, Ahnen D. Primary prevention of colorectal cancer: Diet and drugs. *Gastroenterol Clin North Am* 2002;31:587-623.

471. Anonymous. The role of calcium in peri- and postmenopausal women: Consensus opinion of The North American Menopause Society. *Menopause* 2001;8:84-95.

472. Nakhlis F, Morrow M. Ductal carcinoma in situ. *Surg Clin North Am* 2003;83:821-839.

473. Adamovich TL, Simmons RM. Ductal carcinoma in situ with microinvasion. *Am J Surg* 2003;186:112-116.

474. Graham S, Hellmann R, Marshall J, Freudenheim J, Vena J, Swanson M, Zielezny M, Nemoto T, Stubbe N, Raimondo T. Nutritional epidemiology of postmenopausal breast cancer in western New York. *Am J Epidemiol* 1991;134:552-566.

475. Willett W. The search for the causes of breast and colon cancer. *Nature* 1989;338:389-394.
476. Singletary SE. Rating the risk factors for breast cancer. *Ann Surg* 2003;237:474-482.
477. Welsh J, Wietzke JA, Zinser GM, Smyczek S, Romu S, Tribble E, Welsh JC, Byrne B, Narvaez CJ. Impact of the Vitamin D3 receptor on growth-regulatory pathways in mammary gland and breast cancer. *J Steroid Biochem Mol Biol* 2002;83:85-92.
478. Manni A. Polyamine involvement in breast cancer phenotype. *In Vivo* 2002;16:493-500.
479. Manni A, Grove R, Kunselman S, Demers L. Involvement of the polyamine pathway in breast cancer progression. *Cancer Lett* 1995;92:49-57.
480. Glikman P, Manni A, Demers L, Bartholomew M. Polyamine involvement in the growth of hormone-responsive and –resistant human breast cancer cells in culture. *Cancer Res* 1989;49:1371-1376.
481. Manni A. The role of polyamines in the hormonal control of breast cancer cell proliferation. *Cancer Treat Res* 1994;71:209-225.
482. Shah N, Thomas TJ, Lewis JS, Klinge CM, Shirahata A, Gelinas C, Thomas T. Regulation of estrogenic and nuclear factor ?B functions by polyamines and their role in polyamine analog-induced apoptosis of breast cancer cells. *Oncogene* 2001;20:1715-1729.
483. Thomas T, Gallo MA, Klinge CM, Thomas TJ. Polyamine-mediated conformational perturbations in DNA alter the binding of estrogen receptor to poly(dG-m^{5}dC)poly(dG-m^{5}dC) and a plasmid containing the estrogen response element. *J Steroid Biochem* 1995;54:89-99.
484. Persson L, Rosengren E. Increased formation of N1-acetylspermidine in human breast cancer. *Cancer Lett* 1989;45:83-86.
485. Canizares F, Salinas J, de las Heras M, Diaz J, Tovar I, Martinez P, Penafiel R. Prognostic value of ornithine decarboxylase and polyamines in human breast cancer: Correlation with clinicopathologic parameters. *Clin Cancer Res* 1999;5:2035-2041.
486. Manni A, Astrow SH, Gammon S, Thompson J, Mauger D, Washington S. Immunohistochemical detection of ornithine decarboxylase in primary and metastatic human breast cancer specimens. *Breast Cancer Res Treat* 2001;67:147-156.
487. Leveque J, Bansard JY, Watier E, Catros-Quemener V, Havouis R, Moulinoux JP, Grall JY, Seiler N. Polyamines in human breast cancer and its relations to classical prognostic features: Clinical implications. *Anticancer Res* 1999;19:2275-2279.
488. Leveque J, Foucher F, Bansard JY, Havouis R, Grall JY, Moulinoux JP. Polyamine profiles in tumor, normal tissue of the homologous breast, blood, and urine of breast cancer sufferers. *Breast Cancer Res Treat* 2000;60:99-105.
489. Leveque J, Foucher F, Havouis R, Desury D, Grall JY, Moulinoux JP. Benefits of complete polyamine deprivation in hormone responsive and hormone resistant MCF-7 human breast adenocarcinoma *in vivo*. *Anticancer Res* 2000;20:97-101.
490. Manni A, Wechter R, Gilmour S, Verderame MF, Mauger D, Demers LM. Ornithine decarboxylase over-expression stimulates mitogen-activated protein kinase and anchorage-independent growth of humam breast epithelial cells. *Int J Cancer* 1997;70:175-182.
491. Miller FR, Soule HD, Tait L, Pauley RJ, Wolman SR, Dawson PI, Heppner GH. Xenograft model of progressive human proliferative breast disease. *J Natl Cancer Inst* 1993;85:1725-1731.

492. Glikman P, Vegh I, Pollina A, Mosto A, Levy C. Ornithine decarboxylase activity, prolactin blood levels, and estradiol and progesterone in human breast cancer. *Cancer* 1987;60:2237-2243.

493. Manni A, Mauger D, Gimotty P, Badger B. Prognostic influence on survival of increased ornithine decarboxylase activity in human breast cancer. *Clin Cancer Res* 1996;2:1901-1905.

494. Manni A, Washington S, Griffith JW, Verderame MF, Mauger D, Demers LM, Saman RS, Welch DR. Influence of polyamines on *in vitro* and *in vivo* features of aggressive and metastatic behavior by human breast cancer cells. *Clin ExptlMetastasis* 2002;19:95-105.

495. Manni A, Badger B, Martel J, Demers L. Role of polyamines in the growth of hormone-responsive and –resistant human breast cancer cells in nude mice. *Cancer Lett* 1992;66:1-9.

496. Manni A, Wright C. Polyamines as mediators of estrogen action on the growth of experimental breast cancer in rats. *J Natl Cancer Inst* 1984;73:511-514.

497. Glikman PI, Manni A, Bartholomew M, Demers L. Polyamine involvement in basal and estradiol stimulated insulin-like growth factor I secretion and action in breast cancer cells in culture. *J Steroid Biochem Mol Biol* 1990;37:1-10.

498. Manni A, Badger B, Lynch J, Demers L. Selectivity of polyamine involvement in hormone action on normal and neoplastic target tissues of the rat. *Breast Cancer Res Treat* 1990;17:187-196.

499. Thompson HJ, Meeker LD, Herbst EJ, Ronan AM, Minocha R. Effect of concentration of D,1-2-difluoromethylornithine on murine mammary carcinogenesis. *Cancer Res* 1985;45:1170-1173.

500. Green JE, Shibata MA, Shibata E, Moon RC, Anver MR, Kelloff G, Lubert R. 2-difluoromethylornithine and dehydroepiandrosterone inhibit mammary tumor progression but not mammary or prostate tumor initiation in C3(1)/SV40 T/t-antigen transgenic mice. *Cancer Res* 2001;61:7449-7455.

501. Xue L, Lipkin M, Newmark H, Wang J. Influence of dietary calcium and vitamin D on diet-induced epithelial cell hyperproliferation in mice. *J Natl Cancer Inst* 1999;91:176-181.

502. Shin MH, Holmes MD, Hankinson SE, Wu K, Colditz GA, Willett WC. Intake of dairy products, calcium, and vitamin D and risk of breast cancer. *J Natl Cancer Inst* 2002;94:1301-1311.

503. Knekt P, Jarvinen R, Seppanen R, Pukkala E, Aromaa A. Intake of dairy products and the risk of breast cancer. *Br J Cancer* 1996;73:687-691.

504. Negri E, La Vecchia C, Franceschi S, D'Avanzo B, Talamini R, Parpinel M, Ferraroni M, Filiberti R, Montella M, Falcini F, Conti E, DeCarli A. Intake of selected micronutrients and the risk of breast cancer. *Int J Cancer* 1996;65:140-144.

505. Zaridze D, Lifanova Y, Maximovitch D, Day NE, Duffy SW. Diet, alcohol consumption and reproductive factors in a case-control study of breast cancer in Moscow. *Int J Cancer* 1991;48:493-501.

506. Boyapati SM, Shu XO, Jin F, Dai Q, Ruan Z, Gao YT, Zheng W. Dietary calcium intake and breast cancer risk among Chinese women in Shanghai. *Nutr Cancer* 2003;46:38-43.

507. Van't veer P, van Leer EM, Rietdijk A, Kok FJ, Schouten EG, Hermus RJ, Sturmans F. Combination of dietary factors in relation to breast cancer occurrence. *Int J Cancer* 1991;47:649-653.

508. Katsouyanni K, Willett W, Trichopoulos D, Boyle P, Trichopoulou A, Vasilaros S, Papadiamantis J, MacMahon B. Risk of breast cancer among Greek women in relation to nutrient intake. *Cancer* 1988;61:181-185.

509. Greenlee RT, Hill-Harmon MB, Murray T, Thun M. Cancer statistics, 2001.

CA Cancer J Clin 2001;51:15-36.

510. Willis MS, Wians FH. The role of nutrition in preventing prostate cancer: A review of the proposed mechanism of action of various dietary substances. *Clin Chim Acta* 2003;330:57-83.

511. Vlajinac HD, Marinkovic JM, Ilic MD, Kocev NI. Diet and prostate cancer: A case-control study. *Eur J Cancer* 1997;33:101-107.

512. Berndt SI, Carter HB, Landis PK, Tucker KL, Hsieh LJ, Metter EJ, Platz EA. Calcium intake and prostate cancer risk in a long-term aging study: The Baltimore Longitudinal Study of Aging. *Urology* 2002;60:1118-1123.

513. Chan JM, Pietinen P, Virtanen M, Malila N, Tangrea J, Albanes D, Virtamo J. Diet and prostate cancer risk in a cohort of smokers, with a specific focus on calcium and phosphorus (Finland). *Cancer Causes Control* 2000;11:859-867.

514. Schuurman AG, van den Brandt PA, Dorant E, Goldbohm RA. Animal products, calcium, and protein and prostate cancer risk in the Netherlands Cohort Study. *Br J Cancer* 1999;80:1107-1113.

515. Kristal AR, Cohen JH, Qu P, Stanford JL. Associations of energy, fat, calcium, and vitamin D with prostate cancer risk. *Cancer Epidemiol Biomarkers Prev* 2002;11:719-725.

516. Tavani A, Gallus S, Franceschi S, La Vecchia C. Calcium, dairy products, and the risk of prostate cancer. *Prostate* 2001;48:118-121.

517. Hayes RB, Ziegler RG, Gridley G, Swanson C, Greenberg RS, Swanson GM, Schoenberg JB, Silverman DT, Brown LM, Pottern LM, Liff J, Schwartz AG, Fraumeni JF Jr, Hoover RN. Dietary factors and risk for prostate cancer among blacks and whites in the United States. *Cancer Epidemiol Biomarkers Prev* 1999;8:25-34.

518. Kristal AR, Stanford JL, Cohen JH, Wicklund K, Patterson RE. Vitamin and mineral supplement use is associated with reduced risk of prostate cancer. *Cancer Epidemiol Biomarkers Prev* 1999;8:887-892.

519. Ohno Y, Yoshida O, Oishi K, Okada K, Yamabe H, Schroeder FH. Dietary beta-carotene and cancer of the prostate: A case-control study in Kyoto, Japan. *Cancer Res* 1988;48:1331-1336.

520. Tzonou A, Signorello LB, Lagiou P, Wuu J, Trichopoulos D, Trichopoulou A. Diet and cancer of the prostate: A case-control study in Greece. *Int J Cancer* 1999;80:704-708.

521. Zhang Y, Kiel DP, Ellison RC, Schatzkin A, Dorgan JF, Kreger BE, Cupples LA, Felson DT. Bone mass and the risk of prostate cancer: The Framingham Study. *Am J Med* 2002;113:734-739.

522. Chan JM, Stampfer MJ, Ma J, Gann PH, Gaziano JM, Giovannucci EL. Dairy products, calcium and prostate cancer risk in the Physicians' Health Study. *Am J Clin Nutr* 2001;74:549-554.

523. Giovannucci E, Rimm EB, Wolk A, Ascherio A, Stampfer MJ, Colditz GA, Willett WC. Calcium and fructose intake in relation to risk of prostate cancer. *Cancer Res* 1998;58:442-447.

524. Chan JM, Giovannucci E, Anderson S-O, Yuen J, Adami H-O, Wolk A. Dairy products, calcium, phosphorus, vitamin D, and risk of prostate cancer. *Cancer Causes Control* 1998;9:559-566.

525. Chan JM, Giovannucci EL. Dairy products, calcium, and vitamin D and risk of prostate cancer. *Epidemiol Rev* 2001;23:87-92.

526. Heaney RP, Dowell SD, Bierman J, Hale CA, Bendich A. Absorbability and cost effectiveness in calcium supplementation. *J Am Coll Nutr* 2001;20:239-246.

527. Martini L, Wood RJ. Relative bioavailability of calcium-rich dietary sources in the elderly. *Am J Clin Nutr* 2002;76:1345-1350.

528. Recker RR. Calcium absorption and achlorhydria. *N Engl J Med* 1985;313:70-73.

44. Fc
re

45. Fu
pr
B

46. Fl
C
a

47. S
re

48. C
1

49. F
I

50. I
p
F

51. ?
i

52. ?
(

53.
(

54.

55.

56.

57.

58.

59.

60.

61.

62.

63.

26.

27.

28.

29.

30.

31.

32.

33.

34.

35

36

37

38

39

4

4

4

328. Knight KB, Keith RE. Calcium supplementation on normotensive and hypertensive pregnant women. *Am J Clin Nutr* 1992;55:891-895.

329. Villar J, Repke J, Belizan JM, Pareja G. Calcium supplementation reduces blood pressure during pregnancy: Results of a randomized controlled clinical trial. *Obstet Gnecol* 1987;70:317-322.

330. Belizan JM, Villar J, Zalazar A, Rojas L, Chan D, Bryce GF. Preliminary evidence of the effect of calcium supplementtaion on blood pressure in normal pregnant women. *Am J Obstet Gynecol* 1983;146:175-180.

331. Crowther CA, Hiller JE, Pridmore B, Bryce R, Duggan P, Hague WM, Robinson JS. Calcium supplementation in nulliparous women for the prevention of pregnancy-induced hypertension, preeclampsia and preterm birth: An Australian randomized trial. FRACOG and the ACT Study Group. *Aust N Z J Obstet Gynaecol* 1999;39:12-18.

332. Villar J, Repke J. Calcium supplementation during pregnancy may reduce preterm delivery in high-risk populations. *Am J Obstet Gynecol* 1990;163:1124-1131.

333. Niromanesh S, Laghaii S, Mosavi-Jarrahi A. Supplementary calcium in prevention of pre-eclampsia. *Int J Gynaecol Obstet* 2001;74:17-21.

334. Rogers MS, Fung HY, Hung CY. Calcium and low-dose aspirin prophylaxis in women at high risk of pregnancy-induced hypertension. *Hypertens Pregnancy* 1999;18:165-172.

335. Herrera JA, Arevalo-Herrera M, Herrera S. Prevention of preeclampsia by linoleic acid and calcium supplementation: A randomized controlled trial. *Obstet Gynecol* 1998;91:585-590.

336. Kesmodel U, Olsen SF, Salvig JD. Marine n-3 fatty acid and calcium intake in relation to pregnancy induced hypertension, intrauterine growth retardation, and preterm delivery. A case-control study. *Acta Obstet Gynecol Scand* 1997;76:38-44.

337. Sibai BM, Ewell M, Levine RJ, Klebanoff MA, Esterlitz J, Catalano PM, Goldenberg RL, Joffe G. Risk factors associated with preeclampsia in healthy nulliparous women. The Calcium for Preeclampsia Prevention (CPEP) Study Group. *Am J Obstet Gynecol* 1997;177:1003-1010.

338. van den Elzen HJ, Wladimiroff JW, Overbeek TE, Morris CD, Grobbee DE. Calcium metabolism, calcium supplementation and hypertensive disorders of pregnancy. *Eur J Obstet Gynecol Reprod Biol* 1995;59:5-16.

339. Bucher HC, Guyatt GH, Cook RJ, Hatala R, Cook DJ, Lang JD, Hunt D. Effect of calcium supplementation on pregnancy-induced hypertension and preeclampsia: A meta-analysis of randomized controlled trials. *JAMA* 1996;275:1113-1117.

340. Villar J, Belizan JM. Same nutrient, different hypotheses: Disparities in trials of calcium supplementation during pregnancy. *Am J Clin Nutr* 2000;71(Suppl.): 1375S-1 379S.

341. Carroli G, Duley L, Belizan JM, Villar J. Calcium supplementation during pregnancy: A systematic review of randomised controlled trials. *Br J Obstet Gynaecol* 1994;101:753-758.

342. Villar J, Merialdi M, Gulmezoglu AM, Abalos E, Carroli G, Kulier R, de Onis M. Nutritional interventions during pregnancy for the prevention or treatment of maternal morbidity and preterm delivery: An overview of randomized controlled trials. *J Nutr* 2003;133(Suppl 2):1606S-1625S.

343. Hofmeyr GJ, Roodt A, Atallah AN, Duley L. Calcium supplementation to prevent pre-eclampsia - A systematic review. *S Afr Med J* 2003;93:224-228.

344. Hofmeyr GJ, Atallah AN, Duley L. Calcium supplementation during pregnancy for preventing hypertensive disorders and related problems

(Cochrane Review). *Cochrane Database Syst Rev* 2000;(2):CD001059.

345. Heaney RP, Dowell SD, Bierman J, Hale CA, Bendich A. Absorbability and cost effectiveness in calcium supplementation. *J Am Coll Nutr* 2001;20:239-246.

346. Martini L, Wood RJ. Relative bioavailability of calcium-rich dietary sources in the elderly. *Am J Clin Nutr* 2002;76:1345-1350.

347. Recker RR. Calcium absorption and achlorhydria. *N Engl J Med* 1985;313:70-73.

348. Institute of Medicine. Summary. In: *Dietary Reference Intakes for Calcium, Phosphorus, Magnesium, Vitamin D, and Fluoride.* National Academy Press, Washington, DC, 1997, summary.

349. Institute of Medicine. Uses of dietary reference intakes. In: *Dietary Reference Intakes for Calcium, Phosphorus, Magnesium, Vitamin D, and Fluoride.* National Academy Press, Washington, DC, 1997, chapter IX.

350. Food and Drug Administration. Food labeling; health claims; calcium and osteoporosis. Proposed Rule. *Fed Reg* 1991;56:60689-.

351. Food and Drug Administration. Food labeling; health claims; calcium and osteoporosis. Final Rule. *Fed Reg* 1993;58:2665-2677.

352. Malberti F, Surian M, Poggio F, Minoia C, Salvadeo A. Efficacy and safety of long-term treatment with calcium carbonate as a phosphate binder. *Am J Kidney Dis* 1988;12:487-491.

353. Moriniere P, Hocine C, Boudailliez B, Belbrik S, Renaud H, Westeel PF, Solal MC, Fournier A. Long-term efficacy and safety of oral calcium as compared to A1(OH)3 as phosphate binders. *Kidney Int* 1989;36(Suppl. 27):S133-S135.

354. Tsukamoto Y, Moriya R, Nagaba Y, Morishita T, Izumida I, Okubo M. Effect of administering calcium carbonate to treat secondary hyperparathyroidism in nondialyzed patients with chronic renal failure. *Am J Kidney Dis* 1995;25:879-886.

355. Nolan CR, Qunibi WY. Calcium salts in the treatment of hyperphosphatemia in hemodialysis patients. *Curr Opin Nephrol Hypertens* 2003;12:373-379.

356. Clark AGB, Oner A, Ward G, Turner C, Rigden SPA, Haycock GB, Chantler C. Safety and efficacy of calcium carbonate in children with chronic renal failure. *Nephrol Dial Transplant* 1989;4:539-544.

357. Orwoll ES. The milk-alkali syndrome: Current concepts. *Ann Intern Med* 1982;97:242-248.

358. Adams ND, Gray RW, Lemann J Jr. The effects of oral CaCO3 loading and dietary calcium deprivation on plasma 1,25-dihydroxyvitamin D concentrations in healthy adults. *J Clin Endocrinol Metab* 1979;48:1008-1016.

359. Heaney RP, Recker RR. Calcium supplements: Anion effects. *Bone Miner* 1987;2:433-439.

360. Lagman R, Walsh D. Dangerous nutrition? Calcium, vitamin D, and shark cartilage nutritional supplements and cancer-related hypercalcemia. *Support Care Cancer* 2003;11:232-235.

361. Burtis WJ, Gay L, Insogna KL, Ellison A, Broadus AE. Dietary hypercalciuria in patients with calcium oxalate kidney stones. *Am J Clin Nutr* 1994;60:424-429.

LITERATURE CITED *for Calcium and Kidney Stones Health Claims*

1. Bronner F. Intestinal calcium absorption: Mechanisms and applications. *J Nutr* 1987;117:1347-1352.

2. Peng JB, Chen XZ, Berger UV, Vassilev PM, Tsukaguchi H, Brown EM, Hediger MA. Molecular cloning and characterization of a channel-like transporter mediating intestinal calcium absorption. *J Biol Chem* 1999;274:22739-22746.

calcium intake and blood pressure: a meta-analysis of published data" (letter). *Am J Epidemiol* 1997;145:858-859.

46. Curhan GC, Willett WC, Rimm EB, Stampfer MJ. A prospective study of dietary calcium and other nutrients and the risk of symptomatic kidney stones. *N Engl J Med* 1993;328:833-838.

47. Curhan GC, Willett WC, Speizer FE, Spiegelman D, Stampfer MJ. Comparison of dietary calcium with supplemental calcium and other nutrients as factors affecting the risk for kidney stones in women. *Ann Intern Med* 1997;126:497-504.

48. Lemann J Jr, Pleuss JA, Worcester EM, Hornick L, Schrab D, Hoffmann RG. Urinary oxalate excretion increases with body size and decreases with increasing dietary calcium intake among healthy adults. *Kidney Int* 1996;49:200-208.

49. Nishiura JL, Martini LA, Mendonca CO, Schor N, Heilberg IP. Effect of calcium intake on urinary oxalate excretion in calcium stone-forming patients. *Braz J Med Biol Res* 2002;35:669-675.

50. Domrongkitchaiporn S, Ongphiphadhanakul B, Stitchantrakul W, Chansirikarn S, Dursun N, Dursun E, Yalcin S. Comparison of alendronate, calcitonin and calcium treatments in postmenopausal osteoporosis. *Int J Clin Pract* 2001;55:505-509.

51. Domrongkitchaiporn S, Ongphiphadhanakul B, Stitchantrakul W, Chansirikarn S, Puavilai G, Rajatanavin R. Risk of calcium oxalate nephrolithiasis in postmenopausal women supplemented with calcium or combined calcium and estrogen. *Maturitas* 2002;41:149-156.

52. Domrongkitchaiporn S, Ongphiphadhanakul B, Stitchantrakul W, Piaseu N, Chansirikam S, Puavilai G, Rajatanavin R. Risk of calcium oxalate nephrolithiasis after calcium or combined calcium and calcitriol supplementation in postmenopausal women. *Osteoporos Int* 2000;11:486-492.

53. Leonetti F, Dussol B, Berthezene P, Thirion X, Berland Y. Dietary and urinary risk factors for stones in idiopathic calcium stone formers compared with healthy subjects. *Nephrol Dial Transplant* 1998;13:617-622.

54. Robertson WG, Peacock M, Hodgkinson A. Dietary changes and the incidence of urinary calculi in the UK between 1958 and 1976. *J Chronic Dis* 1979;32:469-476.

55. Heaney RP, Dowell SD, Bierman J, Hale CA, Bendich A. Absorbability and cost effectiveness in calcium supplementation. *J Am Coll Nutr* 2001;20:239-246.

56. Martini L, Wood RJ. Relative bioavailability of calcium-rich dietary sources in the elderly. *Am J Clin Nutr* 2002;76:1345-1350.

57. Recker RR. Calcium absorption and achlorhydria. *N Engl J Med* 1985;313:70-73.

58. Institute of Medicine. Summary. In: *Dietary Reference Intakes for Calcium, Phosphorus, Magnesium, Vitamin D, and Fluoride*. National Academy Press, Washington, DC, 1997, summary.

59. Institute of Medicine. Uses of dietary reference intakes. In: *Dietary Reference Intakes for Calcium, Phosphorus, Magnesium, Vitamin D, and Fluoride*. National Academy Press, Washington, DC, 1997, chapter IX.

60. Food and Drug Admin istration. Food labeling; health claims; calcium and osteoporosis. Proposed Rule. *Fed Reg* 1991;56:60689.

61. Food and Drug Administration. Food labeling; health claims; calcium and osteoporosis. Final Rule. *Fed Reg* 1993;58:2665-2677.

62. Malberti F, Surian M, Poggio F, Minoia C, Salvadeo A. Efficacy and safety of long-term treatment with calcium carbonate as a phosphate binder. *Am J Kidney Dis* 1988;12:487-491.

63. Moriniere P, Hocine C, Boudailliez B, Belbrik S, Renaud H, Westeel PF, Solal

MC, Fournier A. Long-term efficacy and safety of oral calcium as compared to A1(OH)3 as phosphate binders. *Kidney Int* 1989;36(Suppl. 27):S133-S135.

64.   Tsukamoto Y, Moriya R, Nagaba Y, Morishita T, Izumida I, Okubo M. Effect of administering calcium carbonate to treat secondary hyperparathyroidism in nondialyzed patients with chronic renal failure. *Am J Kidney Dis* 1995;25:879-886.

65.   Nolan CR, Qunibi WY. Calcium salts in the treatment of hyperphosphatemia in hemodialysis patients. *Curr Opin Nephrol Hypertens* 2003;12:373-379.

66.   Clark AGB, Oner A, Ward G, Turner C, Rigden SPA, Haycock GB, Chantler C. Safety and efficacy of calcium carbonate in children with chronic renal failure. *Nephrol Dial Transplant* 1989;4:539-544.

67.   Orwoll ES. The milk-alkali syndrome: Current concepts. *Ann Intern Med* 1982;97:242-248.

68.   Adams ND, Gray RW, Lemann J Jr. The effects of oral CaCO3 loading and dietary calcium deprivation on plasma 1,25-dihydroxyvitamin D concentrations in healthy adults. *J Clin Endocrinol Metab* 1979;48:1008-1016.

69.   Heaney RP, Recker RR. Calcium supplements: Anion effects. *Bone Miner* 1987;2:433-439.

70.   Lagman R, Walsh D. Dangerous nutrition? Calcium, vitamin D, and shark cartilage nutritional supplements and cancer-related hypercalcemia. *Support Care Cancer* 2003;11:232-235.

71.   Anonymous. The role of calcium in peri- and postmenopausal women: Consensus opinion of The North American Menopause Society. *Menopause* 2001;8:84-95.

LITERATURE CITED *for Calcium and Bone Fractures Health Claims*

1.   Bronner F. Intestinal calcium absorption: Mechanisms and applications. *J Nutr* 1987;117:1347-1352.

2.   Peng JB, Chen XZ, Berger UV, Vassilev PM, Tsukaguchi H, Brown EM, Hediger MA. Molecular cloning and characterization of a channel-like transporter mediating intestinal calcium absorption.   *J Biol Chem* 1999;274:22739-22746.

3.   Zhuang L, Peng JB, Tou L, Takanaga H, Adam RM, Hediger MA, Freeman MR. Calcium-selective ion channel, CaT1, is apically localized in gastrointestinal tract epithelia and is aberrantly expressed in human malignancies. *Lab Invest* 2002;82:1755-1764.

4.   Fleet JC, Wood RJ. Specific 1,25(OH)2D3-mediated regulation of transcellular csalcium transport in Caco-2 cells. *Am J Physiol* 1999;276:G958-G964.

5.   Barger-Lux MJ, Heaney RP, Recker RR. Time course of calcium absorption in humans: Evidence for a colonic component. *Calcif Tissue Int* 1989;44:308-311.

6.   Cashman K. Prebiotics and calcium bioavailability. *Curr Issues Intest Microbiol* 2003;4:21-32.

7.   Ireland P, Fordtran JS. Effect of dietary calcium and age on jejunal calcium absorption in humans studied by intestinal perfusion. *J Clin Invest* 1973;52:2672-2681.

8.   Gallagher JC, Riggs BL, DeLuca HF. Effect of estrogen on calcium absorption and serum vitamin D metabolites in postmenopausal osteoporosis. *J Clin Endocrinol Metab* 1980;51:1359-1364.

9.   Heaney RP, Saville PD, Recker RR. Calcium absorption as a function of calcium intake. *J Lab Clin Med* 1975;85:881-890.

10.   Heaney RP, Recker RR, Stegman MR, Moy AJ. Calcium absorption in women:

Relationships to calcium intake, estrogen status, and age. *J Bone Min Res* 1989;4:469-475.

11. Heaney RP, Weaver CM, Fitzsimmons ML. Influence of calcium load on absorption fraction. *J Bone Min Res* 1990;5:1135-1138.

12. Abrams SA, Wen J, Stuff JE. Absorption of calcium, zinc and iron from breast milk by five-to seven-month-old infants. *Pediatr Res* 1996;39:384-390.

13. Heaney RP. Effect of calcium on skeletal development, bone loss, and risk of fractures. Am J Med. 1991 Nov 25;91(5B):23S-28S.

14. Bullamore JR, Wilkinson R, Gallagher JC, Nordin BEC, Marshall DH. Effects of age on calcium absorption. *Lancet* 1970;ii:535-537.

15. Wolf RL, Cauley JA, Baker CE, Ferrell RE, Charron M, Caggiula AW, Salamone LM, Heaney RP, Kuller LH. Factors associated with calcium absorption efficiency in pre- and perimenopausal women. *Am J Clin Nutr.* 2000;72):466-471.

16. Pattanaungkul S, Riggs BL, Yergey AL, Vieira NE, O'Fallon WM, Khosla S. Relationship of intestinal calcium absorption to 1,25-dihydroxyvitamin D [1,25(OH)2D] levels in young *versus* elderly women: Evidence for age-related intestinal resistance to 1,25(OH)2D action. *J Clin Endocrinol Metab* 2000;85:4023-4027.

17. Abrams SA, Silber TJ, Esteban NV, Vieira NE, Stuff JE, Meyers R, Majd M, Yergey AL. Mineral balance and bone turnover in adolescents with anorexia nervosa. *J Pediatr* 1993;123:326-331.

18. Abrams SA, O'Brien KO, Stuff JE. Changes in calcium kinetics associated with menarche. *J Clin Endocrinol Metab* 1996;81:2017-2020.

19. Farmer ME, White LR, Brody JA, Bailey KR. Race and sex differences in hip fracture incidence. *Am J Public Health* 1984;74:1374-1380.

20. Kellie SE, Brody JA. Sex-specific and race-specific hip fracture rates. *Am J Pub Health* 1990;80:326-328.

21. Dawson-Hughes B, Harris S, Kramich C, Dallal G, Rasmussen HM. Calcium retention and hormone levels in black and white women on high- and low-calcium diets. *J Bone Min Res* 1993;8:779-787.

22. Drinkwater B, Bruemner B, Chestnut C. Menstrual history as a determinant of current bone density in young athletes. *JAMA* 1990;263:545-548.

23. Marcus R, Cann C, Madvig P, Minkoff J, Goddard M, Bayer M, Martin M, Gaudiani L, Haskell W, Genant H. Menstrual function and bone mass in elite women distance runners. Endocrine and metabolic features. *Ann Intern Med* 1985;102:158-163.

24. Berkelhammer CH, Wood RJ, Sitrin MD. Acetate and hypercalciuria during total parenteral nutrition. *Am J Clin Nutr* 1988;48:1482-1489.

25. Sebastian A, Harris ST, Ottaway JH, Todd KM, Morris RC Jr. Improved mineral balance and skeletal metabolism in postmenopausal women treated with potassium bicarbonate. *N Engl J Med* 1994;330:1776-1781.

26. Bell NH, Yergey AL, Vieira NE, Oexmann MJ, Shary JR. Demonstration of a difference in urinary calcium, not calcium absorption, in black and white adolescents. *J Bone Min Res* 1993;8:1111-1115.

27. Spencer H, Kramer L, Lensiak M, DeBartolo M, Norris C, Osis D. Calcium requirements in humans. Report of original data and a review. *Clin Orthop Related Res* 1984;184:270-280.

28. Jackman LA, Millane SS, Martin BR, Wood OB, McCabe GP, Peacock M, Weaver CM. Calcium retention in relation to calcium intake and postmenarcheal age in adolescent females. *Am J Clin Nutr* 1997;66:327-333.

29. Institute of Medicine. Calcium. In: *Dietary Reference Intakes for Calcium, Phosphorus, Magnesium, Vitamin D, and Fluoride.* National Academy Press,

Washington, DC, 1997, chapter IV.

30. Cooper C, Campion G, Melton LJ. Hip fractures in the elderly: A world-wide projection. *Osteoporosis Int* 1992;2:285-289.

31. Riggs BL, Melton LJ. The worldwide problem of osteoporosis: Insights afforded by epidemiology. *Bone* 1995;17:505S-511S.

32. Melton LJ, Chrischilles EA, Cooper C, Lane AW, Riggs BL. How many women have osteoporosis? *J Bone Min Res* 1992;7:1005-1010.

33. Marottoli RA, Berkman LF, Cooney LM Jr. Decline in physical function following hip fracture. *J Am Geriatr Soc* 1992;40:861-866.

34. Greendale GA, Barrett-Connor E, Ingles S, Haile R. Late physical and functional effects of osteoporotic fracture in women: The Rancho Bernardo Study. *J Am Geriatr Soc* 1995;43:955-961.

35. Laxton C, Freeman C, Todd C, Payne BV, Camilleri-Ferrante C, Palmer C, Parker M, Rushton N. Morbidity at 3 months after hip fracture: Data from the East Anglican audit. *Health Trends* 1997;29:55-60.

36. Oden A, Dawson A, Dere W, Johnell O, Jonsson B, Kanis JA. Lifetime risk of hip fracture is underestimated. *Osteoporos Int* 1998;8:599-603.

37. Forsen L, Sogaard AJ, Meyer HE, Edna T-H, Kopjar B. Survival after hip fracture: Short- and long-term excess mortality according to age and gender. *Osteoporos Int* 1999;10:73-78.

38. Parker MJ, Anand JK. What is the true mortality of hip fractures? *Public Health* 1991;105:443-446.

39. Parker MJ, Palmer CR. Prediction of rehabilitation after hip fracture. *Age Aging* 1995;24:96-98.

40. Amin S, Felson DT. Osteoporosis in men. *Rheum Dis Clin North Am* 2001;27:19-47.

41. Campion JM, Maricic MJ. Osteoporosis in men. *Am Fam Physician* 2003;67:1521-1526.

42. Kado DM, Browner WS, Palermo L, Nevitt MC, Genant HK, Cummings SR. Vertebral fractures and mortality in older women: A prospective study. *Arch Intern Med* 1999;159:1215-1220.

43. Cooper C, Atkinson EJ, Jacobsen SJ, O'Fallon WM, Melton LJ. Population-based study of survival after osteoporotic fractures. *Am J Epidemiol* 1993;137:1001-1005.

44. Center JR, Nguyen TV, Schneider D, Sambrook PN, Eisman JA. Mortality after all major types of osteoporosis fracture in men and women: An observational study. *Lancet* 1999;353:878-882.

45. Heaney RP. Thinking straight about calcium. *N Engl J Med* 1993;328:503-505.

46. Cummings SR, Black DM, Nevitt MC, Browner W, Cauley J, Ensrud K, Genant HK, Palermo L, Scott J, Vogt TM. Bone density at various sites for prediction of hip fractures. *Lancet* 1993;341:72-75.

47. Melton LJ, Atkinson EA, O'Fallon WM, Wahner HW, Riggs BL. Long-term fracture prediction by bone mineral assessed at different skeletal sites. *J Bone Min Res* 1993;8:1227-1283.

48. Dargent-Molina P, Favier F, Grandjean H, Baudoin C, Schott AM, Hausherr E, Meunier PJ, Breart G. Fall-related factors and risk of hip fracture: The EPIDOS prospective study. *Lancet* 1996;348:145-149.

49. Albrand G, Munoz F, Sornay-Rendu E, DuBoeuf F, Delmas PD. Independent predictors of all osteoporosis-related fractures in healthy postmenopausal women: The OFELY Study. *Bone* 2003;32:78-85.

50. Riggs BL, Melton LJ. Evidence of two distinct syndromes of involutional osteoporosis. *Am J Med* 1983;75:899-901.

51. Nguyen TV, Center JR, Sambrook PN, Eisman JA. Risk factors for proximal

and hip fractures: A prospective study among postmenopausal women. *Am J Clin Nutr* 2003;77:504-511.

86. Cummings SR, Nevitt MC, Browner WS, Stone K, Fox KM, Ensrud KE, Cauley J, Black D, Vogt TM. Risk factors for hip fractures in white women. Study of Osteoporotic Fractures Research Group. *N Engl J Med* 1995;332:767-773.

87. Cumming RG, Cummings SR, Nevitt MC, Scott J, Ensrud KE, Vogt TM, Fox K. Calcium intake and fracture risk: Results from the Study of Osteoporotic Fractures. *Am J Epidemiol* 1997;145:926-934.

88. Paganini-Hill A, Chao A, Ross RK, Henderson BE. Exercise and other factors in the prevention of hip fracture: The Leisure World Study. *Epidemiology* 1991;2:16-25.

89. Lumbers M, New SA, Gibson S, Murphy MC. Nutritional status in elderly female hip fracture patients: Comparison with an age-matched home living group attending day centres. *Br J Nutr* 2001;85:733-740.

90. Lau EMC, Suriwongpaisal P, Lee JK, Das De S, Festin MR, Saw SM, Khir A, Torralba T, Sham A, Sambrook P. Risk factors for hip fracture in Asian men and women: The Asian Osteoporosis Study. *J Bone Miner Res* 2001;16:572-580.

91. Varenna M, Binelli L, Zucchi F, Rossi V, Sinigaglia L. Prevalence of osteoporosis and fractures in a migrant population from southern to northern Italy: A cross-sectional, comparative study. *Osteoporos Int* 2003 Jul 10 [Epub ahead of print].

92. Clark P, de la Pena F, Gomez Garcia F, Orozco JA, Tugwell P. Risk factors for osteoporotic hip fractures in Mexicans. *Arch Med Res* 1998;29:253-257.

93. Lau E, Donnan S, Barker DJP, Cooper C. Physical activity and calcium intake in fracture of the proximal femur in Hong Kong. *Br Med J* 1988;297:1441-1443.

94. Chan HHL, Lau EMC, Woo J, Lin F, Sham A, Leung PC. Dietary calcium intake, physical activity and the risk of vertebral fracture in Chinese. *Osteoporos Int* 1996;6:228-232.

95. Kanis JA, Johnell O, Gullberg B, Allander E, Dilsen G, Gennari C, Lopes Vaz AA, Lyritis GP, Mazzuoli G, Miravet L, Passeri M, Perez Cano R, Rapado A, Ribot C. Evidence for efficacy of drugs affecting bone metabolism in preventing hip fracture. *Br Med J* 1992;305:1124-1128.

96. Chi I, Pun KK. Dietary calcium intake and other risk factors: Study of the fractured patients in Hong Kong. *J Nutr Elder* 1991;10:73-87.

97. Cooper C, Barker DJ, Wickham C. Physical activity, muscle strength, and calcium intake in fracture of the proximal femur in Britain. *Br Med J* 1988;297:1443-1446.

98. Varenna M, Binelli L, Zucchi F, Ghiringhelli D, Sinigaglia L. Unbalanced diet to lower serum cholesterol level is a risk factor for postmenopausal osteoporosis and distal forearm fracture. *Osteoporos Int* 2001;12:296-301.

99. Paganini-Hill A, Ross RK, Gerkins VR, Henderson BE, Arthur M, Mack TM. Menopausal estrogen therapy and hip fractures. *Ann Intern Med* 1981;95:28-31.

100. Partanen J, Heikkinen J, Jamsa T, Jalovaara P. Characteristics of lifetime factors, bone metabolism, and bone mineral density in patients with hip fracture. *J Bone Miner Metab* 2002;20:367-375.

101. Johnell O, Gullberg B, Kanis JA, Allander E, Elffors L, Dequeker J, Dilsen G, Gennari C, Lopes Vaz A, Lyritis G, Mazzuoli G, Miravet L, Passeri M, Perez Cano RP, Rapado A, Ribot C. Risk factors for hip fracture in European women: The MEDOS Study. Mediterranean Osteoporosis Study. *J Bone Miner Res* 1995;10:1802-1815.

102. Perez Cano R, Galan Galan F, Dilsen G. Risk factors for hip fracture in Spanish

and Turkish women. *Bone* 1993;14(Suppl 1):S69-S72.

103. Ribot C, Tremollieres F, Pouilles JM, Albarede JL, Mansat M, Utheza G, Bonneu M, Bonnissent P, Ricoeur C. Risk factors for hip fracture. MEDOS study: Results of the Toulouse Centre. *Bone* 1993;14(Suppl 1):S77-S80.

104. Kanis JA, Johnell O, Gullberg B, Allander E, Elffors L, Ranstam J, Dequeker J, Dilsen G, Gennari C, Lopes Vaz AA, Lyritis G, Mazzuoli G, Miravet L, Passeri M, Perez Cano R, Rapado A, Ribot C. Risk factors for hip fracture in men from southern Europe: The MEDOS study. Mediterranean Osteoporosis Study. *Osteoporos Int* 1999;9:45-54.

105. Kalkwarf HJ, Khoury JC, Lanphear BP. Milk intake during childhood and adolescence, adult bone density, and osteoporotic fractures in US women. *Am J Clin Nutr* 2003;77:257-265.

106. Verd Vallespir S, Dominguez Sanchez J, Gonzalez Quintial M, Vidal Mas M, Mariano Soler AC, de Roque Company C, Sevilla Marcos JM. [Association between calcium content of drinking water and fractures in children] *An Esp Pediatr* 1992;37:461-465.

107. Wyshak G, Frisch RE. Carbonated beverages, dietary calcium, the dietary calcium/phosphorus ratio, and bone fractures in girls and boys. *J Adolesc Health* 1994;15:210-215.

108. Nieves JW, Grisso JA, Kelsey JL. A case-control study of hip fracture: Evaluation of selected dietary variables and teenage physical activity. *Osteoporos Int* 1992;2:122-127.

109. Cline AD, Jansen GR, Melby CL. Stress fractures in female army recruits: implications of bone density, calcium intake, and exercise. *J Am Coll Nutr* 1998;17:128-135.

110. Kreiger N, Gross A, Hunter G. Dietary factors and fracture in postmenopausal women: A case-control study. *Int J Epidemiol* 1992;21:953-958.

111. Meyer HE, Henriksen C, Falch JA, Pedersen JI, Tverdal A. Risk factors for hip fracture in a high incidence area: A case-control study from Oslo, Norway. *Osteoporos Int* 1995;5:239-246.

112. Michaelsson K, Holmberg L, Mallmin H, Sorensen S, Wolk A, Bergstrom R, Ljunghall S. Diet and hip fracture risk: A case-control study. Study Group of the Multiple Risk Survey on Swedish Women for Eating Assessment. *Int J Epidemiol* 1995;24:771-782.

113. Tavani A, Negri E, La Vecchia C. Calcium, dairy products, and the risk of hip fracture in women in northern Italy. *Epidemiology* 1995;6:554-557.

114. Wallace LS, Ballard JE. Lifetime physical activity and calcium intake related to bone density in young women. *J Womens Health Gend Based Med* 2002;11:389-398.

115. Wooton R, Brereton PJ, Clark MB, Hesp R, Hodkinson HM, Klenerman L, Reeve J, Slavin G, Tellez-Yudilevich M. Fractured neck of femur in the elderly: An attempt to identify patients at risk. *Clin Sci* 1979;57:93-101.

116. Cumming RG, Klineberg RJ. Case-control study of risk factors for hip fractures in the elderly. *Am J Epidemiol* 1994;139:493-503.

117. Jaglal SB, Kreiger N, Darlington G. Past and recent physical activity and risk of hip fracture. *Am J Epidemiol* 1993;138:107-218.

118. Bendich A, Leader S, Muhuri P. Supplemental calcium for the prevention of hip fracture: Potential health-economic benefits. *Clin Ther* 1999;21:1058-1072.

119. Heaney RP. Calcium needs of the elderly to reduce fracture risk. *J Am Coll Nutr* 2001;20(2 Suppl):192S-197S.

120. Nordin BEC, Horsman A, Crilly RG, Marshall DH, Simpson M. Treatment of spinal osteoporosis in postmenopausal women. *Br Med J* 1980;280:451-454.

12. Abrams SA, Wen J, Stuff JE. Absorption of calcium, zinc and iron from breast milk by five-to seven-month-old infants. *Pediatr Res* 1996;39:384-390.
13. Heaney RP. Effect of calcium on skeletal development, bone loss, and risk of fractures. *Am J Med.* 1991 Nov 25;91(5B):23S-28S.
14. Bullamore JR, Wilkinson R, Gallagher JC, Nordin BEC, Marshall DH. Effects of age on calcium absorption. *Lancet* 1970;ii:535-537.
15. Wolf RL, Cauley JA, Baker CE, Ferrell RE, Charron M, Caggiula AW, Salamone LM, Heaney RP, Kuller LH. Factors associated with calcium absorption efficiency in pre- and perimenopausal women. *Am J Clin Nutr.* 2000;72):466-471.
16. Pattanaungkul S, Riggs BL, Yergey AL, Vieira NE, O'Fallon WM, Khosla S. Relationship of intestinal calcium absorption to 1,25-dihydroxyvitamin D [1,25(OH)2D] levels in young *versus* elderly women: Evidence for age-related intestinal resistance to 1,25(OH)2D action. *J Clin Endocrinol Metab* 2000;85:4023-4027.
17. Abrams SA, Silber TJ, Esteban NV, Vieira NE, Stuff JE, Meyers R, Majd M, Yergey AL. Mineral balance and bone turnover in adolescents with anorexia nervosa. *J Pediatr* 1993;123:326-331.
18. Abrams SA, O'Brien KO, Stuff JE. Changes in calcium kinetics associated with menarche. *J Clin Endocrinol Metab* 1996;81:2017-2020.
19. Farmer ME, White LR, Brody JA, Bailey KR. Race and sex differences in hip fracture incidence. *Am J Public Health* 1984;74:1374-1380.
20. Kellie SE, Brody JA. Sex-specific and race-specific hip fracture rates. *Am J Pub Health* 1990;80:326-328.
21. Dawson-Hughes B, Harris S, Kramich C, Dallal G, Rasmussen HM. Calcium retention and hormone levels in black and white women on high- and low-calcium diets. *J Bone Min Res* 1993;8:779-787.
22. Drinkwater B, Bruemner B, Chestnut C. Menstrual history as a determinant of current bone density in young athletes. *JAMA* 1990;263:545-548.
23. Marcus R, Cann C, Madvig P, Minkoff J, Goddard M, Bayer M, Martin M, Gaudiani L, Haskell W, Genant H. Menstrual function and bone mass in elite women distance runners. Endocrine and metabolic features. *Ann Intern Med* 1985;102:158-163.
24. Berkelhammer CH, Wood RJ, Sitrin MD. Acetate and hypercalciuria during total parenteral nutrition. *Am J Clin Nutr* 1988;48:1482-1489.
25. Sebastian A, Harris ST, Ottaway JH, Todd KM, Morris RC Jr. Improved mineral balance and skeletal metabolism in postmenopausal women treated with potassium bicarbonate. *N Engl J Med* 1994;330:1776-1781.
26. Bell NH, Yergey AL, Vieira NE, Oexmann MJ, Shary JR. Demonstration of a difference in urinary calcium, not calcium absorption, in black and white adolescents. *J Bone Min Res* 1993;8:1111-1115.
27. Spencer H, Kramer L, Lensiak M, DeBartolo M, Norris C, Osis D. Calcium requirements in humans. Report of original data and a review. *Clin Orthop Related Res* 1984;184:270-280.
28. Jackman LA, Millane SS, Martin BR, Wood OB, McCabe GP, Peacock M, Weaver CM. Calcium retention in relation to calcium intake and postmenarcheal age in adolescent females. *Am J Clin Nutr* 1997;66:327-333.
29. Institute of Medicine. Calcium. In: *Dietary Reference Intakes for Calcium, Phosphorus, Magnesium, Vitamin D, and Fluoride.* National Academy Press, Washington, DC, 1997, chapter IV.
30. Bendich A. Micronutrients in women's health and immune function. *Nutrition* 2001;17:858-867.

31. Alvir JMJ, Thys-Jacobs S. Premenstrual and menstrual symptom clusters and response to calcium treatment. *Psychopharmacol Bull* 1991;27:145-148.
32. Bendich A. The potential for dietary supplements to reduce premenstrual syndrome (PMS) symptoms. *J Am Coll Nutr* 2000;19:3-12.
33. American College of Obstetrics and Gynecology. Premenstrual syndrome (ACOG Committee Opinion). *Int J Gynaecol Obstet* 1995;50:80.
34. Daugherty JE. Treatment strategies for premenstrual syndrome. *Amer Fam Phys* 1998;58:183-192.
35. Grady-Weliky TA. Clinical practice. Premenstrual dysphoric disorder. *N Engl J Med* 2003;348:433-438.
36. Ward MW, Holimon TD. Calcium treatment for premenstrual syndrome. *Ann Pharmacother* 1999;33:1356-1358.
37. Okey R, Stewart JA, Greenwood ML. Studies of the metabolism of women. IV. The calcium and inorganic phosphorus in the blood of normal women at the various stages of the monthly cycle. *J Biol Chem* 1930;87:91.
38. Thys-Jacobs S. Micronutrients and the premenstrual syndrome: The case for calcium. *J Am Coll Nutr* 2000;19:220-227.
39. Facchinetti F, Borella P, Sances G, Fioroni L, Nappi RE, Genazzani AR. Oral magnesium successfully relieves premenstrual mood changes. *Obstet Gynecol* 1991;78:177-181.
40. Thys-Jacobs S. Vitamin D and calcium in menstrual migraine. *Headache* 1994;34:544-546.
41. Thys-Jacobs S, Ceccarelli S, Bierman A, Weisman H, Cohen MA, Alvir J. Calcium supplementation in premenstrual syndrome: A randomized crossover trial. *J Gen Intern Med* 1989;4:183-189.
42. Penland JG, Johnson PE. Dietary calcium and manganese effects on menstrual cycle symptoms. *Am J Obstet Gynecol* 1993;168:1417-1423.
43. Thys-Jacobs S, Starkey P, Bernstein D, Tian J. Calcium carbonate and the premenstrual syndrome: Effects on premenstrual and menstrual symptoms. Premenstrual Syndrome Study Group. *Am J Obstet Gynecol* 1998;179:444-452.
44. Thys-Jacobs S, Donovan D, Papadopoulos A, Sarrel P, Bilezikian JP. Vitamin D and calcium dysregulation in the polycystic ovarian syndrome. *Steroids* 1999;64:430-435.
45. Christian RC, Dumesic DA, Behrenbeck T, Oberg AL, Sheedy PF 2nd, Fitzpatrick LA. Prevalence and predictors of coronary artery calcification in women with polycystic ovary syndrome. *J Clin Endocrinol Metab* 2003;88:2562-2568.
46. Heaney RP, Dowell SD, Bierman J, Hale CA, Bendich A. Absorbability and cost effectiveness in calcium supplementation. *J Am Coll Nutr* 2001;20:239-246.
47. Martini L, Wood RJ. Relative bioavailability of calcium-rich dietary sources in the elderly. *Am J Clin Nutr* 2002;76:1345-1350.
48. Recker RR. Calcium absorption and achlorhydria. *N Engl J Med* 1985;313:70-73.
49. Institute of Medicine. Summary. In: *Dietary Reference Intakes for Calcium, Phosphorus, Magnesium, Vitamin D, and Fluoride.* National Academy Press, Washington, DC, 1997, summary.
50. Institute of Medicine. Uses of dietary reference intakes. In: *Dietary Reference Intakes for Calcium, Phosphorus, Magnesium, Vitamin D, and Fluoride.* National Academy Press, Washington, DC, 1997, chapter IX.
51. Food and Drug Administration. Food labeling; health claims; calcium and osteoporosis. Proposed Rule. *Fed Reg* 1991;56:60689-.
52. Food and Drug Administration. Food labeling; health claims; calcium and osteoporosis. Final Rule. *Fed Reg* 1993;58:2665-2677.